HEAVEN ON EARTH

HERE AND NOW

HEAVEN ON EARTH HERE AND NOW

Joyous News from Jesus to His People

Mary Ellen Gilliland

ZoeBooks
Alpenrose Press

Library of Congress Catalog Card Number: 98-93272

ISBN: 1-889385-01-8

Cover design by:
Paulette Livers Lambert
Illustration and Design
4319 Snowberry Court
Boulder, Colorado 80304

ZoeBooks
Alpenrose Press
P.O. Box 499
Silverthorne, Colorado 80498
1-800-579-1179

About the Author

"I am a Rewarder of those who diligently seek Me." God spoke this scripture to author Mary Ellen Gilliland nearly every morning for many months. "Diligent" and "seeker" describe this woman. She spends ample time daily in worship, prayer and studying God's word. During this time, which culminates in listening to the Lord speak, she has received an amazing "reward"--the dynamic message of this book. Day by day, God revealed Himself and then poured out His plan for a seven-year blessing feast during the prophesied seven years of tribulation.

"What an awesome thing this is!" Mary Ellen comments. "It didn't originate with me so I am free to be as excited as any of my readers. The revelation of Yahweh is so simple it's profound. And the wonderful news about the blessing feast is typical of the bounteous, alive, exuberant God the book reveals.

Mary Ellen, an active Colorado outdoorswoman, has written many newspaper and magazine articles. She has ten other published books on various subjects, from art to Colorado gold rush history and hiking guidebooks. *Heaven on Earth* is her first spiritual book, but may not be her last.

Acknowledgements

Credit goes first to the Holy Spirit for the book's content. To those who read and critiqued the manuscript, my warmest thanks. The readers, who worked with enthusiasm and dispatch, are: Mary Greenhalge, Pastor Mark Klingenberg, Mary Windfeldt, Dianne Brekke, Jane Saul and Marilyn Waldrop. My appreciation goes to those who prayed for the book, including my prayer group. Larry Gilliland generously gave his time in typesetting and formatting the text. Paulette Livers Lambert lent her artistic skills and creativity to the cover design.

M.E.G.

CONTENTS

Section One

I AM

God revealed His name to Moses:
I AM WHO AM,
the God Who is Life.

I AM wanted a love bond with Moses
and drew him into His presence.

He flowed His power through Moses
to free His people Israel,
calling them to a prophetic
"feast in the wilderness."

Yahweh's intimacy with Moses led to
a manifestation of God's glory.

Today those who draw close to God's heart
will witness His glory
in dimensions beyond
our asking or imagining.

Chapter 1

Self-Revealing One

We have entered a crucial moment on God's clock. Events in the spirit realm have accelerated. Time has compressed. The prophets proclaim that God has begun to pour out His glory in a way never before seen or equalled.

As He initiates this mighty work, the Lord wants us to know Him again in the personal, intimate way Moses knew Him. Hc revealed Himself to Moses as *Yahweh*, I AM. He told Moses, "I AM WHO AM...This is My name forever, and by this name I am to be remembered to all generations." (Exodus 3:14-15)

The name *Yahweh*, or *Jehovah* as it is also rendered, captures God's essence as Life. He not only causes all life, He **is** all life. The name Yahweh, a primitive form of the Hebrew verb, "to be," means the self-existent one, alive in Himself and the source of life.

God gave Moses His personal name. His earlier-revealed name, El, with its combinations, El Shaddai, Elyon and Elohim, showed forth the might and sublime nature of God. But Yahweh or I AM personifies God's desire for self-revelation. It is a relational name, one that opens a door to intimacy. When Moses called upon the name of Yahweh in Exodus 34:6-7, the word of God says, "Yahweh passed before him and proclaimed, 'Yahweh, Yahweh, a God of tenderness and compassion, slow to anger, rich in kindness and faithfulness.'" Moses bowed down to the ground and asked I AM to accompany the people with a crucial blessing: His presence, or anointing.

God is calling His people today to again know Him as I AM. His call comes because He plans now to achieve a restoration and wide scale work of His glory beyond our imagination to conceive. He will manifest Himself as I AM, His goodness breaking forth into the physical, natural realm. That is His glory—His wonderful presence manifested.

This endeavor will dwarf God's work with ancient Israel. That physical feat will pale beside the spiritual undertaking God has now begun. He challenges each believer to join a Jesus-powered, need-meeting army of witnesses who will say to a hurting world, "I AM sent me."

God wants His people to know Him—beyond His works and attributes—His vital true self. The God who dwells in us is available to His own as **all that He is.** He is available in power to those who know Him to fully restore what Adam lost by sin—closeness with God, abundance, dominion in the earth and God's glory as a covering.

Our role in this mission involves faith. I AM is calling us today to witness that He is and that He is God. A witness differs from a reporter, who communicates facts in an objective, intellectual way. A witness burns with the message, the way Moses' burning bush flamed, because he or she has experienced the message event. Like Moses, we "turn aside" from personal goals and activities to seize the moment when God is revealed as I AM.

A Momentous Work

Before the Exodus and before other great spiritual events, God has heralded His earth-changing work by proclaiming His name, I AM. When God announced through the prophet Isaiah the downfall of Babylon, another momentous undertaking, He first proclaimed:

> You are My witnesses...that you may know Me, believe Me, and remain steadfast to Me and understand that **I am He.** Before Me there was no God formed, neither shall there be after Me.
>
> I, even I, am the Lord, and besides Me there is no Savior.
>
> Yes, from the time of the first existence of day and from this day forth **I am He.** (Isaiah 43:10-11, 13. Emphasis mine.)

When God addressed His spokesman in Ezekiel 6:7 to prophesy Israel's judgement, He said "they will learn that **I am Yahweh.**" When Jesus in John 8:28 told the people He would be crucified, He said, "then you will know that **I am He.**"

God wants us to witness before heaven and earth that He Is and He is God. Today, He manifests Himself anew to His people, saying "I AM." Before the coming messianic age, He wants to give His people a rock-bottom understanding that He is God. His people today must have an intimate, experiential knowledge of their God as together they move into a glorious new era of righteous judgement, vengeance against satanic works and jubilee restoration—the Day of the Lord.

When the long-promised glory of God comes in fullness,

God will use His messengers to declare to the pharaohs of today, "I AM sent me."

This revelation of God for His purified people comes not from this writer's own thoughts but from the mind of God. He is speaking to His people today and those who take the time to listen are hearing from Him. Throughout this book, readers will encounter sections like the one appearing below in italics. These are words that God spoke directly into my mind. He said:

"I AM sent me," is what My children, My messengers, My "sent ones" will say. They will use the words of Moses to Pharaoh, "I AM sent me" because they will be setting nations free, the same as Moses did.

Yes! And I will do the work. I will anoint these words and do all the work as I did anoint the words of Moses and back up with glorious works the word of Moses. Did I not say you would speak the word "with signs following?" Yes! Signs, great signs, will follow the word spoken by My sent messengers.

God will rain down His glory. I AM wants us to know Him as Life. He wants to fulfill the reason He sent Jesus, to bring us "abundant life." (John 10:10) Then He will demonstrate for us the fullness of His life in us—His glory. This word of prophecy is again set in italics to signify a revelation to this writer by the Lord. It echoes God's Babylon-era declaration, quoted a few paragraphs earlier from Isaiah 43:

Yes, I AM! Know today I AM. Eternal existent life force of the created universe and beyond. I am in control. I AM God. Know today that beyond all, beneath all, over all, ***I AM God****. Witness with Me before heaven and earth that I am finally, irrevocably God.*

I AM Wants to Pour Out Life

God's name not only reveals Himself but conveys access to the God behind the name. When He gives a name for His people to know, and they call upon that name in faith, He causes them to witness in power the manifestation of all His name means. His people learn by experience the character that the name unveils.

The living God, the God of Life, is preparing to pour out life upon a dying world. He will fulfill, perfect and complete to its fullest extent Jesus' mission:

> I came that they may have and enjoy life, and have it in abundance (to the full, till it overflows). (John 10:10)

"I Am Who I Am" identifies God as life but also implies the inadequacy of any mere name to define God. "I Am Who I Am" affirms God as eternally alive, living, life itself and source of life. The Hebrew words God used, *ehyeh asher ehyeh*, mean "I Am the One Who Is." The Hebrew name for God, *Yahweh* (also translated Jehovah) means literally "He Is."

God reveals His name not only to prepare the hearts of His people for transition. He also wants to win their hearts, 100 percent.

Why did God say to Moses, " I AM?" Because He wanted to reveal Himself to the Israelites, yes, but also because He wanted a personal relationship with Moses. God is a person. Persons want to relate with others. God wants to be known. He deeply desires to be known to His people. He was saying to Moses, "Know Me, I AM."

God is Life who is a person. His personality spills over with life. He is a person who is so alive that His life fills the created universe. Life, like love, is difficult for our minds to pin down because it is spirit. Yet Life is a person! That person is God. The name I AM mixes God's life, love and light together in one awesome, ecstatic essence.

He wanted Moses to know the same thing He wants us to know: Life isn't a thing. It's a "who."

Chapter 2

He's Right Here, Right Now

How can we better know this God who is Life? As Christians we learn to know God through His word, the Bible. We can find Him in His word. Daily meditating on it is vital for one who wants to know God.

But He also encourages us to know Him as I AM through His creation, the life we see in the earth He made and in other people, the repository of His I AM life.

Here's a secret: just behind natural scenes and happenings, God is waiting. Directing me to notice Him in His handiwork, He told me:

I AM. Hear Me: I AM. See Me: I AM. Know Me: I AM.

What does that mean? To you it means you can experience Me in all of life. In the calm beauty of the morning, find Me. In the bright and beautiful variety of life around you in nature, find Me. In the steadfastness and faithfulness of people, know Me. In the goodness found in people know Me. Experience Me in your life each day, moment by moment, and you will know Me. All that you love, that you delight in, that you find deeply satisfying—that's Me.

The world around us in all its activity and diversity bids for our attention and distracts us from God's continual presence.

But God is saying, "Find Me in the world around you." It requires a wrenching shift of focus from looking **at** things to looking **through** things to find God.

Imagine being locked up in solitary confinement in a prison cell, cut off from communication with the world. A Denver teenager, Adri, age 13, had been locked in a prison of autism since birth. Her parents, Kristi and Rodrigo Jorde, discovered that a hand-held keyboard could fling open the heavy door that blocked Adri from relationship with her family.

They also discovered that Adri had a secret: she communed with God.

Here is her story, described by "LifeWise" columnist Susan

Valaskovic in the October 19, 1995 *Rocky Mountain News*.

> Kristi Jorde says she's a different person since she began communicating with her daughter, Adri.
>
> Adri, 13, is autistic, trapped in a body that doesn't allow her to speak, a body she is often unable to control, that sometimes spins wildly and doesn't respond on cue.
>
> ...She was diagnosed as unable to learn.
>
> When she was 9, they found facilitated communication. This technique unlocked the secrets of Adri's life. With the assistance of a facilitator—friend, family member or teacher—to hold her arm and hand steady, Adri began to spell out words on a hand-held keyboard with her index finger. Soon she was sharing her feelings, needs and desires. And to the amazement of her teachers and parents, Adri began sharing spiritual awareness and wisdom.
>
> ...Slowly Adri began to share a message of universal love: God comforts her.
>
> "God is God. You will see him without seeing him. You will hear him without hearing him. You are touched by him without being touched. You will be comforted by him if you have faith and surrender unconditionally to him. Faith is not rational with our limited knowledge. So when I look out this window I know that we cannot explain our existence or that of the world, the universe or anything, except through faith."
>
> Jorde says Adri taught her to look for love in all things and admits that her daughter's tutoring has affected every aspect of her life.
>
> "When you grocery shop and are looking for God in the people you meet, it changes your marketing," she says.
>
> Kristi is a social worker and learned about the value of empathy in counselor training. She also learned to leave her empathy in the counseling sessions, so she could get on with her real life. Now with Adri's help, empathy is the foundation of her life. She says she's learned to let her intellect rest so her heart can speak.

Using Spiritual Senses to Become God-Conscious

Unlike Adri, most of us operate freely in the world, with full command of our five senses. How do we find God in our surroundings? By staying alert in our spirits, actively seeking God behind the physical reality. We can learn to operate less out of our intellect and more out of our spirits.

But how? One way is by daily prayer using the prayer language that the Holy Spirit gives those who ask for His infilling—what the Bible calls praying in tongues. Somehow, the Holy Spirit forms a bridge between our soul (the mind, will and emotions) and our spirit when we pray regularly in the Spirit.

We can also supervise our seeing, hearing, touching, smelling and tasting with spiritual sensing.

We can govern the data arriving at our physical sense gates to experience all that God is. We can "judge at the gates," as in Biblical times, using God's word as a monitor. We can deny entry to the shoddy, the trivial, the negative, the outright evil. Judgement takes place when we compare sense data with the word of God. For example, when someone makes a hurtful statement during an office conversation, we can disallow the remark's power to cause offense by refusing it entry at the gates of our spirit. On the other hand, we can allow the kindness of a grocery clerk to bathe our spirit in God's love. By allowing only the good and the true access, we allow God to cleanse and refresh us. His I AM life can pass through the physical and mental to bless the spirit.

Judging at the gates also calls for judgement of what comes out of us as individuals. We can learn to respond, not with the mind, but the spirit, allowing it to color the emotional response and shape the thoughts that arise from physical sensory input. I AM's life resides within us. His life as a response can rise out of our spirit to cleanse, refresh and restore as it comes out through our physical expression—by gentle words to an irritable person, a smile, a radiant look or a skip of joy in our walk. Encouraging and allowing this flow cleanses us from the residue of rage, bitterness or greed, any negative that clogs our spiritual aqueduct.

This is living in God, in His life. We can experience God moment by moment if we pause to savor Him in the daily flow. It's guaranteed—life will be more fun!

Chapter 3

Seeing God In Creation

A mountain hike through a creek canyon near Vail, Colorado ends at a 1920s cabin called "the Bighorn Hilton." Behind the cabin lies a large, wet subalpine meadow, brilliant with color in July. Indian paintbrush blooms in fuchsia, rose and cerise. White saxifrage and yellow groundsel all erupt in a riot of hues against the vivid green backdrop. A fast-moving stream cuts the meadow, its tiny green "islands" alive with pink Parry's primrose and pure white brook cress. It's a perfect place to meet God.

I sat down by the stream, watching it bubble and churn over rocks, rushing to its descent to the valley far below. I AM began stirring my mind:

This beautiful place you remembered is Mine, My creation, My handiwork.

I AM. Now hear this: I AM. Know Me. Joy. Peace. Goodness. Beauty. Life. Mercy. Purity. Wholeness, or holiness. Perfection. I AM.

These are what and who and how God is. They're not qualities or traits. They are inherent to Him, natural and inseparable. Joy is Him. He is joy and beauty and life. Like the profusion of wildflowers around me, God blossoms forth all He is, in a beautiful array of goodness.

Consider

...The joy when a couple becomes engaged. A glimpse of God's joy.

...The peace that presides as the horizon brightens before day. A hint of His peace.

...A fertile farm clothed in goodness. A flash into His goodness.

...Beauty that shines forth in a smile. Oh, how He shines!

...An aquarium alive with brilliant fish. He's so alive!

...A forgiving spouse showing mercy. A drop in the ocean of His mercy.

...Purity in a child. A window into God's purity.

...Holiness, in a person like Mother Theresa. A momentary snatch of the holiness we will behold for all eternity.

...Perfection, perhaps found in beautiful music. A fleck from the diamond of His perfection.

We meet God in these moments. He's not far off or unknown to us. He penetrates our lives. Be alert to the sense of awe. For a moment, everything is whole and in harmony. We're sensing the presence of God.

When we watch a spectacular waterfall or view a panoramic sunset, we stand captivated. All our troubles fall away. We are caught up in the glory of the moment and while we take it in we feel alive, aware, charged with life.

When we experience His presence, it is impossible to stay angry at a companion or worried about a child or upset about a credit card balance. We forget that dull headache or sore feet. Everything fades but the loveliness we see. It cleanses us, makes us feel whole and gives us a sense of reverence.

We seek out these experiences. We are really seeking God. We climb mountains to feel that charge of life, travel to a lake cabin to savor its peace, admire the perfection of an ancient Greek sculpture. A Mozart performance captures the voice of God.

These are spiritual things, and God is spirit and life. These moments span the gap between us and God. Our spirits soar in response, flooding us with life, joy, peace. Deep speaks to deep, spirit meets spirit. The life of God expressed outside us breaks through to meet the magnetic presence of God within us.

Life

I am! your life...I am! your love. I am in you all that you cherish as good and sweetly memorable and of your spirit. That's Me! That's My life in you expressed. That's why being human is so important, so valuable. I reveal Myself to you today as the Great I AM. You experience Me in other people as love, as truth, as integrity. That's Me!

When God puts His life, His personhood with its accompanying "personality" into man or woman, He allows one glint of His personhood to shine best through that human being. For example, my father-in-law, Jack, provides a glimpse at the goodness of God. My friend Debbie reflects the purity of God. Her thoughts are pure, uncontaminated with bitterness, suspicion or negativity.

Learning to know I AM is like falling in love. Beyond the

thrill, the romance, the physical yearning of natural love is a deep knowing that it's right. A peace and a sureness come with this knowing. You don't have to be an adult or have an education. You don't have to be someone. Forrest Gump said to his Jenny, "I'm not a smart man, but I know love."

Know Me as I AM, My children, for I long for you to know Me. All that you hold most dear about other people is Me shining out through them.

Discover this! See My life around you and you will have a heightened experience of My presence and a heightened experience of Who I AM. For I permeate all things. I am omnipresent, as you know, but now know in a fuller sense.

Love

We see God revealed in His own creation and also in our human creation, such as fine art or music, but He reveals Himself best through people because they are made in His image and likeness. He has made us persons, as He Himself is a Person, and made us for relationship. Inherent to God and mixed into man's spirit is love. When we experience love, we should consciously heighten our awareness, shift to a higher gear and realize that we are experiencing God.

The God of Love reveals His heart to you, My children, My beloved. God is love, lovingkindness and compassion and blessing. Understand Me, Who I AM. I AM Love.

You have experienced love. Remember what love is like. I am that. That is Me. Understand? I am that love. Know Me as the God of Love. Every time you experience love, know Me better.

This God of ours is passionate, intense, alive and enthusiastic. The enthusiasm for its playmate that He put in a puppy, the passion He put in the heart of an ardent lover, are His nature.

Hear Me, Hear Me, Israel. Hear Me, My children: I AM. Know Me as I AM. Your life. The life in others around you. My expression in flesh. Know the awesomeness, the importance, the preciousness of this. The enemy wants to destroy this expression, mask it, darken it, veil it.

I AM! In you! Believe it and act on it. Love and reach out to that which is Me expressed in others. See that and nothing else. Love one another!

One day God highlighted for me His essence expressed in the people I see daily. Suddenly I saw clearly my friend's tenderness, my father's patience, my mother's graciousness, my husband's servanthood, my son's enduring strength, my daughter's tender love for others, my sister's forgiveness. Though I had noticed these qualities, I had never viewed them as God's own life, His essence expressed uniquely in each one.

God planned for us to understand love. He sheltered children in families so each one could grow up with continual, consciousness-forming experiences of love. He made marriage so we could have repeated, building-block experiences of intimate, forever-love. A person who has a foundation of love, made solid and strong through continual love events impressed on his or her consciousness, is a person prepared to receive and respond to God's love. He wants our hearts so prepared that when we encounter Him, we can say, "I know you. I've known You all my life."

To remain in a state of heightened awareness of Him, where we allow Him to infuse the moments of our lives, we must choose to be alert. We can expect Him at any moment to manifest His presence. Most people won't experience lightning bolts or an angelic appearance. Nevertheless, He's there, breaking through the visible. He breaks through as spirit, not as something physical or material. That's why we earth-minded folks miss our divine moments.

One of His Biblical names is Jehovah Shammah, "God Is There." It implies being present and available. He is present, like the stag in the Song of Solomon 3:9.

> My beloved is like a roe or a young hart; behold he stands behind our wall, he looks forth at the windows, showing Himself through the lattice.

The language is intriguing: our ardent God stands behind our personal walls. He looks forth when we open a window. He shows Himself through our lattices, partial openings that allow His presence to be perceived.

Any time we open up entry to our spirits, due to a life event, a touching book or piece of music, He looks forth saying "See Me, notice Me, I want to talk with you." He is waiting to love, despite our fences. "Here I am," He's saying, "I want to have a relationship with you. I love you and I want you with Me now and for all eternity, loving and rejoicing with Me."

Chapter 4

All That We Cherish About Life Is Him.

Encounters with God

Early this morning, November mist rose along the Blue River. Vapor is a rare sight in Colorado's dry alpine climate. It occurs only when night's icy grip squeezes warmth from lake or stream and forces it into the atmosphere.

The river, whispering and babbling in conversation, exhaled frosty breath. Just then three mallards startled. They rose to the south into mist suffused by morning light. Stair-stepped in sharp ascent, unforgettable in beauty, they imprinted a memory.

Beauty is a spiritual thing, undefinable. When we pause to recognize and savor beauty, it enervates our spirits and brings us closer to God.

During a December cross-country ski tour into the snowy back country, the skis cut through diamond-dazzle snow, arcing a wave of white sea spray. The snow is fresh, the sky intense blue, the pines frosted like Christmas cookies. Snow nestles in the branch crooks of tawny aspen trees. Streams, yet to freeze, gurgle beneath the eiderdown snow. The hard work of breaking trail cleanses mind and body. Like a painting where each brush stroke is right, like a symphony with every note blended, the winter scene reflects God's harmony.

We Know God Better Than We Think

From God's point of view, we meet Him around every corner. He says we know Him better than we think.

I have experienced God through counseling work with young women.

...I am conversing with a girl my grown daughter's age. She's doing drugs and has a sexually transmitted disease. She has had two abortions. These leave her full of fear, bitterness, anger.

God's love rises up in me and she is my daughter. I find love pouring out for her, even though I don't know her well. It's God's love and sensing it I "know" God.

She feels it too and it softens her.

Love is mysterious because it is spirit. It's real, more real than natural earth-things, but it is not tangible. In the everyday setting of my office, God's love has touched two lives.

The key is to **recognize** I AM in these encounters. God wants us to know Him in the Biblical sense—intimate, experiential knowing. How many of these moments with God do we miss? His glory, His presence, the manifestation of His person breaking through the barrier of the ordinary, makes these times holy.

The scripture in Genesis says that Adam walked with God in the cool of the evening. God walks with us today, but we must recognize Him. Adam's sin has veiled our eyes to His presence. God wants to rip off that veil and show Himself as alive and real to us as He was to Adam.

God Desires To Be Known

I AM, hallelujah. I AM. Receive I AM. Perceive and understand I AM. Know Me as I AM. I am revealed to you now as I AM. Know Me.

I desire to be known. It is my strongest desire because I love you. "Please understand Me"—this plea is the cry of your heart, and of Mine as well. Please look at Me and **see** *Me. Please know Me. You would like Me. I am all that your heart desires, for I made you. You are My child.*

Please don't be just acquainted with Me, like Martha who entertained Jesus in her home and made herself so busy that she never listened to Him, never learned from Him.

She missed the most important thing because she took on worldly concerns and cares in the presence of the Lord. Mary, on the other hand, sat at Jesus' feet and listened. She gazed up at Him and studied His face. She watched His hands move. She drank Him in. As the Bible says, when we "behold Him we are changed from glory to glory." (2 Corinthians 3:18)

Know, My children, that there is a better way. Worldly concerns—work, home care, demands—are important. Just don't put them first. When there is an opportunity to be in My presence, snatch it and "work it" for all it's worth. Don't miss the day of your visitation. Always put me first, put knowing Me first, and the other things will be o.k. Start your day with the scriptures and with prayer, and see things work out better. In other words, "Seek first the kingdom of God and all these things will be given to you." (Matthew 6:33)

People in prosperous countries of the world enjoy full and free access to the things of God but fail to seize their opportunity. They rush past Him to their next pursuit.

Some people on this earth have never heard the name of Jesus. When the story of His life, including His crucifixion, is portrayed on screen in the villages of India, people weep openly. Their hearts are touched by the story of a savior they never knew. In Mongolia, Nepal, Sri Lanka, Malaysia, the Sudan, Algeria, Albania, there are people who have never heard the gospel. These people may never have the chance to know God. In China, a fire storm of revival is sweeping the land. People are willing to be martyred for Jesus Christ. They sacrifice everything to know Him.

Like the Chinese, a remnant people across the globe is now seeking God. Psalm 24:6 describes them:

> This is the generation of those that seek Him (who inquire of and for Him and of necessity require Him), who seek your face (O God of) Jacob.

This people yearns for God. They are hungry and thirsty for Him. They have fallen in love with Him. This people would die for Him (and have) because they have died to self, letting go all their hopes, dreams, ambitions espouse His hopes and dreams.

God Rewards Those Who Seek Him

When we seek God, really pressing in to know Him, we find Him. His word tells us, "He is the rewarder of those who earnestly and diligently seek Him." (Hebrews 11:6)

He will reward anyone who persistently seeks Him. His reward will be a revelation of who He is. Jesus emphasized this when He said, "Seek and you shall find. Knock and it will be opened to you." (Matthew 7:7)

We don't have to be whole or holy to seek Him. In the Book of Revelation, Jesus addresses the "L" church, the lazy, lethargic, lukewarm, last days Laodicea church, saying, "Behold, I stand at the door and knock. If anyone hears my voice and opens the door, I will come in and eat with him. (Revelation 3:20 RSV) He is humble and real. He says "Just reach out and knock. Don't focus on your sin or your hurt, focus on Me. I am available."

Like the man who obtained the pearl of great price in Jesus' parable, we have to "sell all we have" to get the great treasure. The seeking cannot be sporadic, half-hearted, second-rate or second-place. We must set aside time every day to seek His face, to read His word, pray and spend time gazing upon Him. We must let go of other activities to make time for Him. And we must give Him our best, most alert time of the day. Jesus offered practical, how-to instruction for us to live by when he said:

> Seek first of all His kingdom of God and His righteousness and then all these things taken together will be given you besides. (Matthew 6:33)

For many, first thing in the morning is the best time to seek God. The mind is fresh, a clean slate after sleep, and the pressures of the day have yet to begin. It takes self-discipline to rearrange the schedule to "diligently" seek Him. It takes faithfulness to do this seeking every day. Not a burst of two or three days now and then, but daily, diligent pursuit. That kind of seeking brings reward and the reward is a person, the I AM. God says, "I am...thy exceeding great reward." (Genesis 15:1 KJV)

How do we tap into this reward?

We know God the same way we know any other person: through conversation, observing, being together. We can trust God to talk to us. He uses His word to reveal Himself. He gives us impressions about Himself. (A spirit impression involves intuitive knowledge that happens in our inner person, a non-analytic "knowing" characterized by assurance and peace.) He gives us visions (mental pictures) in waking hours and dreams during sleep. He makes His presence known to us at moments during the day.

The Holy Spirit Will Reveal Jesus

The Holy Spirit will highlight the word of God, making it vivid and real. He will use the scripture to reveal Jesus. One day, the Holy Spirit spotlighted for me God's name as "The Lord of Hosts" or *Yahweh Sabbaoth*. I learned that the Lord of Hosts administers legions of angels, major groups of people and massive, large-scale works of God. Not only is He the Lord of Battles; I discovered that He is also Judge. Then I found in Isaiah 44:6 that the Lord of Hosts is our Redeemer, Jesus. The Lord of Hosts is the Lamb who redeemed us at the cross. He has earned the right to judge.

In His role as judge He uses refiners' fire. Malachi 3:1-5 explains that in these last days the Lord of Hosts will refine the priests and the Levites (those who have entered into the holy place to worship and minister to Him) and make them into pure gold, burning out dross and impurities.

Since refiner's fire burned hot for me at the time, I wanted to understand the Lord of Hosts who presides as refiner. The Holy Spirit opened my eyes to the person of the Lord of Hosts. It helped me accept the painful refining process, knowing that the Lamb who died had earned the right to judge sin in me.

The Holy Spirit made this facet of Jesus' personhood real to me through His word, the Bible, and also His personal *ramah* word to me. He revealed to me the wide scale work the Lord of Hosts, Yahweh Sabbaoth, is doing in the earth today.

We Can Know Father, Son and Holy Spirit

God delights in revealing Himself to His loved ones. He knows about love because He **is** Love. He knows His way around relationships, friendship, bondedness, intimacy and family belongedness because He originates love.

He is like a father home from a busy day at the office who takes his baby son up on his lap. The little one puts his hand on daddy's cheek and explores his face with chubby fingers. The baby looks into daddy's eyes. He is "knowing" his daddy. He is in his daddy's presence and his daddy is available to him. Even if the daddy is an important man at work, he is humble and patient with his son. In the same way, our Father puts aside the majesty of the throne room to make Himself, relaxed, real and available.

Jesus is Redeemer and Judge, but He is also the Bridegroom, fresh, ready and eager for His bride.

The Holy Spirit is the Spirit of Might. Yet He humbly works in people's hearts, slowly, patiently, quietly restoring wholeness, rejoicing at each sign of progress. The Holy Spirit rolls up His sleeves and gets in where it's smelly, dark and dirty, to clean up those places that still fester with hate, unforgiveness, pride, resentment, lust, addiction or idolatry. Our God is humble!

If we faithfully seek Him, we will find Him. But He won't cast pearls before swine. He won't indulge a fad or fancy or a burst of pseudo-spirituality. He honors consistent, sacrificial seeking. He says, "I am available and so ready for those who diligently seek Me. What I offer is an intimate relationship with Me."

Throughout scripture, God invites this kind of relationship. He said to David, "Seek ye My face." David replied, "Thy face, Lord, will I seek." (Psalm 27:8-9 KJV) He promised to reveal His secret self to those who hold Him in awe. His word says, "The Lord confides in those who fear him." (Psalm 25:14 NIV) God says of Himself, "I am no respecter of persons. What I will do for one, I will do for another." The qualifying factor is to apply careful, persistent effort.

How do we get started?

The same way we learn to ride a bicycle. We get on the bike. We straddle it. We begin to balance and pedal, despite feeling awkward and uncertain. We stick with it, no matter how unsuccessful our first try is. As with riding a bike, it's good for some beginners to have a patient helper to steady the bike while we get the hang of it. A patient friend can call out suggestions and give a firm push when needed. Other beginners do best on their own with a few simple instructions from the manual (in this case the Bible). The Holy Spirit is a patient counselor and guide, especially to those who have given Him full access by accepting the baptism of the Holy Spirit. (See Acts 2 for more). They discover new insight reading the word as He actively teaches them.

How I Heard From God

My personal experience took place alone in my room. Daily seeking God in scripture had yielded beautiful revelation of Him. I learned much about Him. But I wanted to sit and talk with Him. I had read about people who claimed to "hear" from God like a close companion would. Adam, the Book of Genesis says, fellowshipped with God. I wanted to experience His presence.

So one morning I informed the Lord, "I'm going to sit here and wait for you to speak to me. I'm going to do this every day until I hear from you."

The first and second day not much happened except a serene time of quiet—fine for a busy wife and mother of school-age children.

On the third day, I had a vision, one of only two He has given me in now over a decade of listening. The vision in March, 1985 pictured a glorious golden downpour. Heavy golden raindrops poured like a fountain of liquid light. I later understood it to be a vision of the rain of glory God has long promised to pour out.

Day by day, He began to speak to me, in words that burst into my mind. I wrote furiously to get them down on paper in the journal I had prepared for that purpose. Often the words I received from the Lord were tied to the scripture I had read during that morning's prayer time.

Now years later, what began as a daily sentence or two in my journal has emerged into profound revelation—prophecy, wisdom, bursts of insight into scripture, encouragement, elaboration on His word, cautions, direction on how to pray for family, friends, generation groups and geographic locations.

What I continue to do is diligently seek. No matter what the day brings, be it a rush to the airport or a relaxed Saturday morning, I set aside the time to seek Him first.

What God continues to do is reward me with precious experiences of Himself, with words that I cherish. They are my sapphires, rubies, diamonds and pearls. He has given me knowledge of Him, a treasure that will last for all eternity.

Chapter 5

I Am Available

God knows us and loves us. He is with us forever. He wants us to know Him now as the one who is present to us, "close to us as our skin," always present and available. He says, "I am here! I love you!"

One of Yahweh's Old Testament names, the names that begin with "I AM," is Jehovah Shammah, expressing the meaning, "I AM present and available to meet needs." We don't have to strive to enter the presence of Jehovah Shammah. We are already with our need-meeting God and He makes Himself available to us because He loves us so intensely.

Now I AM God. Instantly, closely present, intimately bound up with you, right here, right now. This is Jehovah Shammah in the fullness of His name. That is I AM, your present, available God, "Close as your next thought," they say, but I say even closer. Immediate, not next.

So rejoice that I AM and that I AM is as present to you as your own consciousness (or even more present because you can lose consciousness). But as present as what you are aware of and sensing right now. Each instant I AM with you, present and available.

You don't have to seek Me! I AM here and now! you can be aware of Me each instant if you turn your thoughts and attention to Me. You can "be with" Me at a higher level by heightening your awareness of Me.

God made man in His image so He could relate to each one of us. He wants us to know Him now as a God of Love in relationship with His people. He says:

Know Me as Moses knew Me, a person of greatness and glory, but knowable and humble in relationship because of love. There! I have revealed Myself to you. The Father's love is intimate and humble. And Jesus is the same with His bride—fresh and ready and eager. So know Me. And know the Holy Spirit of Might, humbly working in men's hearts, slowly, patiently, quietly waiting and rejoicing at each sign of progress.

Think of "knowing" God's availability using the Biblical meaning of the word "knowing": intimate experiential knowing. Think of this knowing as "coming to know"—progressively understanding. We perceive and recognize, gradually gaining a better and clearer knowledge of Him.

As we come to realize that He is truly always with us, we become aware that, conversely, we are truly always with Him. For us to experience this, we must actively chose to be with Him.

> Indeed I am with you, but you will never know the power of this 'withness' unless you are also with Me. Withness means to walk with, to talk with, to be with. Be with Me, as a child, and I will be with you, as a Father. (*Your Move God*, Sister Francis Clare, New Leaf Press, 1982)

The Father says, "I am available. I want you to yield to Me, to allow Me to be Father to you."

Jesus says, "I am available to My bride, bonded to you in love."

The Spirit says, "Just ask Me and I will do all that needs to be done to make you holy. No, you can't do this on your own, but I can and will do it. I am available to you to comfort, encourage, build up and sanctify."

God is present and available. He has everything to give and He wants to give it. He is with us, full to bursting with love, wisdom, peace, joy, blessing. We need only to "be with" Him. We need to make ourselves present and available to Him in order to participate in His availability. He is a person of great love who delights in loving. He has made you and me the object of His everlasting love. He seeks to be all in all to each of us. His invitation is, "Enter into My presence. Become conscious of Me, moment by moment. Walk with Me through your days. Sleep in My arms during your nights. Talk with Me, as a beloved father and friend. I will be just as present and open to you as you have faith to expect Me to be."

His love is not restrained or proper. It is passionate.

I love you with an everlasting love. I ache for you, long for you, yearn for you, as the lover yearns for the beloved. I will make Myself open and available to you because of this love. I will not stand on My position as Lord of All.

No! I will be ready to meet you and to meet your every need, as a lover is ready to meet the need of the loved one, as a father desires to meet the need of His precious child. So know Me as real, present and available ***to you****.*

God Offers Himself

Though God offers Himself to us in many ways that meet our deepest needs—as Father, as healer, as shepherd, as our rescuer—He wants most to offer Himself. He wants to be closer than a best friend, always ready in relationship to share time together, to talk, to just be with us.

God is the Great I AM. He is saying, "All that I am, I am **for you**. I exist to you and for you; that is, I am available."

We need to open our eyes and see Him. He is available, first, in relationship. He is as close as our next thought, pressing against the windowpane of our lives, ready to interact and be with us. Think about that. Almighty God is eager and ready, waiting to relate and talk and "be" with us.

Now I AM! Right now, right here, I AM. In your face, though you do not see Me, I AM. Right here present, right now available, giant and more real than your surroundings, I AM. Very big, I am, all encompassing. I AM right here, right now. Jehovah Shammah, the present and available God, like a mother dog with her puppies. (See, I have put pictures in nature.)

Now know Me as vitally present, excitingly alive, more right-here than you think or imagine. I am Life! I am alive! Intensely, actively alive, not remote, and not dead, as the world thinks of Me. I am vibrantly alive. What happens around you is not important because I am that real.

Oh, My people, I am pressing in on you, I am appearing at all your windows. I fill the space of every door. Notice Me! See Me! I am here!

What the Father is offering is "the pearl of great price," an intimate relationship with Him. When we experience that bondedness, with its intimate communication, it becomes the greatest treasure in our personal lives. Vital connection with the Living God makes us fully alive.

The Father is tender, gentle, unflappable and available. He is like a sweet Dad. We can go to Him with anything.

Afraid to seek Him because of sin? We can run to Him with a sin situation. He's open and gentle. The moment we confess the sin isn't the first time He becomes aware of it. He already knows. And He's waiting.

When our minds are bombarded with thoughts of anger and revenge or thoughts of rejection and abandonment, we can run to

Him. We can ask Him to give us His perspective on our situation. When we notice we're offended by someone, we can take it to Him. He will always set us on the right course. We can present to Him the very real and valid-seeming thoughts we're having and ask Him to judge them—are they authentic or not? He will guide us into truth and tell us how to respond. We should run **to** Him, not from Him.

Take hurts to Him. Don't dwell on them. Give them to Him to deal with. He will resolve them—if we let go and allow Him to do so.

Share joys with Him. He loves simple conversation such as, "Father. Look at the son you've given me. I'm so proud of him today." It's a balm to His heart as well as our own.

"Father, this car has a fine engine. Listen, Father, how it responds to the accelerator. Look how it handles this hill. Thank you Lord." He'll be pleased. He is interested in our interests because He loves us.

God loves to do what he does best. An athlete wants to use his body. A runner wants to run. He's got the training, the energy, the muscle power, the fitness and the desire to run. He wants to taste the joy of running. He knows he excels at running and he seeks every opportunity to run.

God is like that. He's full of love and power, abounding in wisdom, rich in mercy. He wants to exercise and use these qualities because He knows He excels at blessing His people. He is a Father with overflowing resources at His disposal and He wants to give to His children. When we ask, He is delighted to give.

Drawing on God's Goodness

He's a good God and He yearns to make His goodness available to us.

God is good; in fact, He is goodness itself. He expresses the essence of goodness, pure, unblemished goodness, expansive, abundant goodness. But we need to know His goodness before we can begin to draw upon it.

His goodness is better than the world's good and operates on a higher level. For example, righteousness and right living bring wholeness and integration to the human personality. Righteousness makes a person whole. But sin fractures the personality, bringing confusion, disorder and unhappiness. Sin may seem good, but it brings only temporary, short-term "good" while righteousness brings eternal, lasting, indestructible good.

God is goodness who is a person. He wants us to look for Him, as goodness, in the world around us. That's one way we will know Him as goodness. He also wants us to express His goodness to others. Goodness resides inside us as a fruit of the Spirit. Deep calls to deep; goodness seeks to link up with goodness, magnetically drawn to another's goodness. Combined you have a bit of God's glory.

The one who knows God's goodness receives His goodness and His mercy. The one who relates to God as goodness plugs into Him. Recognizing God as good activates His flow of goodness toward us. His name is *Jehovah Shammah,* the present available God, or literally "The Many Breasted One." To humbly acknowledge our need and draw near in faith to the Many Breasted One activates the flow.

Though He seeks to be available to us first in person-to-person relationship, He also yearns to be the one to meet our needs. He is sufficient and He knows it. He wants us to draw on Him.

Our Need-Meeting God

Today I AM in your life all that you need. Avail yourself of Me, for I Am your protection, your strength, your provision, your wisdom and your unfailing close companion. Drink from Me. Draw from Me. Learn from Me, for I will show you "great and mighty things which you know not." (Jeremiah 33:3)

I promised it in My word for those who worship Me. So today know and learn of Me, My child, for I am your Shepherd who will lead you into repose.

The God of our hearts stands before us saying, "I am all that you need. Avail yourself of Me." Because we are so earth-minded, it's difficult for us to accept and believe His words. So we continue to look for love, comfort, wisdom and security in all the wrong places.

We seek love from people. They let us down. We seek comfort from alcohol or pills. Wisdom from the world's gurus, talk shows and media stars. Security from money and position. Joy from buying beautiful things. We try to drain life from people we love. We're never satisfied.

God says, "Drink of Me. I will satisfy you with life, love, light."

How we need that life to overwhelm and transform our death, our clinging to negativity, our never-ending attempt to suck life from deadness. If we could yank our gaze off the world's shallow resources and fix it onto God, we would see our needs met.

God's ways are not our ways. His satisfaction of our need

may not be instant. A man suffering grief from the loss of a son may pray and find that God's comfort just doesn't seem real, tangible or available. God's word promises comfort, but we don't really believe Him.

Alcohol, on the other hand, offers quick relief.

Creature comforts appear real and available. The problem is they fail. The comfort they offer is temporary and there's always a negative payback involved, often in the form of addiction. Addiction leads to idolatry. Whenever we direct an abnormal amount of thought, imagination, planning and activity toward something other than God, it becomes a false god.

If we have the courage to undergo the gut-wrenching change of gears, to take our eyes off the natural and to focus on God, and if we can forego instant delivery in exchange for genuine, long term, real deliverance from the problem, we will get the genuine satisfaction we crave.

Of course, it takes faith and patience. Like quitting smoking, it takes hanging in there during the hard times. The end result is freedom from dependence on false need-meeting devices, but the weaning process requires persevering trust.

When we see our prayer as unanswered, we feel tempted to give up on God. We believe that it "doesn't work for us." But the problem lies with us. Ignorance of His ways, and our familiarity with the quick-fix way humans operate, causes us to mistrust Him and His faithfulness.

The way to overcome is to believe in His goodness, *no matter what happens.* Often He needs to first change us to be able to properly answer our prayer. That may take time. But when we continue to trust in His character as a good God, the answer comes. God's answer may not be what our shortsighted request entailed; His answer will probably be bigger and better than we imagined.

The answers God offers are true and eternal and lasting. He wants us to experience His goodness, not the world's. In the end, He Himself is the answer. He Himself is the provision, the wisdom, the comfort or the joy we seek.

When we seek Him, we find Him. What a reward we earn!

I Am and I am a rewarder of those who diligently seek Me. See that word "rewarder." I am your Rewarder. I am your Recompense.

Think about it! Your reward is a person, the Most High God! I will increase your greatness and comfort you on every side. Receive, receive of all that a Father's hand desires to give from the God of Love.

God offers us intimacy with Him.

Intimate, Present God

"Intimate" implies physical, emotional, intellectual and spiritual closeness. An intimate is allowed into the private place where others are shut out. One properly enters that inner circle of intimacy via a love relationship.

"Present" means readily available, at hand, in the immediate vicinity. A stronger meaning, one that we will use here, is "occurring in or existing in."

In His words to His disciples just hours before His death, Jesus defined the intimate present relationship God has with us.

> At that time (when that day comes) you will know (for yourselves) that I am in My Father and you (are) in Me and I (am) in you.
>
> The person who has My commandments and keeps them is the one who (really) loves Me; and whoever (really) loves Me will be loved by My Father, and I (too) will love him, and will show (reveal, manifest) Myself to him. (I will let Myself be clearly seen by him and make Myself real to him.)
>
> Judas (not Iscariot) asked Him, Lord, how is it that you will reveal Yourself (make yourself real) to us and not the world?
>
> Jesus answered, If a person (really) loves Me, he will keep My word (obey My teaching) and My Father will love him and We will come to him and make Our home (special dwelling place) with him. (John 14:20-23)

Jesus and the Father dwell in us. His presence can't get much closer. The Lord of eternal glory lives within us.

The Son of the God of Love, perfect representation of the Father of Love and of the Father's love, says: know Me. Know My heart. Understand Me. Recognize Me. Witness to and of Me. For I AM great and lovely and glorious to My people.

Passionate Love

The Holy Spirit uses the "Song of Solomon" to express the passionate yearning of this intimate relationship.

> Behold, you are beautiful, my love!...You have ravished my heart...How beautiful is your love, my sister, my (promised) bride....Set me as a seal upon your

> heart...Rise up, my love, my fair one and come away... Make haste, my beloved, and come quickly, like a gazelle or young hart (and take me to our waiting home) upon the mountains of spices. (Song of Solomon 1:15 2:10, 4:9.10, 8:6, 14)

The Shulammite woman, a figure of the bride of Christ, declares, "My beloved is mine, and I am his." That intimate sense of belonging to one another characterizes our relationship with God.

This closeness between persons united by love and dwelling as one is a vital, exciting relationship. Those who really love Him and seek out this intimate relationship have it as a treasure in their lives. Intimacy is available to more than a special few. Jesus declared, "Whoever (really) loves Me will be loved by My Father and I too will love him and will show (reveal, manifest) Myself to him." (John 14:21)

Whoever means whoever. The qualification is to love Him and show it by keeping His commandments.

Jesus instructed, "You will know (for yourselves) that...you are in Me and I (am) in you." Remember, the Biblical word "know" implies intimate, experiential knowledge. We gain that closeness by spending quality time with Him.

Evangelist James Robison tells a story of his close friendship with Jesus. Even as a teenage boy James Robison knew through repeated experiences that God was present with him and in him. As soon as high school classes ended in the afternoon, he would run to a place in the woods where he met Jesus. "He always got there first," James remembers. "He was waiting for me."

Jesus talked to a fatherless boy raised in poverty and rejection, telling James how God viewed him and giving him a mission as an evangelist. God became the father James never had. The Lord built a strong foundation in a boy who grew up on little parenting and less love. Jesus was intimate, present and available to a young man hungry for God.

James fell in love with his future wife, Betty, during those late teen years. He once told her, "Betty, Jesus is more real to me than you are." That an 18-year old boy in love could say this communicates one fact: Jesus was really real to James.

The Lord is intimate and present to me and my Christian friends in the same way. He talks to us daily. He gives insight for our jobs, our family relationships, our service to Him.

God Wants to Tells Us About Himself

I know what God Almighty is thinking about today because He told me. Sometimes He rejoices with me so exuberantly that I am astounded, even a bit embarrassed, by His unfettered expression of joy.

Sometimes He tells me what's on His heart for me or my loved ones. Often He explains the broad moves of the Almighty across the earth or His present work in the body of Christ. (He has formed a purified, faithful people for Himself and He is overjoyed about it.)

Occasionally He asks me to grieve with Him over the Judgement coming on the world, weeping with me for His errant but nevertheless beloved children who will suffer in this Judgement. He has repeatedly wooed them from their ties to the world, but they have refused to come to Him and His place of safety. He expresses His need for solace from His beloved, the comfort He draws from those who truly know Him and know His heart. He asks for support, even praise, during the time of Judgement.

He reveals to me unseen realms, unlocking for me the mysteries in His word. He often takes a passage of scripture and explodes my understanding. Then He will elaborate on it, showing me its connection to other truths in the word, giving me a glimpse of the "big picture". He leaves me amazed. And humbled.

Jesus said in the John 14 passage quoted earlier, "At that time you will know for yourselves that...you (are) in Me and I (am) in you." That day, the day of intimate, present God relating to His people, has fully come. It is still fully available to anyone who seeks it. Jesus invites all in the Book of Revelation saying, "Behold, I stand at the door and knock. If any man opens to Me, I will come in and fellowship with him." (Revelation 3:20)

That fellowship means intimate friendship with an available, present God.

God Is Available In Fullness

God is I AM. His is **all** that He is. And He makes that fullness available to us.

Jesus came to bring life in abundance. We have reached the end of time and entered the harvest season when we will see fullness, mature ripeness, repleteness and abundance. The word of God will yield its full power anointing. Prophecy will be fulfilled. The maturity and full-fruit season of God's people has arrived and God has a time of harvest blessing planned for His righteous. He is available in the abundance of life Jesus came to bring, the abundant life reflected in His name, I AM.

I am your Recompense.

Oh, yes! Know Me now, today, as your Recompense, for I will show you fullness of all that that name means. Oh, I will show you "great and mighty things you know not of." Things you didn't dream or imagine or know to wish for I will do for those that love Me.

Reward. Now is the time of reward, My people, O My beloved people. My own. So get ready now for massive reward coming on the body of Christ, My people, My own reward.

Your inheritance. There's a will. There's been a death (My own). My will is validated. And now, the inheritance in full shall be yours. Rejoice! The abundance that I, Jesus, came to bring is here, on the brink of arrival, is come, just about come.

Behold, I stand at the door and knock. If any man will open the door and let Me in, I will ***fellowship*** *with him.*

I'm ready! Open that door to real personal relationship with Me and see what happens! Life! Life more abundantly. I will be life to him. Abundant life!

God says, "I am all that you need Me to be in your life today." His title, I AM, is a vitally present-tense name. He is an immediate, now God. He is Life, vibrant, genuine, lasting Life. He is available right now to be all that we need. The question is, can we accept His offer?

> Wait and listen, everyone who is thirsty! Come to the waters; and he who has no money, come, buy and eat! Yes, come, buy (priceless, spiritual) wine and milk without money and without price (simply for the self-surrender that accepts the blessing). ...Eat what is good and let your soul delight itself in fatness (the profuseness of spiritual joy.) (Isaiah 55:1-2)
>
> To the thirsty I (Myself) will give water without price from the fountain (springs) of the water of Life." (Revelation 21:6)

His offer is authentic. Do we realize our need? Will we yield to take advantage of His availability?

I am today, now, all that you need Me to be in your life today. I am to you what I Am, available, present, waiting to be needed and asked.

It takes a shift of gears, an attitude change, to be "thirsty" before God. We must recognize our needs and bring those needs to Him. In the Book of Revelation Jesus rebukes the smug Laodicean church, located in a city which produced a popular eye balm, advising them to buy eye salve from Him because they were blind and didn't realize it.

The Amplified Bible wording of Isaiah 55:1 brings out the idea of "self surrender that accepts the blessing." Yieldedness to the blessing.

God says "now, today." When we are thirsty, when do we ask for a drink? Right now! When we are hungry, when do we want the restaurant to seat us? Now! (Remember Pharaoh. When Moses' asked when he wanted to be rid of the plague of frogs, he replied, "Tomorrow.")

He is promising to answer our need today. He's saying, "Ask Me! Bring it to Me. I'm here waiting to meet your needs. You don't need to qualify (have money) to buy the priceless spiritual provision I will give. I will give you what I am. From out of Me, I will give you peace, truth, goodness."

NOW I AM God; there is no other. Rejoice that I will show My Self forth as I AM NOW. Right now I AM, RIGHT HERE. Oh, hallelujah, you will see it and "know" it.

Go and do likewise: be alive, like Me. Choose life in every case, the choices that don't seem good or natural to you but are My way. Choose life as I see it, not as you, in your flesh, see it. Remember the Beatitudes—they are My way. The meek (gentle and humble) shall inherit the earth.

My ways are not your ways, but My ways win! Choose life. Choose Me and My ways to succeed—the way of peace over turmoil, the way of joy over deep, deep sorrow. In rest is your peak efficiency. In surrender is power. In yieldedness, victory. See things from My perspective, then go and do. This is faith--living belief. Take the risk. It will pay off.

• • •

At the core of our personhood, God dwells.

He is, in us, our Life.

He is Love. His love persists, yearning for closeness.

He is Light. He shines resplendent through our surrendered lives.

All that we find exquisite...quintessence of spirit...goodness we cannot grasp...is in I AM.

Section Two

I AM Life, Love, Light

God wants us to behold Him

as Life

as Love

as Light.

In beholding Him, we are changed.
Awake to His presence within us,
we become like Him,
fully alive, loving, radiant.

Then we shine Him into the lives of others.

Moses beheld I AM
and witnessed Him to God's people.
We will experience the fullness of I AM
Who is

Life

Love

Light

and we will change the people we touch.

Chapter 6

I AM Life

God is alive! His personality exudes vitality, freshness, reality, animation, passion, spirit, energy and newness. This exuberant person lives in us. He wants to express His life through us.

Though it may shake up our theology, we need to know our God as a person brimming with life and fun. Yes—fun! He loves to laugh. He likes to joke and play. Listen to Him describe Himself:

Now I AM God and I will reveal Myself to you personally. Yes, personally. I desire to be intimate with My people, as I said when I instructed Noah to build the ark. Now I AM God. Listen to Me: I AM God. What does that mean? Living God. Life-God. Life is God; God is Life. Alive! I am Fullness of Life. Think of what life at its ultimate peak would be—aliveness in full. That's Me. Brimming with Life.

Attractive? Yes! Beautiful and exciting to you? Yes! That's what and who I AM! Get it? That's Me!

The genie pictured in the film "Aladdin" wasn't so far off. The joy, the multiplicity, the variety, the peak perfection the life and aliveness—yes, that's like Me.

You are going to enjoy Me. I am fun, lots of fun. Holy, righteous, majestic, yes. But fun, pure plain fun. Who do you think invented fun! Me! I did. I am fun. I like to laugh (I made that, too).

I am majestic and holy, an awesome God. But with My intimates, like a family man, I laugh and have fun. Heaven is going to be very fun for you. I like play. I do! I made it up. Play is from Me. Oh, hold onto this: play is from Me. Fun is from Me. Relaxation and joy are from Me. That's why you feel at your best and highest then because these things are from Me.

Oh, how I desire to give My best to My children—just as you do. You're made in My image and likeness—except what's twisted. Know that we are a lot alike. I can relax and play as well as be holy and sit upon My throne. Let's have fun together because I am a fun, a real fun, God.

All what you love best—that's Me. The greeting card stuff, that's Me. The enthusiasm of a puppy—that's Me. The passion of romance—that's Me.

God Stirs Life from Our Dormancy

God has planned for nature to reveal His nature. Earth's best revelation of God's life happens in springtime when insistent life stirs dormant roots in dead earth. Life pushes and presses, stirring sap and swelling the bud to burst. In the earth-grave, life explodes the seed case, a birthing eruption.

Our flesh is like the seed case, imprisoning God's vibrant life within.

British poet T.S. Eliot wrote, "April is the cruellest month, breeding lilacs out of the dead land...stirring dull roots with spring rain." Yanked from sleep, the pale sprout must bulldoze its way through blackness to burst forth into the light.

In a similar way, God's life within us must break through the darkness of our mind, will and emotions, even our physical bodies. How many times have we wanted to reach out to someone and held back? How many times have we decided to invest more time in prayer, then failed to do it? That is the flesh resisting life.

Springtime's urge, persistent and inexorable, pushes toward growth, flourishing and profuse. Exuberant life is the kind Jesus came to bring. His mission statement, "I came that they might have and enjoy life, and have it in abundance (to the full, till it overflows)" (John 10:10) will be perfectly and completely fulfilled. When God brings it to pass in us, this abundant, thriving, profuse life will seem to us like **heaven on earth.**

His life hidden inside us also has a springtime. Our own life has to yield, our thoughts, feelings, attitudes surrender to Him. As our flesh dies, the seed case bursts open and the cataclysm of springtime in the Spirit brings forth life.

The seed of self must die in darkness first. Just as Jesus died and entered a tomb, we also die, die to ourselves and our own self-interest. During that time in the valley of death, we need to let go and die, so the seed case of His life can break open and burst forth life. Like the life-burst of His resurrection, the life of God bursts within us, in His perfect timing. His life within us grows, multiplies, sends forth shoots, reaches for the light.

Yes! I AM. I reveal to you Myself as I AM. The very life of God springing up in all directions in your life. Springtime urge. pressure, insistence to life. Understand it is I who makes you alive. I AM your life. That's who I AM. I reveal myself to you as life, as I AM today.

We shouldn't despise the winter of our souls. The time spent in darkness stirs us to seek Him. We press in to His presence, as the spindly white shoot rushes to grow sunward. There we find life. His presence, like the seedling's burst into the spring sun, makes life leap within us.

Becoming Alive, Like Him

God wants us to become intimately acquainted with Him as Life so we can witness His life. His cherished dream for each of us is to give us abundant life. Our job is to surrender to the process and support it with praise. He wants us to continually praise Him as He works within to make us fully alive, as alive as a God-infused human person can be. That praise needs to flow, even in the dead season.

God's vision for each unique son and daughter to be fully alive is more than we can now imagine, but it will be revealed in fullness. (He will perfectly fulfill His word—and soon!) God is so alive that His name can raise the dead. Jesus IS the Resurrection and the Life. I AM dwells in His people in fullness, as all He IS.

Whether we're conscious of it or not, most of us do experience moments of God's presence. The way most people respond to a May morning illustrates the way people respond to His breaking through our boundaries. When we're in His presence in a time of quiet communion with Him, in worship with others or alone with Him in His creation, His life and energy make us feel intensely alive.

When we step outdoors on a sunny May morning, the world seems right. We're energized. People start jogging, gardening, throwing frisbees around in May. God's presence invigorates like that. Once sensitized to His presence, we enjoy a heightened daily awareness of Him, joy and a consciousness of the harmony that His Life-presence brings. Problems melt away. Peace washes over us. This blissful sense of wholeness transmits from God's manifest presence. It's fun and so refreshing to spend time with Him. It's also life-changing.

I AM. The excitement of it, the dynamism of it, the sheer life that I AM is being revealed to God's people. I am Life! Oh, that My people would understand that I AM, who I am. I long for it, to reveal Myself to My beloved. I AM.

God wants us to recognize Him as the exuberant, alive,

divine person who indwells us. The joy and power in that realization can change the world. He is the life that makes alive all the created universe and beyond. He wants His people to know Him and to acknowledge Him before angels, demons and men, with our unshakeable conviction that He is God. He is Life and death cannot stand before Him. He aches for us to really hear Him say absolutely and irrevocably, "I AM." Every problem and obstacle melts under the power of that statement. He aims to overcome His last enemy, death, in and through us.

God's life resurrects. He can take death and turn it to life. Our spirits are reborn in Him. God wants to take our dead souls, that is, our mind, will and emotions, and give us new life. Through His ministering Holy Spirit, He restores souls numbed by grief, stunted by loss, deadened by despair, damaged by abuse, Even our bodies He will purify, resurrect and clothe in glory. He wants us to surrender all to Him so He can infuse all we are with His life. He wants His people alive!

I am the life in you. I am in you alive and bursting with life energy. My life energy released in you will make you better, stronger, more alive because I AM lives in you and is your life.

Know Me in life. When you see it and its accompanying joy, rejoice! Life in abundance, abundant God-life, is what Jesus came to bring.

Life Generates Life

How do we reproduce the life of God within us?

In the natural sphere, we release soul life by expressing life. Our body language expresses it and it's contagious. We let it flow, touching other's lives with its vitality and joy. Who can watch a delighted toddler rush to greet his daddy without feeling delight? If we remain joyously aware that I AM resides at the core of our personhood, our facial expression, our walk, our behavior will spill over with life.

Spiritual things reproduce just as natural things do. Life brings forth more life. Love reproduces new love. Light regenerates as light.

For example, life flows from a good teacher to a student when words of encouragement, challenge and inspiration bring forth life in the student. Potential actualizes; skills blossom; a variety and profusion of growth results. A parent loving a child, for example, creates love within him or her and the child shares that new love with others. Light spreads. In the natural world, light from the sun is regenerated on earth as warmth, life, growth and energy. On a human intellectual level, the light of truth springing from the genius of Albert Einstein brought new light to scientific minds around the globe.

But God's creative I AM life in us can bring forth more life than we can ask or imagine. Just as a peach produces seed to reproduce something much greater, a peach tree, His life brings forth according to its kind—spirit life. Its vitality, diversity and multiplicity are beyond our ability to understand.

Our Words Create Our Worlds

Richer than physical expression is verbal expression. God's life emerges from our spirits, coming through the soul (mind, will, emotions) with words. Made in the image of God who spoke life into creation, we speak life. God's life takes on flesh via these natural expressions.

Our natural words of comfort, healing, truth or love can bring wholeness to another human being.

In the spiritual realm God offers an even more powerful way to recreate the world around us with words. One way is to speak God's own words, those found in the Bible, in faith. These words from I AM, who is Life, bring forth life.

Another way we can use words as spirit-expression to bring forth life relies on the words of the Holy Spirit to achieve a pure flow of God's life. We can pray in the Spirit. Jesus spoke about giving us springs of living water.

Jesus told His listeners, "...if you ask the Father, He will give you the Holy Spirit." (Luke 11:13) and "He who believes in Me...From his inmost being shall flow (continuously) springs and rivers of living water." (John 7:38) Those rivers of living water are words of life, uttered through us by the Holy Spirit who dwells within.

As we drink this water, we come to know Him intimately, experience Him for ourselves. Not book knowledge, but experiential knowing, "being with" knowing, as intimates know one another. We experience His life, resurgent life, dynamic life, I AM life.

Jesus told the Samaritan woman at the well:

> The water that I will give him shall become a spring of water, welling up (flowing, bubbling continually) within him unto eternal life. (John 4:14)

Our Life Is A Person

The scriptures identify Jesus as our life. "He who possesses the Son has this life." (1 John 5:12) Our life is a person and that person is Jesus Christ. "Christ who is our life" (Colossians 3:4) abides in us. He makes us alive and He IS our life. We are so identified with Jesus that He is the very who of who we are. When the Spirit works to release in us more life, He is working to establish and release Jesus, to allow Jesus to shine through our flesh veil. Our life is in Him. He is at our core, our essence. We are expressions of His aliveness, His life and personhood.

When we see natural life, our response is joy. When we plant a tree and it takes hold, we're delighted. Birds at the feeder fascinate us. Just being around someone full of vitality makes us glad.

In a fireworks display, people ooh and aah when a large explosion of light explodes, then quickly another light fountain pours out from the first. That's how joy pours out of life.

The Great I AM reveals Himself as Life to each of us. We respond with joy. Psalm 16:11 proclaims, "In your presence is fullness of joy." In response to a genuine, personal experience of God as Life, and understanding His work in our lives to reproduce life abundant, we are filled with joy.

I AM. Know Me as I am, source of Life! Life! Life! Eternal life, life itself. Essence of life. What life is—is Me! Know Me in life, when you see it, and its accompanying joy. Rejoice!

Life in abundance is what Jesus came to bring. Not death. Life! Anything that's death is not of Him. Know this. Prepare your heart in joy for My coming. Change your thought in each situation to joy. Don't look at your teenager, your spouse, your job and be depressed. Rejoice in My ability to restore—and My desire to do so. Come into a new kind of prayer life in praise and joy, not praying the problem but praying the joyous blessing heart of the Father and His ability in power, wisdom, love, to bless and restore. I am Life!

Nothing can shake or disturb this joy because we know that the God who is Life is present and available to us. He is ready to be Father, to protect, feed, guide and nurture. We come to Him with our needs, which are often aspects of death. Financial lack, physical illness, mental instability, danger, destructive relationships—all wear the face of death. We can prophesy life into death areas as Ezekiel prophesied to the dry bones of Israel in Ezekiel 37. When we raise our vision to look upon Him and see life, those death problems fade. When God's life breaks through our surrendered flesh and is allowed to flow freely, we can put it to work touching death around us with vibrant life.

I've seen suicidal depression in a 20-year old overcome, cancer in an old friend eradicated, a critically ill baby instantly healed, a fatally brain-injured young woman restored, all overwhelming obstacles that faded when we looked at Jesus.

Witness the Resurrection and the Life. He doesn't author death. As Life, He cannot negate Himself. No lack, sickness or failed love comes from Him. Instead, His life flows in to restore. His life brings forth life. Confronting this, we must respond with joy, despite negative circumstances. This is faith at its peak level.

Jesus Is Life

Jesus, who is Life, exemplifies joy. His joy is exuberant. Hebrews 1:9 says, "God (the Godhead) has anointed you with the oil of exultant joy and gladness above and beyond your companions." He foresaw the life that His death would release. "He, for the joy that was set before Him, endured the cross." (Hebrews 12:2)

The great joy of Jesus' heart is to fulfill His mission in coming to earth. His mission statement, given in John 10:10, was "I came that they might have and enjoy life, and have it in abundance (to the full, till it overflows)." Jesus rejoices as the day of God's fullness dawns and the time for Him to give all He promised has arrived.

The joy level in heaven is reaching a peak. Jesus is exuberant with joy because He comes to rule the land. He is coming into the fullness of His reign. This is a time of great, great joy. All the life outflowing from His cross is now springing forth in absolute fullness. He is filled with joy.

As we yield to His work in us, we become a witness to I AM, demonstrating His vitality and life. In His continual presence, our joy will become full.

What's the secret of obtaining joy? Hang around Jesus.

Chapter 7

I AM Love

I AM is a God of love. He aches for us to really know Him as Love. When we experience love, we need to leap to the realization: that's Him!

We've all experienced love. Real love is of the spirit. Do we understand that love is out of God? God is love. Conversely, Love is God.

This awesome person named "I AM Love" will soon do some I AM-ing. Prepare for the Age of the Father's Love. His love abiding in us will set the captives free. His anointing of compassion in us will overcome all the world's hate. His love will not die in this dark world but will leap from heart to heart. His love will transform lives and usher in His glory.

Love will motivate us to reach out in the anointing. Love overcomes the fear of men which causes us to hold back. Jesus, the Anointed One, came because of love. God sends us in the name of I AM to be living witnesses of His love.

Deep speaks to deep. Our love can reach deep with love into the person we want to touch. When our loves connects with the "image and likeness of God" love inherent in that person, we will see God's anointing flow.

The God who is Love wants us to experience His love now, as He pours out His love like never before.

The Father's love is so great that He sent His only Son for us. What is an only son worth? Would any of us send a cherished child into a scene of brutal rejection? Would we allow him to be cat-called by religious leaders, struck, scourged, spit on and crucified?

The Father, Lord of Heaven and Earth, disentangled His precious Son from the embrace of His heart and ordained His birth in a Bethlehem stable reeking with livestock dung. He allowed His Son's life blood to be spilled on Calvary's dusty soil.

This love made Almighty God vulnerable. His heart was broken in love for His errant children. Would His offer of salvation through His Son be rejected? Would He send the very image of Himself, His best expression, and be scorned?

The Father's humble, giving, self-sacrificing love is mirrored in the love of Jesus. He suffered a pain that experts say is the human body's most excruciating. The Romans made crucifixion an art, hammering the hand nail into a critical nerve of the wrist, the human body's most sensitive. Yet the scriptures say He *gave* His life.

Jesus wanted to give more. The Father and the Son together gave those who asked Their own spirit, the Holy Spirit. Imagine giving one's own spirit—how intensely personal and intimate that gift is. Humble, sacrificial giving characterizes the love of God expressed in Jesus.

Growing In Love

Experiencing God's love is a process. Our knowledge of God expands and deepens as we progressively know Him. As we observe, recognize and understand God's love, we become increasingly aware of it and believe in it, putting faith in His love in real life situations.

God is longing for us to enter His embrace. He says:

The God of Love waits. Behold, I stand at the door and knock. Anyone who opens to Me, I will go in and fellowship, commune, share intimacy and love with that person. Know Me as the God of Love who waits expectantly for My people to say "yes." The Song of Solomon pictures the stag coming to the window, the lattice, any opening in the beloved's heart, waiting there expectantly. Yes! That is how I am with My people, waiting expectantly to enter into full communion with each one.

As we move closer into the embrace of the God who is Love, our shared love comes to completion and perfection. Is that exciting? Yes! All the delight, keenness, passion, eagerness, zest and joy of natural love and more characterize a growing love relationship with God.

I AM THAT I AM. I AM WHAT I AM. I AM WHO I AM and I AM LOVE. Love is Me, God, and I am love. Know love—that's Me.

Ask to know Me as the love person. I AM WHO AM LOVE.

"Know Me as love" is a call to come up higher. I call you to approach this mountain as Moses did, without fear or trembling but with trust and joy and a sense of adventure, a sense of joy in the exciting process.

Love begets love. As we grow in love with God, we just

naturally love those around us. We see God in them. And knowing Him as love, we understand how He loves each one of us. We participate in that love.

> Beloved, let us love one another, for love is of God and he who loves is born of God and knows God. He who does not love does not know God; for God is love. (1 John 4:7-8 RSV)

Jesus commanded:

> You shall love the Lord your God with all your heart and with all your soul and with all your mind (intellect)...You shall love your neighbor as (you do) yourself. (Matthew 22:37, 39)

Jesus explained that the begetting process began with the Father: "As the Father has loved Me, so I love you." The next natural step came in this directive: "This I command you, to love one another." (John 15:9, 17)

Love makes dying to the flesh easier. For example, forgiving someone who has hurt us may seem unthinkable. But when we make a choice to love that person, daily blessing them and daily praying for them, the forgiveness flows. Witnessing our faith to someone might seem to call for a boldness we don't possess until love melts away the fear of men. We can step out, across and over fear of rejection when love motivates us to tell someone else about Jesus.

The person who is Love lives within us and is our very life.

> So we know and believe the love God has for us. God is love and he who abides in love abides in God and God abides in him. In this is love perfected with us... (1 John 4:16 RSV)

God's big dream is that His presence, expressed in each of us as Love, would be a unique, unrepeatable, one-of-a-kind witness of Him.

Progressively knowing Him as love is a process that we must initiate now. Just think: once begun here on earth, our vital love relationship with God will intensify forever.

Intimacy, the Power Source

To "know" means power-in-love. It implies an intimacy that guarantees favor. God taught the ancient Israelites that to know His name and all that it signified gave them special access to

Him. Mary, the mother of Jesus, understood this privilege when she prevailed on Him to do the miracle of the wine at the Cana wedding, even though He protested that it was not yet His time.

Jacob also had developed a relationship with God. Because he contended with God, Genesis 32:28 says "you...have power with God and with man and have prevailed." After his all-night encounter with a figure that scholars identify as Jesus, Jacob became a changed man and God changed his name to signify the transformation. "Thy name shall be called no more Jacob but Israel..."

Jacob contended with God and knew Him. Jesus prayed about this intimate knowing to the Father when He said, "I have manifested your name (I have revealed your very Self, your real Self) to the people who You have given Me..." In that knowledge is favor. "My Father will grant you what you ask in My name (as presenting all that I AM)." (John 16:23)

God is no respecter of persons, but our love relationship with Him yields power in intercession. When two or more who love Him are gathered together in His name, the corporate prayer power synergizes. The corporate anointing accomplishes things.

Jesus said He only spoke what He heard the Father saying. His listening to the Father took place in the "secret place of the Most High" (Psalm 91:1), the love abode where two spend time together. When He did one of His greatest miracles, raising a three-day dead Lazarus, Jesus didn't have to beg or plead with the Father. He simply said, "I know that you hear Me." And then, "Lazarus, come forth!"

A loved one has only to whisper a request and the need is met by the beloved. When we sit at the Father's feet, listening and talking with Him daily, we know whether or not He hears us. We're **certain** He does.

The power anointing comes from the presence of God and deep, intimate knowing Him. As we gaze upon Him, we become more and more like Him, in love and in power. The power flows when His Spirit stirs us, by impressing us with someone's need, burdening us with prayer or searing a truth within for us to proclaim. We remain surrendered and available to speak or act in the way He directs.

> Do you not believe that I am in the Father and that the Father is in Me?...the Father Who lives in Me does the works (His own miracles, deeds of power). (John 14:10)

Intimate love and knowledge yield a surpassing trust in the

availability of His power to save, heal, deliver. Intimacy produces:

> the (deep and intimate) knowledge of Him...(so that you can know and understand) what is the immeasurable and unlimited and surpassing greatness of His power in and for us who believe... (Ephesians 1:19)

Nevertheless, this power doesn't originate with us. "Power belongs to God." (Psalm 62:11) It resides in His word and His anointing. "We have this treasure in earthen vessels, to show that the transcendent power belongs to God." (2 Corinthians 4:7) Our humanity, our ability to goof up, our weakness, all accompany the awesome power of God within. In fact, God likes it that way. He told Paul, "My power is made perfect in weakness." (2 Corinthians 12:9 RSV)

Today, God's people walk in power. The authority of the spoken word coming from the hearts and mouths of God's people breaks down strongholds and ushers in the glory of God. This is power-in-love. The Holy Spirit, speaking in Psalm 110:3, declares, "Your people will offer themselves willingly in the day of your power." This yieldedness to His power is done in love. Those who choose to go through refining fire because of their sacrificial love receive anointed power.

What God is preparing us for is a kingdom of love. We say God is Love. Conversely, Love is God. If the two are interchangeable, which they are, we can also put "Love" into other phrases describing God. Instead of "God reigns," try "Love reigns."

That's just what God has in mind, a reign of love through His Son, Jesus, and through His worshipping people.

Obedience, the Evidence of Love

How do we know whether we have that kind of love? Simple. We check our obedience. Jesus demonstrated His love for the Father in a simple way: He obeyed Him. "...I love the Father and do only what the Father has instructed Me to do. (I act in full agreement with His orders.)" (John 14:32) He asks the same of us. "If you really love Me you will keep (obey) My commands." (John 14:15) The disciple of love, John, wrote in his letter to his brothers:

> But he who keeps (treasures) His word (who bears in mind His precepts, who observes His message in its entirety) truly in Him has the love of and for God been

> perfected (completed, reached maturity). By this we may perceive (know, recognize and be sure) that we are in Him;
>
> Whoever says he abides in Him ought (as a personal debt) to walk and conduct himself in the same way in which He walked and conducted Himself. (1 John 2:5-6)

God is giving us more and more glimpses of His love. Just glimpses, for fleshly beings cannot fully see His face and live. Though it is still veiled, He is showing us enough of His love for us to grow in love and service.

Like Moses, we ask to "see His face" of love. As we seek Him, we will find Him in the faces of those He calls us to serve.

Moses Love Prefigured Ours Today

We saw how God revealed Himself to Moses. God not only gave His name to Moses; God allowed Moses to see His glory. (Exodus 33:19) Moses fell in love with God. I AM wants the same for His beloved today: He wants to show us His glory.

As Moses progressed up the mountain, Sinai shook visibly. Shaking, flashes of lightning and darkness scared the Israelites down to their sandal straps. But Moses ascended the mountain unafraid because he knew and trusted his God. This, too, presents a parallel for today. As God shakes the heavens and the earth, His people who know Him will walk unafraid.

Moses, in His intimacy with God, gained both favor and power. In the knowledge of God, beholding Him, and then loving Him, Moses gained a power anointing. And the Lord said, "My presence shall go with you..." (Exodus 33:14)

Exodus 33:21 portrays Moses standing on a stone promontory prepared to witness God's glory. The Lord gave my prayer group a vision of a man positioned on an outcropping with a mighty wind blowing his robe and hair. The Lord told us:

The picture I gave you of a Moses-like figure standing on a rocky pinnacle in the roaring wind is you. For I see you as Moses, a man who knew Me, knew My heart, and a man of anointed, Godly power. He had no fear. And yet he was a humble man, the most humble except for My son Jesus, who excelled Moses in humility.

Today the wind of judgement and the wind of holiness will blow and who can stand in the wind? Who can stand except the one who abides in the shadow of the Almighty? Even the glory and blessing that the God of Love promises (see Section Seven) will come like a deluge to knock us off our feet if we're not firmly standing on the Rock. Like Moses whom God hid in the stony cleft as His glory passed by, we will dwell safely in the secret place of the Most High. (Psalm 91:1)

God told Moses, "Behold, there is a place beside Me and you shall stand upon the rock." God reveals His name to us, like Moses. He reveals His heart to us: He is the God of Love. We enter in to Him, responding to Him with love. And He secures our place beside Him on the Rock where we can face any wind with the zeal and joy of Moses. God wants us to witness the excellence of the God of Love. We will descend from that holy-place encounter, our faces radiant with His love, a shining witness to I AM.

Chapter 8

I AM Light

Yahweh reigns from a throne surrounded by a brilliant emerald rainbow. Before Him spreads a clear crystal sea. He Himself shines with the fire and luster of precious gemstones. "You wear light as a garment," Psalm 104:2 says of Him.

"God is Light," 1 John 1:5 tells us. A man who saw His glory, Moses, emerged from His presence with a shining face. His countenance radiated light. He was a one-man light show!

John in Revelation proclaimed that the radiance of Yahweh will illuminate the entire New Jerusalem, which measures a massive 1500 miles in each direction.

God is Light. It flows from Him. In the earth's genesis, God commanded, "Light, be!" Light was.

Yet the Father has ordained that He Himself will not manifest the excellence of His glory. Instead He relinquishes that privilege to His beloved, obedient Son.

Jesus is Light. He is "the sole expression of the glory of God," Paul relates in Hebrews 1:3. Jesus is the Light Being, a Person Who IS Light, the out-raying of His divine Father. He is the radiance of God's glory.

Jesus, pictured in the early books of the Old Testament as the Angel of God's Presence, reappears in the Bible's final book as the mighty Angel of Revelation 10. Robed in a cloud of diffused light, He comes down from heaven, crowned with a dazzling rainbow. His body radiates light. His legs appear as columns of flame; His face shines like the sun.

God sent a dark world His best revelation of Himself as the Light. "In Him was Life and that Life was the Light of men," John 1:4-5 declares, "and the Light shines on in the darkness for the darkness has never overpowered it." Jesus confirmed that to the crowds following Him in His public life, saying "I am the Light of the World. He who follows Me will have the Light which is Life."

Jesus, who is called "the Light of the nations," now speaks to us by His Spirit, calling "Arise! Shine, for your light has come, and the glory of the Lord has risen upon you." (Isaiah

60:1 RSV) Now that the world approaches its midnight, God is getting ready to unleash the Light burning in His people. Watch out, world!

Darkness Prevails Now—But Wait!

Spiritual darkness engulfs the earth. God wants us to know Him now as light because He's getting ready to overcome the darkness. The darkness will deepen but to His people He speaks these words, "I AM Light."

To the human soul, to the poet, artist and composer, light symbolizes life, freedom, truth. Darkness implies death, unhappiness, enslavement, misery, delusion. Darkness is a negative; it is the absence of light. In the spiritual realm, darkness results from sin. One kind of sin that especially causes darkness is sorcery. God speaking through Isaiah said:

> When the people (instead of putting their trust in God) say to you, Consult for direction mediums and wizards...they will behold only distress and darkness, the gloom of anguish, and into thick darkness and widespread, obscure night they shall be driven away. (Isaiah 8:19)

Unbelief and sorcery shadow America and other nations of the world today. The resulting darkness is a looming problem. Men like George Washington sought God on their knees for the future of their country and won freedom. Today, our leaders rely on their human wisdom—with ludicrous results. We throw money at problems like racial discord, teen pregnancy and drugs. The roots of these spiritual problems go deeper than government cash can reach.

The New Age movement teaches men, women and children to seek their spirit guides for light. These spiritual entities are actually demonic beings who get a foothold in people's lives with the illusion of light. In the beginning they delight and enchant. In the end they enslave.

Because nations have yielded to sin and sought light from human intelligence, idols and demonic beings, darkness covers the earth. Our governmental leaders walk around like blind men, bumping into walls, unable to take effective action. Because we have abandoned God, who is Light, our nations lay in gloom and distress.

But our God, who has no darkness in Him, has a solution. His light will arise in us.

I AM. Know Me as I AM.

Clouds and darkness now cover the whole earth. Gloom and night cover the people. Rejoicing in the earth, the glad voice of the bridegroom, the festival of the people will cease. Merriment will cease, for the whole earth will come under trial or tribulation. See it with the eyes of faith in Me. See it in the Spirit. Shafts of light will come through and bathe in light those in My Spirit. But know that clouds and darkness cover the whole earth.

Is this a weather report? No! It is an assessment of the spiritual condition of the earth. And yet My people bring light. They are light bearers, bearing Jesus Christ, the Light of the World. And their light will shine. Know today that darkness and gloom cover the earth and night the peoples. But My people will now ***arise and shine.***

Let God arise in His people and ***shine****. Light is greater against a background of darkness. You will see it* ***shine!***

The I AM presence we bear within is Light. This Light overcomes spiritual darkness. The darkness cannot comprehend or overcome this light. God's people will arise to shine in this day of darkness and cause light to come forth as surely as the day of creation when God said, "Light be!" God spoke the light into being in this material world with His word of faith. Likewise, we create light in our individual worlds by words spoken in faith.

God wants us unfazed by death and darkness. Grounded in the intimate experiential knowledge of Him as Light, we simply and surely overcome the darkness as we encounter it. What can darkness do but flee when confronted with the absolute, unrefutable I AM who is Light?

We can speak to darkness. We can address darkness rooted deeply in our past or in another's past and say, "Darkness, go in Jesus' name. Let there be light." We can exert authority over the darkness in our cities and command it to flee. New York City's crime rate, especially murder, has plummeted because of this kind of authority in prayer.

I cry out, allow Me to be in you all that I AM in you! Let my life shine in you, My people, for I am the Light of the World. Let's set the world on fire with My light to overcome the darkness which cannot quench or overcome it.

We take light with us wherever we go because we have Christ, the Light, alive within us. Pumping gas, checking out at a convenience store, playing frisbee in a park, we can speak His light.

Go forward in the things of God, taking the spiritual land. The darkness will increase but, because of My people, the light will increase also. I am the Light. The Light is a Person, Christ in you. You bring the Light because you are a Christ bearer.

So! Light, be! Light shine in My people to overcome the darkness. And what force will win? The darkness cannot comprehend or conquer or overcome the Light. One match, one small candle, drives out darkness. So it is with My people. One little light begins to shine and more comes and the darkness is defeated. I am the Light!

Go forward into the Light. Take the spiritual land by declaring My Light. Say, "Light, be!" Demand it. Command it. You have the authority. Rise up now and demand, command, light.

Now go, go into these territories I have given you. Enter, enter the land I lead you to and point out to you. Despite what you see. Despite the enemy fortress rising right before your eyes. Despite the enormity of the darkness. Despite the sewer run of filth. Rise up, go and do battle for the Lord and see what happens. Say "Light, be" in the grocery store, in the auto repair shop, in the movie theater. Say "Light, be" and see what happens.

Light and Life, A Symbiotic Relationship

God's essence is light and light is Him. "God is Light, and there is no darkness in Him at all." (1 John 1:5) His light flows out of His life. "In Him was Life and that Life was the Light of men." (John 1:4) Life and light have a symbiotic relationship, even in creation where light prompts the seedling to thrive. He declared, "I am the Light of the world. He who follows Me will not be walking in the dark, but will have the Light, which is Life." (John 8:12)

The perfect expression of God's essence as Light is Jesus, the radiance of the Father. And the Father gives Jesus as light to us, establishing Jesus as the Light of the World. Jesus is the Light who overcomes this present darkness.

Isaiah prophesied of Him:

> But (in the midst of judgement there is the promise and the certainty of the Lord's deliverance and) there shall be no gloom for her who was in anguish. The people who walked in darkness have seen a great Light; those who dwelt in the land of intense darkness and the shadow of death, upon them has the Light shined.

(Isaiah 9:1-2)

Millions suffer in captivity and bondage today, whether from the horrors of war in places like Rwanda and Bosnia, or tyrannical regimes in China or North Korea, or the degradation of domestic violence in the U.S. The rate of abuse of innocent children within the shelter of their own homes and families has skyrocketed. Our world is filled with evil. Darkness hangs like a pall over our land.

But God, who is Light, has a plan. It is the reign of the Lord Jesus Christ, who is Light. Those who dwell in the land of intense darkness and shadow of death will see a great Light. Let's consider the remainder of the Isaiah scripture prophesying the Light and see what it says:

> For unto us a Child is born, to us a Son is given; and the government shall be upon His shoulder, and His name shall be called Wonderful Counselor, Mighty God, Everlasting Father (of Eternity), Prince of Peace.
>
> Of the increase of His government and of peace there shall be no end, upon the throne of David and over his kingdom, to establish it and to uphold it with justice and with righteousness from the (latter) time forth, even forevermore. The zeal of the Lord of hosts will perform this. (Isaiah 9:6-7)

Governed by Light

Isaiah links the Light with the reign of the Lord Jesus Christ. "The government shall be upon His shoulder...of the increase of His government and peace there shall be no end." Christ's messianic reign will subject all things to the authority of the Light of the World. The darkness will submit to His reign of light, the reign of God's righteous son, the Sun of Righteousness.

I am the Light, Light of the nations. I am light. No darkness can comprehend or overcome Me. I am the light of the world. Darkness, flee! The light is come! Know now, My children, that "the people who walked in darkness have seen a great light."

Does "darkness" seem to apply to your nation and the world? Yes! This people, walking in darkness today, will see a great light. The Sun of Righteousness will rise with healing in His wings! And the yoke shall be broken as in the day of Midian, of Gideon (Isaiah 9:4) because of the anointing.

The Anointed One who is the Light and His anointing will go

forth in power to change our world. The Isaiah passage brings this out:

> For the yoke of (Israel's burden), and the staff or rod for (goading) their oppressor, You have broken as in the day of (Gideon with) Midian.
>
> For every (tramping) warrior's war boots and all his armor in the battle tumult and every garment rolled in blood shall be burned as fuel for the fire. (Isaiah 9:4-5)

Notice that verse 4 speaks of the yoke of burden or bondage. Isaiah traces that yoke (in this case bondage to Israel's Assyrian captors). The yoke occurred because of sin, which led to darkness and captivity. In the next chapter, Isaiah 10:27 proclaims, "The yoke shall be destroyed because of the anointing."

The anointing of God's presence released from millions of Spirit-filled Christians, His full anointing in men, women and children, will destroy the yokes that enslave them. Jesus was anointed to set the captives free. God's people, fully alive in Him, will destroy every yoke through the anointing. Every vestige of oppression by the enemy will melt away under their blazing light. "...every tramping warrior's war boot, every garment rolled in blood shall be burned."

Because of the zeal of the Lord of Hosts, the people of light will drive back the darkness. His orchestrated campaign will establish the messianic reign of the Lord Jesus Christ in our time, the latter time. "Of the increase of His government and of peace there shall be no end...from the (**latter**) time forth, even forevermore." (Isaiah 9:6) (Boldface mine)

How can we help bring about Christ, the Anointed One's, messianic reign?

We can begin enforcing His reign in the earth, begin bringing light to overcome the darkness. We hold within us the presence and anointing of the God who is Light. We must begin to focus laser-like beams of that light on situations of darkness—sin, lack, bondage.

The people who walked in darkness have seen a great light. Does the darkness of today qualify? Arise, shine, for your light has come. Darkness showcases the light.

Oh, know now, children of Mine, that darkness will increase, physical and spiritual darkness. Know that I have sent you a great light, Jesus, My Son, and His government will increase until all the world is filled with His light. "Shine, Jesus, shine!" are prophetic words in song. Yes, call forth that light everywhere you look—postoffice, grocery store, computer, church. Call forth His government of integrity, righteousness and joy. Enforce it in the Spirit, a grassroots, groundswell movement. Oh, yes! Oh, yes! And I will do all when My people call it forth, says the Lord.

Enforcers of Light

God wants us to call forth His reign. We do it with God's word, spoken as a command from our mouths. Our faith words will shatter the darkness we see in our daily lives. How do we break out of the concrete overshoes of lethargy and unbelief that weigh us down?

Breaking loose requires an **attitude shift.** What shackles us is actually unbelief. We listen to God's word, we study God's word. We see that He has commissioned us to heal the sick, cast out demons and spread the good news of Jesus and His anointing to break every yoke. But we don't really believe it. We never apply it to ourselves.

Sometimes we do accept the commission, for God's people in general, but we remain convinced that our personal weakness cancels God's specific call on our own lives. Our low self esteem shouts "You can't!" Our sinful past cries out, "You aren't really forgiven." Our less than perfect life circumstances deceive us, saying, "When things are just right, then you can properly serve God." (This counsel comes from a religious spirit. God uses people where they are.)

These attitudes hinder the reign of the Lord Jesus Christ.

An attitude shift demands 1. recognizing unbelief. 2. repenting of the sin (unbelief) and 3. embracing belief in God's word. Genuine belief naturally conceives action. We will be both believers and doers of the word.

We are anointed to do the work of Jesus. Let's stop doubting that anointing. We must stand sure in it and use it. As God's people, let's stop hindering and start initiating the messianic reign of the Lord Jesus Christ.

Go forth knowing today, My child, that "thy light has come." (Isaiah 60:1) The light of the nations has risen upon thee, even the glory of the Father, the Son. So know now that things will change ***for the better.***

Lo, He is risen! The resurrection glory of Our Lord Jesus Christ has "risen upon thee!" So arise! Shine with that glory, My people, My church, and walk in the awareness of it and the full authority of the anointing.

And what is that anointing? To set the captives free, to break every yoke, in intercession and prayer, in ministry from the body, the body of Christ. So go forth with a new anointing of light today. Yes, I have anointed My people with life and with love. Now with light. And that full anointing will fully destroy the yoke. For the darkness will submit to it, succumb to it, fail to comprehend it, and be overcome by it. Rejoice!

This is the fullness of the anointing that was on Christ Jesus. Rejoice! This message will be on the body of Christ. Hallelujah!

Jesus, the Sun of Righteousness, will arise and shine like the sun. The prophet Malachi, last of the Old Testament writers, spoke of His rising to heal.

> But unto you who revere and worshipfully fear My name shall the Sun of Righteousness arise with healing in His wings and beams, and you shall go forth and gambol like calves (released) from the stall and leap for joy.
>
> And you shall tread down the lawless and wicked, for they shall be ashes under the soles of your feet in the day that I shall do this, says the Lord of Hosts. (Malachi 3:2-3)

Wholeness! Victory! Joy!

Just before this prophecy of Malachi, God's word speaks of a refining fire designed to purify God's people. The Lord of Hosts, it declares, "is like a refiner's fire" (Malachi 3:2) When God's people allow Him to refine them with fire, they will become like pure gold, so pure that it is no longer opaque but translucent. Like their maker, they will be people "with no darkness." When individuals submit 100 percent to this refining process, their light will shine! This is the intense desire of God. He pleads with us in this final hour to yield.

It's our choice. One way we choose is by recognizing and believing that His light resides in us. Another way is by walking in the light of His word, the truth. A third is by calling forth His light into everyday situations. Just as God's word is "a lamp unto our feet and a light unto our path," so our words bring light to those who hear them.

Arise Means Get Up and Do It

Finally, we **arise.** Jesus, the Sun of Righteousness, will rise with joyous healing light—in us. When we arise we express our choice to be light as He is Light.

How do we do that? By throwing off the death attitude that we are just poor old sinners, too sick, too weak, too imperfect to be used by God. "Poor old me. Ain't got nothin' to give."

What kind of a valiant bride of Christ is that? If we wait till our marriage is right, till we find the right church, till we overcome that bad habit, we'll miss our moment to shine for Him. Our shining moment comes in darkness. Now is the time, the hour and the instant, to arise to God-in-us and shine for Jesus Christ.

Remember Peter who walked on the water with Jesus. He had to first get up and get out of the boat!

Let's go back to Isaiah who had the honor of prophesying this pre-messianic moment in his words, "Arise, shine, for thy light is come, and the glory of the Lord is risen upon thee." (Isaiah 60:1 KJV)

The Amplified Bible spells it out:

> Arise (from the depression and prostration in which circumstances have kept you—rise to a new life)! Shine (be radiant with the glory of the Lord) for your light has come, and the glory of the Lord has risen upon you!
>
> For behold, darkness shall cover the earth, and dense darkness (all) the peoples, but the Lord shall arise upon you (O Jerusalem) and His glory shall be seen on you. (Isaiah 60:1-2)

"Arise" means arise. "Shine" means shine. We take the bushel basket off our light and let it shine. Choose to do it—then do it!

God wants us to fulfill His word. We must yield.

Yes, I AM! I am with you. I am in you. I am you. You are Me at the deepest part of your being and that Me-life will be lightened, light infused, made light by the light within you. It will conquer, override, supersede the flesh and you will SHINE! Yes, you will shine! I am excited about this.

Oh, yes, you will shine. I will do it as you surrender your flesh to Me. Amen! I have spoken and promised it and it shall be done!

God's light will shine like never before to quench the present darkness. As the darkness grows, look for His light to break through. Isaiah's call to shine links the light to God's glory. "Shine ...and the glory of the Lord has risen upon you." (Isaiah 60:1) Like the pillar of fire that illumined the darkness for the Israelites in the desert, an evidence of His glory and presence, so God's light will shine with His glory in coming darkness.

I took the picture on this book's cover on a day of sorrow.

Our family had gathered to discuss and mourn an onslaught of suicide against a loved one. In the midst of this tragic conference our attention was arrested by an immense, light-filled cloud that slowly traveled eastward to settle along the Continental Divide above shimmering Lake Dillon. We jumped into the car to follow this phenomenon and watched later as the sunset diffused the mounded cumulus puff with gold, peach and wine. A full moon arose to enhance the glory cloud panorama. God had shown us His light in an hour of intense darkness.

Again one gloomy spring morning when sun broke through stormy skies for a few moments, He spoke this to me:

Glory. My glory will be as welcome as the light shining this dark morning, a light-deprived morning suddenly bursting into light. My glory will come like that, emphasized by the darkness. My light in darkness will shine, shine, shine!

The darkness will be broken by shafts of light more beautiful because they illuminate darkness. Hallelujah!

God has a powerful antidote to darkness. His son, the King of Glory, will light up our world. As gate keepers in His seat of government, Jerusalem, His people must be the ones to open the doors. This translates to opening our personal closures and letting His anointing flow.

Now know, and consider in your heart, and apply to your ways that I am coming. This is an awesome thing in the history of creation. I want My people's hearts fully prepared. I AM is coming in glory.

"I will come again," Jesus said. He is coming again in a way unprecedented, in His people, and the whole earth will see His glory, in His people. Christ in you, your hope of glory.

The glory to be shown forth, the excellence and need-meeting love of our God, will be at its brightest in the midst of darkness. Know this, it will be in darkness that the Light shines best.

Jesus came in simplicity to a world full of religious spirits, a viper's nest. Show forth My glory, My people, by allowing Jesus in you to shine. Open the gates, Jerusalem, and allow free intercourse—the flow of the anointing. Allow the King of Glory free access. (Psalm 24)

Yes, I am speaking of mighty things My people must be willing in the day of My power. Willing.

Touch Me and Receive

I AM is Life, Love, Light. We've looked at these separately.

Now watch as God blends these three aspects of Himself:

Think of the Resurrection—intense light at work, which is energy, moved by love, brought life. I am a person of ***intense*** *Life, Love, Light. The light is energy, dynamos energy. When you think of energy, think of Me. I am that. Touch Me and absorb that intense life-love-light. Jesus said to Mary, "Do not touch Me," for the time for transfer of glory was not full. But today I say, "Touch Me and receive." I will overshadow you. All of it will happen by faith—without a perceptible "experience."*

God has assured us that He is present and available. What He wants to give us in fullness of Life, Love, Light—in fullness of Himself—is beyond our ability to conceive. It is vital to know Him in these aspects because this is how He will manifest His power-presence in us. We need to reach out and touch our available God, in daily worship in His presence, and we will receive that fullness. He wants us to be for Him all that He is.

He gives us marching orders.

The Holy Spirit expressly commands and directs this day: go therefore into all the earth and bring the gospel to all nations. Go therefore and tell the good news of salvation in Christ Jesus. Go. Be My arm, My branch today, says the Lord Jesus speaking to His body. Be for Me all that I AM—life, love, light.

Go forth! *Arise and shine for now is the moment for My glory to be released into* ***all*** *the earth. Go forth as light bearers, love bearers, life bearers, My people. Go now, says the Lord. Go now to a hurting world.*

A key word in this message is "now." There is no more time. Either we rise to the challenge now or we miss it for all eternity. He has made us alive with life, love, light, the fullness of His presence on us and within us. His fullness will increase, multiply and fill the earth **if** we choose to release His Life.

The sheer excitement of the God of Life, Love and Light emerges in this final word from the Lord describing Himself. Being around Him is like experiencing first love. What ecstasy to spend eternity with this person:

Eternally, I AM. Know Me ***as I AM****. What is life, love, light when mixed? Think of the ecstasy of romance—yes! An intense experience of love, with joy and zest and brightness of attitude or outlook. That is as* ***I AM.***

Life, Love and Light fuse in Him. When we touch Him, we find ecstasy.

Section Three

Mixed Spirits

We are so integrated with God,
He in us and we in Him,
that we are closer than married.
We're fused.

Holy God dwells within us.

Jesus, transfigured, shown resplendent
with the glory of God, His Father.

Light from within suffused His body.

When we say a full yes to God,
the glory of His presence within
will clothe us in light.

Chapter 9

I Am In You

Beneath flesh, beyond soul, at the deepest part of who we are, is God. He **IS** in us. He has infused I AM into our very essence. We are mixed spirits.

In Jesus, ordinary flesh concealed Yahweh, the I AM. We, too, camouflage the Great I AM in flesh. We **have** bodies, which we wear as an earth suit, but we are more than flesh. We **have** a soul (mind, will and emotions), but our souls are not our essence.

We **are** spirits. God indwells these spirits.

The "who" of who we are is God. He makes us the individual we are. The I AM in each of us is the core of our personhood. So the very basis of our unique and unrepeatable self is God.

Please understand, we are not God. We have life; He IS life. He has enabled us to share in the life of the Godhead, but that life originates with Him. He lends life to us—on permanent loan!

We are not little gods. We are created beings; He has always existed. But He amalgamates with us, making us what we are, making us who we are.

This sets us apart from all creation. At the center of us is the holy I AM. Deep inside is His life and personality. His personhood permeates us and that is holy. This holiness is not of us. It is of Him. His life confers holiness on what He made from garden soil.

All that you are I Am in you. My life expressed uniquely in you. You are flesh...dust. I Am in you your life and the who of who you are. The imprint of My Spirit is upon your spirit which I made. I Am through you, in you. Know this: I am you; you are Me. I am in you but not only in you. I Am through you. I Am My life expressed in you.

Know who you are. I know who I AM. Know your value, great value, but only in Me. That's why the angels were in awe of My creation of man, of Adam. They knew what I am sharing with you now. They understood fully and stood in awe at the greatness of the thing: man made in My image. Value yourself but only in

Me. Earthen vessels, yes, but more than that, you see. Words can't express what I am telling you today. It can only be experienced and "known."

Until the Lord spoke those words to me, I imagined that I originated my personhood. At the core of my being lay me, my nature as a unique human being. I believed that after God had given me life He withdrew His hand. I then shaped my existence by imposing my self-determination on the life God had given me. I saw my God-given life as a generic aliveness that I could form. Heredity, environment, parenting and experiences played a part, but I imprinted my life with my own developing "me."

In contrast, God says, "I am the who of who you are." His identity stamps us. We are not just ourselves; we are unique expressions of Him. Each individual is mixed with God and God is mixed with each one.

Our flesh veils God-in-us. I AM wants us to allow the flesh to die, to be crucified under His delicate, watchful and protective care so that He can shine through. He wants us to embrace the cross, under His leading and direction, so that our true personhood, God-in-us, can break through the flesh barrier. The tight seed case must burst for His life to break through.

I AM you; the very essence of you is Me. I am in you. You are Me because I have put My Life, My AM, My essence in you. My very Life, My Me, is in you. That's who you are! An expression of Me.

At the deepest core of your being is Me, I AM. Know the power of this. Let it shine before men. Release it! Allow it to be seen and be visible to the world. You have it and the flesh veil has been lightened, lifted and dealt with so that the world can see. "Shine, Jesus, shine through me!" Understand? It's big.

This is resurrection: the glory of My presence in you shining out. The flesh veil changed, transformed. That's why My people will be ready to go in a twinkling—because the flesh veil has died and is ready for instant resurrection to full expression of glory.

The I AM in us is well-disguised. Our creative imaginations recognize the disguise and we speak of it in our tales. The powerful genie hid in Aladdin's ordinary lamp. Beneath Old Scrooge's crusty exterior lay a kind-hearted British gentleman. Cinderella was no char girl. Our spirits know what's true—that we humans hide a treasure in a common clay vessel.

Always, eternally I AM. I AM. I AM. I hold you in existence by "I AM." We are one. Our life is merged. Our life is inter-

twined, "mixed spirits." Would God mix with man? (The angels were astounded.) The answer is "Yes!" See it in My son. It is manifest in Him.

Jesus, the Great I AM, humbled Himself to take on flesh. And it was real flesh, not the idealized image glowing from a Renaissance painting. Jesus was a male Jew who lived in a hot, dusty climate. He perspired and probably smelled like sweat. His feet, walking in sandals, grew grimy by day's end. He looked like his family and his people, probably olive skinned with dark hair and eyes. He dressed in a simple robe with a single-piece undergarment and a cloak for cool days. He had worked as a village carpenter.

> He has no form or comeliness (royal, kingly pomp), that we should look at Him and no beauty, that we should desire Him. (Isaiah 53:2)

Yet He spoke as one sent from God.

His majesty hidden, He received scorn from Pharisees. Mockers spit on Him. The Scribes and Pharisees remained blind to Him, just as we today fail to see God's vital presence in ourselves and others. But the disciples "knew" Him. They sensed something special in Him and listened for clues to it, watched for signs of it, tingled in alertness to the expression of God-life in Jesus.

Jesus makes a good example of our identity in God. Most of us can see clearly that the Gospel Jesus, who walked, talked and behaved like a man, concealed majestic God. Jesus was wholly God and wholly man. He had both natures. (See Romans 1:3-4)

On earth He lived out of His human nature. Born of a woman, He grew up like any other Jewish boy and called Himself "the Son of Man." Like us, He needed the infilling of the Holy Spirit for His power anointing which resulted in miracles. He operated out of His God-infused man spirit and Holy Ghost power anointing to accomplish His ministry. He died a real physical death.

The Holy Spirit Mediates Between Spirit and Flesh

Jesus lived out the fullness of I-AM-in-flesh. He fulfilled it perfectly. He did it in the same way you and I can do it: by allowing the Holy Spirit to mediate between the I AM and the flesh.

The Holy Spirit came into Jesus at His Jordan baptism. (We too can receive the Holy Spirit. All we need to do is ask, with our whole heart and in faith.) The Holy Spirit comes in to translate between the flesh and our I-AM-infused spirit. He makes the I AM to shine through our flesh veil. He labors within us, to purify and change us, so the flesh veil becomes more and more transparent. As He works, more of God's life shines through the flesh.

The ultimate expression of the I AM shining through flesh occurred at the Transfiguration (Mark 9:2) when Jesus shone with the radiance of the glory of God. His God-life broke through the flesh barrier. The I AM who is Light shone through in radiance. Jesus, displayed in the fullness of His glory, conversed with Moses and Elijah.

> Six days after this, Jesus took with Him Peter and James and John and led them up on a high mountain apart by themselves. And He was transfigured before them and became resplendent with divine brightness.
>
> And His garments became glistening, intensely white, as no fuller (cloth dresser, launderer) on earth could bleach them.
>
> And Elijah appeared (there) to them, accompanied by Moses, and they were holding (a protracted) conversation with Jesus.
>
> And Peter took up the conversation, saying, Master, it is good and suitable and beautiful for us to be here. Let us make three booths (tents)—one for You and one for Moses and one for Elijah.
>
> For he did not (really) know what to say, for they were in a violent fright (aghast with dread).
>
> And a cloud threw a shadow upon them, and a voice came out of the cloud, saying, This is My Son the (the most dearworthy) Beloved One. Be constantly listening to and obeying Him!
>
> And looking around, they suddenly no longer saw anyone with them except Jesus only. (Mark 9:2-8)

Scripture says the New Jerusalem, consecrated city and bride of the Lamb, is made of pure gold. But the words imply "transparent" gold, light-permeated gold. Jesus' flesh became transparent in that way and the glory of I AM permeated it, transforming it to such beauty, life, light and love that Peter wanted to put up a tent and stay.

(Overtaken by this impulse, impetuous Peter actually interrupted the Transfiguration.)

Why did Jesus, our example and role model for full spiritual maturity, allow His flesh to reveal the glory of God hidden within? Because this same transfiguration will occur in us.

Paul describes it as a progressive change:

> But we all...beholding...the glory of the Lord are changed into the same image from glory to glory...by the Spirit of the Lord. (2 Corinthians 3:18 KJV)

The Amplified Bible elaborates Paul's meaning, using the word "transfigured."

> And all of us, as with unveiled face (because we) continue to behold (in the Word of God) as in a mirror the glory of the Lord are constantly being transfigured into His very own image in ever increasing splendor and from one degree of glory to another; (for this comes) from the Lord (Who is) the Spirit. (2 Corinthians 3:18)

This same Holy Spirit dwells in us now. He remains intent on making God's glory shine in us. He works in those relinquished to Him to make their surrendered flesh translucent, to show forth the presence of God within. He beautifies that flesh, just as Hegai directed the year of myrrh oil and perfumes on lovely Esther of the Old Testament before her marriage to the king. He transforms our flesh, with holy fire refining, so that it comes out transparent. Then the Light of the World can suffuse our flesh veil as surely as it did in Jesus' flesh at His "shining," His Transfiguration.

Arise, shine, for your light has come, church! "The glory of the Lord has risen upon you!" (Isaiah 60:1)

I AM dwells in us and desires to so encompass us that His life-light shines for all to see. He wishes to permeate us with Himself. We are not gods. But God has infused our created spirits with I AM. At the moment of our creation, He stamped us with His imprint, His likeness. We never were, even for an instant, not of Him. He formed us in the womb. We are "fearfully and wonderfully made." (Psalm 139:14) Even in our fallen state before receiving salvation, we are, like God, spirits who will live forever.

We need to know and understand the sanctity of our life in Him. At the center of each of us lives God, I AM WHO AM, the One Who Is Life.

That's why we reverence each human life as sacred. Because God has fused Himself to each individual. Each person is a unique and unrepeatable hand-made spirit creation of God. Every phase of human life on earth, from the earliest moments of life after conception to the waning years before death, challenges us to reverence, caring, protection and love.

Because God has permeated our spirits with His life, our human lives are unique in the spirit world. The angels gasped in awe when God announced the news of man's impending creation The archangel Lucifer rebelled because he saw his high position usurped. The anointed cherub, son of the morning, saw that his God-presence (his anointing) had become a lesser God-presence (or anointing) than man's.

God was **on** Lucifer with His anointing. Lucifer shone in the beauty of God which made him brilliant. He was gifted with God-like creativity, especially in music, and with Godly authority and splendor. But God planned to be both **on** and **in** Adam. God proposed to infuse His GREAT I AM life into Adam's created life, God mixing with man.

Lucifer saw this plan and hated God. As his nature changed from light to darkness, so did his name. Satan rebelled. A great war in heaven ensued. Michael and his angels drove Satan from his heavenly place. Jealousy and hatred then drove him to attempt to destroy God's dream for man.

Through deceit, Satan stole Adam's dominion. He took authority in the earth when Adam and Eve sinned. Eve, being deceived, ate the apple. Adam, who was not deceived, ate also. (Did he disobey because he loved Eve? Perhaps he could not bear to lose his beautiful companion, so he deliberately joined Eve in sin.) Satan still relies on deceit, lies and counterfeit. He counterfeits every move of God.

I AM Challenges Us to Recognize His Presence Within

God plans to do a mighty work in these last days. He wants a prepared people to take dominion in the spiritual promised land. He wants this people ready to be transformed in the twinkling of an eye to meet Him in the air when He comes for His church. (1 Thessalonians 4:15-17) To prepare the hearts of His people so they will rise up to this high calling and purpose, He needs us to know who He is and the fullness of His life in us.

He wants us at least as awed as the angels over the reality that I AM has mixed His life with ours. Each of us is an unrepeatable spirit-in-flesh person. God has so many facets to His magnificent person that He can express Himself uniquely in billions of individuals. God has intertwined His life with our life to create a synergism that is unparalleled in creation.

The angels who remained faithful to God in Lucifer's rebellion act as servants and messengers to God and ministers to us who are heirs of salvation. They looked down the annals of time as God revealed His sovereign plan. They are just as committed to our success in carrying out God's plan as demonic beings are to destroying that same destiny. They saw after the Resurrection the infilling of the Holy Spirit, first at Pentecost and then throughout history in the body of Christ. They learned that God would indwell, anoint, equip, transform and sanctify surrendered men and women to such a degree that a new-Adam race would emerge. They saw that God would fulfill the purpose He established with Adam. His plan would come full circle. He is the Alpha and the Omega, the beginning and the end.

Brokenness, even crucifixion, releases His life in us. The Holy Spirit, given total surrender, will sanctify us, "spirit, mind and body." (1 Thessalonians 5:23) When at last even our bodies are made holy, subject to the full reign of our Lord Jesus Christ and no longer driven by the lusts of the reprobate mind or physical body, then I AM will fully shine through us. His radiance will come forth through us as a light to a troubled world. That "world" may be our grocery store, office or plant, neighborhood or school, but we will be a light to it. Through us, the whole world will see light. Those with eyes to see will witness in us the glory of God.

Fullness

The Lord has ordained that we should be the fullness of Jesus Christ. In the Body of Christ will live the full measure of Jesus' divine presence. We will know Him full spectrum, in breadth, length, height and depth, and become a body wholly filled with God Himself. (Ephesians 3:17) This happens in love; intimacy with Him makes us full like Him. Our knowing the Lord will develop by experience, a first-hand acquaintance, for ourselves.

We will know Him full-spread, from His birth to His cross to His glory, the breadth. We will go the entire length, overcoming the last enemy, death, according to His word. We know Him in the height, seated with Him in heavenly places, reaching our full spiritual stature. We know Him in the depth, where Spirit calls to spirit in communication beyond words. When Jesus comes in the clouds to take His church home, we will be transformed in an instant, because we will be fully ready.

God expresses His own fullness in Jesus.

> For it has pleased (the Father) that all the divine fullness (the sum total of the divine perfection, powers and attributes) should dwell in Him permanently. (Colossians 1:19)

In a similar way, God ordained that the fullness of Jesus be expressed in His body.

> ...His body, the fullness of Him Who fills all in all (for in that body lives the full measure of Him Who makes everything complete and Who fills everything everywhere with Himself). (Ephesians 1:23)

All this sounds wonderful but vague. Will these misty notions crystallize sometime far off in heaven?

Actually, it's happening now.

The Holy Spirit is working this fullness, meaning the fullness of Jesus-in-us, right now. It's happening as we draw closer to Him in love. The Holy Spirit is now wooing the church with a message: "Press in. Know Me. I want to be known. Enter into the secret place of intimacy with Me, the place of love."

Christian leader Kenneth Copeland sent His ministry partners the following message in early 1998. It reaffirms God's plan for fullness:

> *Fullness of joy. Fullness of Faith. Fullness of healing. Fullness of everything God's word promises.*

Kenneth continued:

> As our family was praying together this past Christmas, the Holy Spirit dropped those words into my heart. We, as a family, took hold of that Word and set our faith-track for the coming year. We are reaching for Ephesians 3:16-19..."To be filled with the fullness of God."
>
> I believe it's time for Jesus to do exceeding, abundantly, above all we can ask or think. All of us here at Kenneth Copeland Ministries are boldly asking, believing and expecting the fullness of Christ—fullness of the Anointed One and fullness of His Anointing. Agree with us and go for it.

Love Will Perfect Fullness in His Body

Here lies God's purpose for His people today: when we know this love, we will achieve the richest measure of His presence in us. We will know His fullness.

> May you be rooted deep in love and founded securely on love, That you may have the power and be strong to apprehend and grasp with all the saints (God's devoted

> people, the experience of that love) what is the breadth and length and height and depth (of it);
>
> (That you may really come) to know (practically, through experience for yourselves) the love of Christ, which far surpasses mere knowledge (without experience); that you may be filled (through all your being) unto all the fullness of God (may have the richest measure of the divine Presence, become a body wholly filled and flooded with God Himself)! (Ephesians 3:17-19)

In intimacy, in knowing intimately and in loving intimately, the presence of God becomes full in us. It happens only in those who are love-bonded. That relationship is what "in Christ" means.

We, His people, need cleansing and purification, by judgement and fire, to gain pure and undivided hearts. He must be established as our God. We must have no other god, no dream or desire bigger than Him, even nothing cherished as equal to Him. Then we can know Him and love Him freely and fully. When we know Him in His cross, then we will know Him in His glory. When we know Him in His glory, we will be transformed, even transfigured, with Him.

Let's look at transformation and see how God is using it now to prepare us for the Rapture.

First, let's expand the idea of fullness.

We know that God has mixed His own life with ours. King David, awed by God's creation of man, wrote: "Thou hast made him a little less than God and dost crown him with glory and honor." (Psalm 8:5 RSV)

Do we have a little spark of God's flame? A bit of glory dust deposited in our spirits? A glimmer reflected from the Light of the World?

No! God's **fullness** is available to us. He has said, "All that I AM is available to you." (See Chapter 5) He has declared in His word that He wants to develop us into nothing less than the perfection of the Lord Jesus Christ:

> ...(that we might arrive) at really mature manhood (the completeness of personality which is nothing less than the standard height of Christ's own perfection) the measure of the stature of the fullness of the Christ and the completeness found in Him. (Ephesians 4:13)

*I AM THAT I AM. I AM **all** that I am. Fullness, to an extent you never imagined. This **fullness** is available to you. Not to be* *as full as I am but to be as full as you can be.*

Do you know what this fullness is? It is God **fully** *inhabiting man. I AM-in-you. I am your you. It is Me! Allow Me to be full in you, in all areas of your life and you will experience that fullness. Who you are is Me. I am in you. My expression is you. My Me shining out through you is the glory of God, the fullness of My presence or life in you expressed fully and completely.*

Can we be as full as God is? No. He is God; we are not God. But we can be as full as created God-infused beings can be.

How big is our vessel? Demitasse? Tea cup? Coffee mug? Soup tureen? Vat? Tanker? As big as we allow the Holy Spirit to stretch us. That's how full we can be with God's life and presence. We determine the size. When we yield to the Holy Spirit's work, He makes us full and shining with God's own life. The completed work results in our expressing God's glory.

The Glory of God

God manifested His presence in Old Testament times by His *shekinah* glory, the glory of His presence. Moses stayed in the presence of God on Sinai and descended with a face so radiant that he had to cover it. The Israelites could not stand to look on the glory. When the priests dedicated Solomon's temple to God, shekinah filled the sanctuary so the priests could not minister.

Shekinah glory appeared as the bright cloud that overshadowed Jesus at His Jordan baptism and later the radiance emanating from Him at His Transfiguration. Jesus Himself is called "the radiance of the glory of God."

The Amplified Bible explains:

> He is the sole expression of the glory of God (the Light Being, the out-raying or radiance of the divine), and He is the perfect imprint and very image of God's nature... (Hebrews 1:3)

(The words "imprint" and "image" echo the words used in Genesis, "Let Us make man in Our image...")

When John, who knew Jesus well in His earthly life, saw Him in His glory, he wrote, "His face was like the sun shining in full power at midday. When I saw Him, I fell at His feet as if dead." (Revelation 1:16-17)

Around the world, in prayer meetings, church gatherings and individual's quiet times, worshippers are sensing the weight of His glory, as His presence manifests. It yields an awareness of His transcendent holiness. We bask in the blessedness and sweetness of His presence, His glory.

The Apostle Paul wrote, "Christ (the Anointed) in you, your hope of glory." (Colossians 1:27) We progress in this glory process. According to the passage quoted earlier from Ephesians 1, the progress occurs when we are in His presence—"as we behold Him, we go from glory to glory." Just as Moses returned from His presence with a radiant face, so we absorb glory from His presence.

Awesome, but eternally purposed in the heart of God, is the fact that this glory is available to us today in this present world.

My Me shining out through you is the glory of God. The fullness of My presence or life in you expressed fully. This is quite a big thing. Man fully alive is the glory of God. The glory of God is man fully alive. Shekinah-presence glory. God expressed in flesh. Hallelujah! It will unite all things in Christ. and unite creation to Me—as one.

Go back and read that again. Did its meaning hit home for you? This is cause for joy. This is what creates heaven on earth, right here, right now. We celebrate God's glorious presence in us, His life and His revealed glory. God's people, full of His glory and power, take up the dominion on the earth that Jesus reclaimed. As we take that dominion, we surrender back all to Him. We become the pivotal players in God's big plan, for this surrender will unite all things under God. It will effect our full spiritual stature, doing what Adam did and more.

Are you ready for this? Get ready, because this fulfillment of all things in the earth is imminent.

In Colossians Paul reveals God's plan for fullness in Christ:

> And you are in Him, made full and having come to fullness of life (in Christ you too are filled with the Godhead—Father, Son and Holy Spirit—and reach full spiritual stature). (Colossians 2:10)

When the body of Christ reaches that full stature, its work on earth will stand finished. Then will come the exciting event God has promised in His word: the catching away of the church.

Fullness Prepares the Church for Rapture

> For the Lord Himself will descend from heaven with a loud cry of summons, with the shout of an archangel, and with the blast of the trumpet of God. And those who have departed this life in Christ will rise first.

> Then we, the living ones who remain (on the earth) shall simultaneously be caught up along with (the resurrected dead) in the clouds to meet the Lord in the air; and so always (through the eternity of eternities) we shall be with the Lord! (1 Thessalonians 4:16)

The popular term for this catching away is the rapture. This differs from the second coming of Christ, which occurs at the end of the Tribulation. What God has promised to do at the catching away of the church is to change us in a twinkling from earth-bound flesh-encased spirit beings to spirit beings with glorified bodies, similar to the resurrected glory-body of the Lord Jesus Christ.

How can this happen? It is happening now. As we allow more and more of God's life to shine through us, our bodies become less and less opaque. Here's how Jesus describes it:

Listen today as I speak to you as the God of the Book of Revelation, the glorious, glorified Jesus, Son of Man, now glorified. I speak to you of resurrection glory, raised-from-the-grave glory.

Death has no sting, no power now, for the people of God. You will not die! This is the generation that will not undergo physical death! Think about it. Glorified bodies for you—with no death to pass through. What joy! Your bodies will be progressively glorified—your spirits already are—and the glory will shine, shine, through the flesh-lamp of your bodies. Glory!

When I come, the change will be in an instant, a twinkling, but most of the change will already have been done. Think about it! No death. A people for Myself, a new-Adam people who ***know*** *Me, who don't have to die. What glory! Rejoice with Me!*

I am coming in glory to My people, Israel, in a way unprecedented, never seen before, "like nothing ever seen or heard." Yes, I am coming in glory upon My people. Know Me. Know Me finally in My glory.

The Apostle Paul refers to a resurrection from the dead that can occur while those who really know the Lord Jesus are still in their physical bodies. Paul pointed to the cross as a route to resurrection fullness in his letter to the Christians at Philippi:

> …that I may know him and the power of his resurrection, and may share his sufferings, becoming like him in his death, that if possible I may attain the resurrection from the dead. (Philippians 3:10-11 RSV)

Paul is not referring to the general resurrection of the dead here. *The Amplified Bible*'s wording clarifies his comment:

> (For my determined purpose is) that I may know Him (that I may progressively become more deeply and intimately acquainted with Him; perceiving and recognizing and understanding the wonders of His Person more strongly and more clearly) and that I may in that same way come to know the power outflowing from His resurrection (which it exerts over believers) and that I may so share His sufferings as to be continually transformed (in spirit into His likeness even) to His death (in the hope)
>
> **That if possible I may attain to the (spiritual and moral) resurrection (that lifts me) out from among the dead (even while in the body).** (Boldface mine.)

Can we gain a glorified body while still in the flesh body? Jesus experienced this transformation at His Transfiguration. He became resplendent with divine brightness. At the catching away of the church, both those already dead and those still alive on the earth will receive an instant resurrection for their bodies. In both cases, resurrection will happen instantly because both groups, those dead and those still alive, have already died. One group lies dead in the grave. The other has "shared his sufferings, become like him in his death" and has, in a real sense, "died" to its own flesh and its demands. Both groups are prepared in spirit, mind and body to receive a glorified body.

The way Jesus shone at His transfiguration and the way Moses' face radiated glory after spending time with I AM may begin to evidence among those who spend time in His glory. They may shine with a radiance not seen on them before.

This awesome transformation will happen in those 100 percent committed to Him. No low-cost, big-reward glory occurs here. In fact, it comes at great cost. A difference exists between being born again and taking the road to the cross. The new birth is just that—rebirth. The past is cleansed and the old nature is gone. We receive the accompanying free gifts of salvation and entrance to heaven. The road to the cross is the narrow way to spiritual maturity. It is not for newborns still feeding on milk. We must lose our lives in order to save them.

Those who walk the road of suffering with Him and undergo death in Him will also see this resurrection in Him. They have paid a price. They took up His cross and shared in His sufferings. This is not a popular concept today when an instant-gratification gospel is preached, but it is true.

This is the church that will go in the rapture. This is what it means to be ready. We pay a price. Jesus said:

> I will tell you, in that night two will be sleeping in one bed. One will be taken and the other will be left. There will be two women grinding together; one will be taken and the other will be left. (Luke 17:34)

God challenges us to know Him in His glory. His word asks "Who shall ascend the mountain of the Lord?" The answer is, the one with "clean hands and a pure heart." (Psalm 24:3-4) "Clean hands" means cleansing our works, which sometimes requires burning up "hay, straw and stubble." "A pure heart" means removing long-held twistedness deep within our hearts—pride, jealousy, rebellion, greed, all forms of perverseness.

An absolute prerequisite for knowing Him in His glory is to know Him in His suffering. Jesus said:

> If any man would come after Me, let him deny himself and take up his cross and follow me. (Mark 8:34 RSV)

Those who have suffered with Him and allowed their flesh to be transformed will share in His resurrection glory while still in their earthly flesh body. Paul said that he himself hadn't attained it yet, though he pressed on to lay hold of that perfection which the Lord Jesus desired for him. (Philippians 3:12) It means shining with God's glory now and in-a-twinkling completion of the glory process at the Rapture.

We might question this idea, saying "Won't the whole body of Christ be caught away at the same time, not just those who have shared His cross?" Jesus didn't teach that the whole body of Christ would go at once. He showed us in the parable of the ten virgins that only five went with the Bridegroom, though all ten were assuredly virgins, symbolizing being cleansed from sin.

Or we might caution, "Isn't this too much to ask? Hoping for the glory before we go to heaven—is it pride? Is this idea idealistic beyond human possibility? Is it man vaunting himself and striving to be like God?"

Glory is what God has purposed for those who love Him. Jesus said that He has given us His very own glory:

> I have given to them the glory and honor which You have given Me... (John 17:22)

The Apostle Peter reminded church elders that he, Peter, was "called to testify of the sufferings of Christ, as well as to share in the glory (the honor and splendor) that is to be revealed (disclosed, unfolded)." (1 Peter 5:1)

But it is a pearl of great price. It costs. It cost Jesus and we must take up our cross and follow Him—to death, that is, dying to ourselves, our flesh. To gain this in-a-twinkling transformation at the Rapture we must have already passed through the valley of the shadow of death. We must have looked death in the face, with all its finality and loss, and chosen to die for one reason—love of the Lord.

That glory is now disclosed: God's life, light and love within us can shine through a transparent flesh veil to glorify Him.

I have spoken to you regarding My Son, My Son in whom I will restore all things. Adam-like glory, walking in glory. As Adam was cloaked in glory so shall you be clothed in glory. He knew not he was naked for he wore glory as clothing. It covered him like a robe, like a light garment. You will wear this light garment, only it will shine from within. Just as Jesus shone when He was transfigured, so the glory will shine out. It will shine out and be as clothing, as a covering. Believe for it. Pray for it for yourselves and others and you will see it.

This is why I said, "Arise, shine, for the glory of the Lord is risen upon thee." Night covers the earth and darkness the people, but it will just make the glory shine more.

You have paid the price. The price is laying down the flesh.

Glory Clothes

Jesus wore glory clothes at His transfiguration. He became resplendent with divine brightness.

> And His garments became glistening, intensely white as no fuller (cloth dresser, launderer on earth) could bleach them. (Mark 9:3)

God wants us to believe Him for this kind of glory to arise from within us and shine. Instead of protesting in false humility that this prophesied glory covering is too great for us old sinners, God wants us to pray for it and receive it with joy.

We have this treasure, the life of God and His glory, in earthen vessels. The God-life comes from Him. The glory presence doesn't originate with us; no human will, capacity or resource birthed it. But God said we have it as His gift. It's false humility to deny the truth of what He has said and the reality of the I AM-life He has given. Will we rob God of the part He planned for us to play in the great messianic plan He has established since time began?

In fact, we must take our place and occupy our position in the authority and dominion He has given us as bearers of His life and glory. Psalm 110 says, "Your people will offer themselves willingly in the day of your power, in the beauty of holiness and **in holy array**..." We must rise to God's vision of us as holy and arrayed in His glory.

Chapter 10

You Are In Me

From the beginning God ordained our awesome position in Christ. In Christ means "in the Anointed One and His anointing." By abiding in Him, in love, yielded to Him, we assume His authority. We are called to believe in the high position God's word gives us and to walk it out in our daily lives.

Following is a long prophetic word given to the author. It lays bare the mind and heart of God for His church right now. It also details our power-in-intimacy position in Christ:

In the Anointed One

Ephesians Chapter 2 says you are seated with Christ in the heavenly spheres. This is what it means to be "in Me." Yes, you rest in the "secret place of the Most High" (Psalm 91:1), yourself inaccessible to the attacks of the enemy. I call this place My "war room," for you are hidden with Me in a secret place impenetrable to attack from the evil one. I have put you there "in Me." And you operate "in Me" in Christ Jesus.

Notice the word "Christ" comes first. That is to emphasize His name, "the Anointed," for He is Christ, the Anointed Jesus. And like the sacred oil ran down from the priest Aaron's head and over his beard to his body, so the anointing of Christ Jesus flows onto and into the body of Christ.

In the Anointing:

"Seated with the Anointed and His anointing in heavenly places." Where is Christ seated? Why, in the throne room of God, at the Father's right hand, so the scriptures say. Where are you seated? Beside Him. What does "beside" mean? It means alongside, working with, just as Jesus is seated beside (at the right hand of) the Father. It flows from the Father to the Son to you. It is Godly authority in the divine sphere. It is kingship on a level with (although not in the fullness of) Jesus.

Now know, My children, that this authority ***belongs*** *to you. I have given it. I bequeathed it as the testament or will at the death* *of My Son and gave it to you and Jesus. Now receive it. Receive it, My children, for the time is short.*

There is much to do and My body, My bride, refuses to walk in the full vision of who she is. I have clothed her in bridal dress, garlanded her in jewels and precious gems, adorned her in every way, but she walks in the vision of the maidservant, the scullery girl, the char.

She is My bride! She walks in authority, using the full privilege of My Name, which I give to her to order what she needs for herself and her household.

She is My bride! She walks in full authority over the enemy who tried to kidnap her from Me, to steal from her. He is incarcerated by her Godly authority—and yet she fails to use it.

She says, "No, God. I am not the valiant and perfect bride described in your word. I am still a scullery maid. I am humble."

No, you are not humble, else you would hear My word regarding your authority and anointing in Christ Jesus and heed it.

You are all I say you are—in Me. Spotless, without blemish or wrinkle. Perfect before Me and conferred with Godly authority, royal authority because of our betrothal. (2 Corinthians 11:2 and Hosea 2:19-20)

Now walk in it, My bride. Honor and obey Me. Love, honor and obey Me.

In the Secret Place of the Most High:

"He who dwells in the secret place of the Most High shall abide under the shadow of the Almighty." What do you think this means? Of course, it means protection. But much more.

Know ye then, son of men, that I am El Shaddai, the Mighty One. Know then, son and daughter of men, that I am Ruler of the Universe. There is no other. Know then, child of Mine, that I am your papa, your daddy, your fond and doting daddy.

How I will protect! How I will bless! "With long life I will honor you and show you My salvation." (Salvation means My wholeness, healing, deliverance, blessing.) Come into the secret place of the Most High. Come daily, regularly, and with a fresh, open, seeking heart, and I will hide you in Me. From this safe place you can observe the world in rest, in peace, in joy. Nothing shall in any way harm you.

But there is more. You will be hidden in Me, in a place of secret conversation, in a love bower. I will speak My most intimate thoughts to you and you will respond to Me there. I will touch your heart there in the secret place and you will be forever changed. You will be "in Me."

Hidden in Me. Cherished in Me. Beloved in Me. Having open access to Me. In Christ. In the Anointed and His anointing. So My presence conveys power. Oh, yes, being in My presence conveys power.

The anointing is My presence-with-power. You carry Me from the throne room out into your everyday world because you are ***in Me.***

Everything I have in power and glory in Christ Jesus is available to you. Yes, I said, "available to you " Know how precious this is and how you should avail yourself of Me.

In Me, In Love

I am in you. Imprinted on you. Mixed spirits with you. But you are also in Me. ***You.*** *In Me.*

How does that happen?

When you seek Me, invest yourself in Me, surrender to Me, yield yourself to Me, you find access to My heart. You are truly in Me. Now, a child is in the heart of the mother. That child-mother bond will never fail. Whether the child is alive or dead doesn't alter that presence of the child in the mother's heart. The vision never fades. It's a spiritual thing, difficult to explain but easily "known."

So it is with you. I hide you in My heart. You are there. You are in Me because of love. Love creates linkage and bonding that you don't even begin to understand. The beloved is "in" the loved one. The two are one. So we are one because of love. That unity, that oneness, will never be broken. Jesus and the Father are one. You and Jesus are one. You are "in" the Father. We are one because of love.

Now I have explained it to you. (It is unexplainable!) You are in Me. Love does the bonding. You are in Christ, flowing with anointing power. Bonded so deeply that you are one flesh, His body.

Would He not care for and love His body? Groom and discipline His body? Test and use His body's wondrous strength? Does not a true husband love and care for his wife?

Yet a nagging, dissatisfied wife sees none of this. She rails against her husband. She misses seeing his love. So the attitude of the bride is one of lack. She focuses on what appears to her as missing.

She fails to see and appreciate the love and care the husband provides—because it doesn't meet her personal expectations and specifications. She has an unwritten list, a hidden agenda, that she expects and insists he live up to. He is himself. He can only love in his own way. She fails to see and cherish the uniqueness and splendor of his love.

So the bride of Christ has unrealistic expectations of the Bridegroom. She expects Him to relate to her in certain human ways and He relates to her in a higher way that she fails to perceive or understand. He wants only her love. Then all else follows. He wants only her surrender, 100 percent surrender and yielding to Him. That's all. That's everything. He desires a virgin yielded only to Him.

When she yields 100 percent to His love, she is "in Him" so strong that nothing, no one, can break that bonding, that fusion. She is complete "in Him" and He is fully in her. He flows through her; she flows into Him.

The ultimate expression of being "in Christ" will take place at the Marriage Supper of the Lamb. It is consummation. But in Old Testament betrothal the two are already one, committed only to one another and they operate as one. So it shall be with My people as they dedicate and consecrate themselves to Me in love. They reside in Me. They dwell in the secret place of the Most High. They sit in heavenly places of authority because of relationship with Me.

Accept this. Embrace it. Don't deny the truth in false humility. Receive the vision I have for you and walk in the fullness of "You Are In Me."

We Abide in Christ by Faith

We accept the fullness of God's vision for us by faith. We refuse to live out of the old nature. We practice and act out our belief in our new nature.

> For if any person is **in Christ** he is a new creation; the old has passed away. Behold the fresh and new has come. (2 Corinthians 5:17) (Boldface mine)

Have we embraced this new identity in our attitudes and "put on the new self, created to be like God in true righteousness and holiness"? (Ephesians 4:24) We must absorb and accept this truth, then act it out in our daily lives by faith. We must recognize that though this new life is fully available, it remains a choice. By conscious acts of our will we choose or refuse to operate in Christ's anointing.

Dominion Through Surrender

God chose to use the sacrificial love of Jesus to completely reconcile all things back to Himself, "whether things on earth or things in heaven, by making peace through His blood shed on the cross." (Colossians 1:20 NIV)

Our shared dominion depends on this blood-bought reconciliation. It happens in our hearts when we let go of our own lives to love Him. We yield to Him in love and intimate relationship. In that closeness, we see and say what Jesus is doing and saying, just as Jesus did only what the Father was doing and spoke only His words. His authority operated in surrender.

When we yield to Him and behold Him in love, we begin to know His ways. They are so different from our ways. Our minds view as incongruous His ways of peace over turmoil, rest into peak efficiency and joy in the face of deep sorrow. We are reconciled to Him as we enter into the free-access to God's presence that Jesus' cross gained for us.

The Creator planned from the beginning, when He gave Adam dominion, that man would walk in Godly authority. Though Adam lost it, Jesus has wrested that prerogative back from Satan and shared with us His heavenly rule.

We flow in His anointed power. It works by love and yieldedness.

Some Christian men have problems identifying with the notion of their role as part of the bride of Christ. The image of the bride denotes surrender and yieldedness, qualities associated with the feminine psyche. Jesus, who was as manly as man can be, demonstrated how a man can surrender to the Father.

Christ Jesus reigns over all. But His subjection of all things encompasses far more than wielding an iron rod. He is Love. He has reconciled all things to God in peace and love. "He abolished in His (own crucified) flesh the enmity...making peace." (Ephesians 2:15) There is no longer any separation between us and God. Now God wants to reconcile everything to Himself and He has chosen to use us and the position He has given us in Christ to do it.

God challenges us to rise to our full stature **in Christ**. He needs us to believe in and walk in the spiritual maturity He has emphasized in the scriptures. A new and clarion call comes forth now, at the end of the age and in the fullness of time, for God's people to fulfill His majestic vision.

The body of Christ must develop

> ...until we all attain oneness in the faith and in the comprehension of the (full and accurate) knowledge of the Son of God that (we might arrive) at really mature manhood (the completeness of the personality which is

> nothing less than the standard height of Christ's own perfection), the measure of the stature of the fullness of the Christ and the completeness found in Him...-Enfolded in love, let us grow up in every way and in all things into Him Who is the Head (even) Christ (the Messiah, the Anointed One). (Ephesians 4:13, 15)

Do we accept and believe this picture of fullness in Him? Do we accept the full status of our position with Him in heavenly places?

The fact is that we as God's people neither accept nor believe the truth that scripture hammers home to us—that we can achieve the height of Christ's own perfection. We choose to ignore the subject, treating it as a fantasy. Or we collapse into phony humility, thinking "that's not for poor old me." The opposite extreme, of course, lies with those who seize the idea and twist it into an earthly kingdom gained by political power or guns.

Because of unbelief, the people of God fail to walk in the fullness of their position **in Christ.** We restrain His holy work in submitting all things beneath the feet of Christ Jesus. We delay the millennial reign of the Lord Jesus Christ. We can reverse this rebellion by deciding to search God's word, meditate on it, repeat and absorb it into our minds and hearts. We can stand up in authority and declare it.

We can make a decision to seek daily intimacy with Him. Out of that relationship comes the flowering of Christ, the Anointed's, life in us. We then can venture out and practice walking in this full stature, just as a young girl practices walking in high heels or a teenage boy adjusts to new-found height and physical strength.

God calls His people today to declare His word into negativity such as lack, sickness, perversion and death. Knowing the reality of I AM in us, we can rise up in our authority, calling forth life out of dead situations. We are called to witness I AM before heaven and earth.

We are so rooted and grounded in Christ, the Anointed One, by our shared love that we can prophesy to death in His name. He is the Resurrection and the Life. We can call forth spirit and life. We, too, can address death from our position in Christ. Because we are "in Him," who is Life, who is I AM, we can command death to yield to life. The dead areas in our lives and the lives of those we pray for will yield when we witness before heaven and earth that He is I AM.

We can prophesy to depression and suicide. We can prophesy to lack, to lost joy, to a broken spirit, to hopelessness, to the spirit of death. Ezekiel commanded life to enter the spiritually-dead:

> Therefore prophesy and say to them, Thus says the Lord God: Behold, I will open your graves and cause you to come up out of your graves, O My people; and I will bring you (back home) to the land of Israel.
>
> And you shall know that I am the Lord (your Sovereign Ruler), when I have opened your graves and caused you to come up out of your graves, O My people.
>
> And I shall put My Spirit in you and you shall live, and I shall place you in your own land. Then you shall know, understand and realize that I the Lord have spoken it and performed it, says the Lord. (Ezekiel 37:12-14)

The Jerusalem Bible uses God's name Yahweh (translated I AM WHO AM) in the above passage, which lends impact to the declaration, "You shall know that I am I AM."

In prophesying His word, we participate in Christ's mission to subject all things, even death, to His rule. What an honor, to be seated with Him in heavenly places and share in executing His word of righteousness upon His enemies.

Power also resides in His people to repent for our nations and pray down high towers of greed, deceit, lust, pride and materialism. Hell reels when we declare over our land that "our God reigns." We have a mandate to proclaim joy, peace, righteousness and light into our troubled world and reap a rich harvest of God's sown word.

When we fulfill God's vision, we assume our full status "in Him."

Celebrate this power-in-love. Psalm 149:5 proclaims, "Let the saints rejoice in this honor!" The Psalm describes our victory:

> Let the high praises of God be in their throats and a two-edged sword in their hands;
>
> To execute vengeance upon the heathen and punishment on the peoples;
>
> To bind their kings with chains, and their nobles with fetters of iron.
>
> To execute upon them the judgement written. This honor have all His saints.
>
> Praise ye the Lord!

Section Four

Storm, Refining Fire and Judgement

Tempest wind stripped.

Shaking jolted apart our flimsy houses
and exposed rot in our foundations.

Impurity and idolatry
permeated the bedrock of our lives.
Fire came to melt and separate out the unholy.

Now, a new purity strengthens us to withstand

the Day of the Lord,

a Day of Judgement,

a Day of glory and power.

Chapter 11

I Am God of the Storm

It began as a pleasant day on the lake, so relaxing that one of the men snoozed as the others rowed across the wide expanse of water. Almost unnoticed, the atmosphere changed. A leaden stillness that fishermen know as foreboding charged the air and crept into their consciousness. The sleepy one dozed on as wind came from behind the stillness, stinging faces and causing the rowers to strain against its force.

While Jesus slept in the sailboat, a full-scale tornado swept down on the Sea of Galilee, causing the waves to swamp the boat. His friends realized that "they were in great danger."

Not imagined danger. The men were experienced sailors and fishermen, at home on the water. Fear seized their imaginations. It crowded out the trust in the one who slept calmly beside them in the boat—the Great I AM. He had sent them across the water and He controlled their circumstances. Wakened, Jesus rebuked the wind and raging waves. Calm came. Then He said to them, "Why are you so fearful? Where is your faith, your trust, your confidence in Me—in My veracity and integrity?"

• • •

How could the disciples have calmed the storm themselves? The storm within them would have quieted if they had begun praising God. The storm surrounding them would have succumbed to their word spoken in Jesus name. The fact is, however, that even with Jesus in the boat, storms arise. What should we do when suffering comes?

Some will say, "I don't have to suffer because Jesus suffered for me." It's true. He bore our grief and carried our sorrow. By His stripes we are healed. He was chastised for our peace. His cross paid the price for our sins.

But it is also true that every Christian is called to "take up his cross daily and follow Me (cleave steadfastly to Me, conform wholly to My example in living, and, if need be, in dying also.) (Luke 9:23)

What has to die is the flesh, the dominance of the old nature. Its death involves pain. And let's face it, pain hurts.

Those who participate in Christ's cross will participate in His glory. As we saw in Chapter 8, in knowing His suffering, we become "continually transformed to His death" so as to share in His resurrection glory. Paul underscores in Philippians 1:29 that we have been granted the *privilege* "to suffer in His behalf." Jesus Himself encouraged us to take up our cross and follow Him. (Matthew 16:24) While churches in nations such as China instruct new Christians that they will experience suffering, and possibly martyrdom, American pulpits fail to echo this message of the cross of Jesus. In Jesus' life, suffering was the path to glory. And He told us that no servant is greater than His master.

Storm

Trouble will come. Jesus told us that the storms of life are inevitable. When we yield to God as Lord of the storm and die to ourselves, we will see our regenerated spirit strengthened and the "me first" attitude of the flesh diminished.

Most of us can handle daily troubles. But when the disturbance escalates to storm, then hurricane stage, we get rattled. "Where is God?" we ask. The answer is, He is in the storm.

I am hidden in the storm. I am hidden in your storm. Just as the hurricane has an eye, a center of calm out of the raging wind, so I remain at the center of your storm, a bastion of peace.

Psalm 18 describes a mighty storm lashing out hailstones, lightning, smoke, coals of fire, earthquake, distress and darkness. Mountain foundations trembled.

But the psalm reveals that God is the Lord of the storm. He is hidden in the chaos.

Verse 11 in *The Amplified Bible* declares, "He made darkness His secret hiding place; as His pavilion around about Him were dark waters and thick clouds of the sky."

Those in a storm now need to know: Jesus is Lord of the storm.

The storm probably began with some gusty wind, the kind that strips leaves from trees, breaks a weak branch, blows away anything not anchored.

The wind comes as a surprise. It arrives in squally blasts that trouble our composure. Maybe the car breaks down, a child gets into trouble at school, hostility disrupts things at work. Loud neighbors continually disturb our peace.

Soon thunder and lightning begin. A loved one becomes seriously ill. A crises develops in a pregnancy. A scandal involving our name arises.

A stinging gale-force wind begins to blow. It gathers strength, refusing to let up. A teenage son attempts suicide. A job is lost. A marriage is on the rocks.

The wind strips from us things we thought we needed. Sometimes it takes a while, but we begin to realize the things we held onto so tightly have lost their value. Family reputation is no longer important when a son's life is at stake. Being right in a marital battle matters no longer when the marriage appears lost. Self-centeredness melts away when pain stirs empathy for others who are suffering.

Psalm 18 describes a storm so cataclysmic that "the beds of the sea appeared and the foundations of the earth were laid bare." Our storms can culminate in shaking so severe that the very core of our being lies exposed. Having lost everything—possessions, people we love, strength, dreams, hopes—our foundations lay exposed.

At the center of the maelstrom we find God waiting. Despite the raging hurricane around us, He is peace. He is sure, calm and quiet. And His peace is sufficient. He's saying "Let all this go and make Me first in your life."

If we stand in the storm on the rock that is Jesus Christ, we will remain anchored.

Psalm 18 calls Him, "my Rock, my Fortress, my Deliverer." When we stand on Jesus, the Rock of our salvation and take a stance to face the wind, we will outlast the storm in safety. Stand on His goodness, integrity and faithfulness. We need to turn our face toward the wind and allow the stripping to occur. We need to shout His praise above the scream of the storm. We need to plant our feet so securely, by standing on His word and His promises, that our feet are cemented to that Rock.

The Lord allows the storm because He needs wind to strip us, rain to cleanse us, thunder to make us finally hear His voice. He uses lightning's flash to illuminate our sinfulness and chaos to make us anchor ourselves securely to Him. He needs us to get serious and make Him Lord of *everything*.

During low moments, we might consider Him a harsh judge. However, He has an urgent reason to get us into right standing with Him. He has a vital need to cleanse us from entrenched bad attitudes, idolatry of things, unrepentant sin.

Mercy in Judgement

As the Bible prophesies, He is bringing judgement on the

earth. It's coming soon. His justice demands He judge sin wherever He finds it. He desires to cleanse us from sin during His time of mercy-in-judgement. He is still sitting on the mercy seat. When He stands up to judge the world, His mercy will not soften His wrath. He needs to bring us to repentance and cause us to come totally under His Lordship. Then He can restore us to beauty, wholeness, radiance beyond our ability to imagine. Then He can, in His justice and fairness, protect us in the time of trial to come upon the whole earth. This is His desire and His plan.

The Father is saying:

I am in control. Know, believe and understand that I am in control of your life, right now in this storm. Glorify Me. Glorify Me in the storm. Repentance, healing and restoration are My goals. Shock treatment is sometimes necessary for some individuals, but know that I am in control of the turbulence and judgement blast.

Jesus was in the boat that rocked in the storm on the Sea of Galilee. Jesus was the fourth man in the fire with the Hebrew children in Babylon. I have given you My Son, Jesus, to stand in this storm with you. So relax. Be comforted and consoled and go on, go forth with praise.

When God brings a whirlwind of judgement into our lives He is saying, "Learn now to trust in Me, My character, My goodness, My integrity." All the props are gone, all the stops are out. The situation is truly serious and possibly life-threatening to ourselves or a loved one Can we trust, despite all natural evidence to the contrary, that He is a good God and that He will not hurt us but will see us safely through?

I will speak to you a word that forms your heart, one that changes your life in a daily way. Entreat My word in your heart. Tell your heart to be changed by My word, for I speak a great and mighty word to you today: Alleluia! The Lord God reigns! Know this: I am in control. Know this beyond a shadow of a doubt for you will need to know this in the days to come. Was I in control of the Gulf War? Yes! I am and will be in control of future events that will unfold very quickly. So know this and comfort your heart when it happens.

"Know that I am in control" means that all things will work together for your good. Know that a loving compassionate God is pulling the strings. Know that I will not lose one of My little ones. Remember the Apostles and their grief after Jesus' death—and remember their joy and incredulity at the resurrection. They were warned, but they didn't know how to

believe it, for God's plan, God's ways, so countered their expectations. So it is with you. I will destroy all that is not from Me to raise up what is eternal.

God has said in His word that He will destroy "hay, straw and stubble." The storm reveals all the rickety structures we've built and lays bare their false foundations. Anything that can't stand for eternity must be destroyed. At the foundations of our lives we find the false—idol worship. We see that we have poured out our lives and strength on creatures rather than on the Creator.

The tornado lays bare the foundations of our lives. Our security devices, comfort sources, reliance on shaky supports, all break apart under the lashing. Destruction and loss occur. Stripped of our protections and comforts, we confront our own negativity and sin. Whatever absorbs our energy, imagination and thought life, along with much of our time, is revealed to us as an idol. Is it food and drink, sex, physical fitness? Houses, cars, possessions? Is it pride-driven power in business or social position? Is it rebellion? Whatever it is, the pursuit that dominates our thinking and activity, if it's not of God, will be judged.

Know ye this, son of man, know ye this, daughter, know all who dwell on the face of the earth:

The Lord thy God is one God.

He will not efface another or compete with another god in your lives. He will be one God. The destruction of your gods is coming because the Lord will be one God.

A chorus of praise and worship has gone up from the earth, a sacrificial praise and worship in suffering, enough to appease our God and have Him say, Yes, I will reign. I will inhabit the praises of My people. I will take over and reign, according to their prayer and declaration.

Now then, what does that mean? Change must come. Every high tower brought down, every low thing raised up (every deficiency repaired), every mountain leveled, every valley filled in, so to speak.

I am God and I will do it.

From our viewpoint, God's effort to establish Himself as one God in our hearts may appear devastating. He understands our pain. This prophecy was spoken at a local prayer meeting in Breckenridge, Colorado:

I weep, contrite and sorrowing, at My judgement which brings pain to My beloved. Know that I am in control. The trou-

ble of the troublous times has begun. Judgement will fall like the wink of an eye. Sometimes I have to tear down an altar of idolatry to raise up an altar of worship. Don't be afraid, for I am in control. I will bring good from judgement.

Our idols are false gods. *False*. We're using our God-infused human spirit, our God-life, which makes us able to worship Him and relate to Him person to person, and pouring it out on something false. In the end, this pursuit of emptiness will bring death.

Fully Alive

God wants us to live up to our fullest potential and to walk in His glory. He wants us fully alive. We get that by beholding Him, knowing Him, relating to Him, drawing from Him, blossoming, growing and maturing in Him, becoming whole and holy as He is holy.

Death comes before resurrection. Jesus had to go to the cross to rise in glory. We have to die to ourselves to live in Him. This death is ugly and brutal just as the cross was ugly and brutal. It hurts. It's final. But it is the route to resurrection.

Jesus went before us.

God is saying:

Gethsemane is My word for you. Drink. Drink deeply of the cup of judgement for it will be health to your body and solace to your soul in the end. Drink the cup I give you for I AM in control, says the Lord.

And I will do it. I will accomplish all things I have in mind for you. It is easier when you are submitted, but I will do it, says the Lord.

For I am committed to you and your future and I say, "'Nothing but the best for My child,' says the Lord of Love." Though it's hard, accept this from Me.

When sin entered in with Adam and Eve, God had already sacrificed the Son of His heart for man. He is called the Lamb slain from the foundation of the world—before Adam. Jesus drank the cup in the Garden of Gethsemane. He went to the cross, a sinless lamb slain from the foundation of the world. Jesus, who paid the price for our sin, has earned the right to be our Judge. He is worthy to judge. It is Jesus, our Redeemer, who is the Lord of Hosts. (Isaiah 44:6) And it is Jesus , the Lord of Hosts, who sits in these last days with a refiner's fire.

We can trust Him to do the job in us.

Chapter 12

Fire

> The Lord (the Messiah, the Anointed One) whom you seek will suddenly come to His temple...says the Lord of Hosts. But who can endure the day of His coming? And who can stand when He appears? For He is like a refiner's fire... He will sit as a refiner and purifier of silver and He will purify the priests...refine them like gold and silver that they may offer to the Lord offerings in righteousness...
>
> Then I will draw near to you for judgement...says the Lord of Hosts." (Malachi 3:1-5)

Malachi clearly identifies Jesus, the Messiah, as the Lord of Hosts and the Lord of Hosts as the one who sits as a refiner and judge.

After His judgement comes restoration. Pressure on "lively stones" (1 Peter 2:5) makes precious stones or jewels. The New Jerusalem, representative of the bride of Christ, has a foundation of twelve splendid jewels.

Which stones in a structure receive the greatest pressure? The foundation stones, of course. Pressure makes natural vegetation into coal and coal into diamonds. To those of us who are "storm-tossed" Isaiah prophesies:

> ...behold I will set your stones in fair colors and lay your foundations with sapphires. And I will make your windows of agates and your gates of carbuncles and all your walls of precious stones. (Isaiah 54:11-12)

The Lord uses every ounce of the pressure He allows in our lives to make us His own gems.

> And they shall be Mine, says the Lord of Hosts, in that day when I publicly recognize and openly declare them to be My jewels. (Malachi 3:17)

God is telling His people that the refiner's fire is "a controlled burn." Jesus, the Lord of Hosts, the Messiah, watches over it. But those who fail to seek Him and refuse to submit to cleansing fire will undergo another kind of fire. That fire destroys utterly.

> For behold, the day comes that shall burn like an oven and all the proud and arrogant, yes, and all that do wickedly and are lawless, shall be stubble; the day that comes shall burn them up, says the Lord of Hosts...
>
> But unto you who revere and worshipfully fear My name shall the Sun of Righteousness rise with healing in His wings and His beams, and you shall go forth and gambol like calves released from the stall and leap for joy. (Malachi 4:1-2)

Foundations Exposed

The storm strips away anything not tied down, anything flimsy, anything or anyone not planted firmly on the Rock. It exposes foundational attitudes. But the fire goes deeper than the storm, melting away bedrock iniquity fused so securely that only a crucible can break its hold. The fire judges sin's hold on us.

For example, rejection may lie at the core of one's personality. Is rejection sin? Or is it woundedness? Both. Rejection may begin as a wound when someone is abandoned, betrayed or hurt. The rejection experience is not sin. It certainly doesn't qualify as a conscious will toward wrong-doing. Springing from the bad seed of the hurt, however, come wrong choices. We choose inner vows, thoughts and a pattern of emotional reactions that twist our thinking and behavior. These pervert our responses to others. They block our relationship with God. Acting out this hurt becomes a life-long mode of operation, based so deep that it eludes conscious awareness. But God sees it. Rejection equals iniquity. It has to go.

The goal in setting us free is to release joy. We are free of sin and bondages to be whole and restored before our King. We are set free to worship as "priests" (Malachi 1:3), having received clean hands and a pure heart.

Personal judgement of idolatry and sin may cost everything. The idol worship and deep-rooted sin lie unperceived until stripped. Wind finally lays it bare and fire consumes it. In the end, the worldly things we strive after, work for, give our prime attention, are false. They're not the God we seek, who will satisfy that underlying, motivating need for love and comfort, peace and joy, beauty and harmony. Only God can fill these human needs. We waste our time trying to squeeze satisfaction from other people, drugs or alcohol, expensive toys or physical strength, beauty, pleasure. When everything is gone and God is sufficient, the work of the Lord of Hosts is finished.

After a night of storm, the sun rises bright over a fresh-scrubbed earth. The air is clean. Grass sparkles in the sunlight. Nature appears new and charged with hope. Even the damage—a downed tree limb, a mangled shed roof—seems more manageable than during the night. Energy comes for the cleanup.

Judgement costs all, leaving us empty. Then God presents Himself to fill the void. He wants us to seek Him first. If we truly do that, He gives Himself. When He becomes enough, then He can lavish on us the blessings that accompany a right relationship with Him.

His purpose is to prepare us to receive His restoration and blessing. But He has an even brighter aim—to prepare us to manifest His glory.

> Beloved, do not be amazed and bewildered at the fiery ordeal which is taking place to test your quality, as though something strange (unusual and alien to you and your position) were befalling you.
>
> But insofar as you are sharing Christ's sufferings, rejoice, so that when His glory (full of radiance and splendor) is revealed, you may also rejoice with triumph (exultantly). (1 Peter 4:12-13)

Chapter 13

Judgement

The Day of the Lord has arrived and is well underway.

Judgement began first in the house of God. The Holy Spirit has exposed sin in believers' lives. The Holy Spirit began with gentle conviction. Some quickly yielded, actually inviting Him to send fire. Others needed more conviction. For those who needed it, storm and fire followed. The Lord's goals—repentance, salvation and restoration—have been accomplished by His Spirit in a fast-paced, disciplined and determined effort because the time is short. Now judgement has appeared on the world scene as well. Jesus, the Lord of Hosts who sits with a refiner's fire, supervises this mighty wide-scale work.

Scripture affirms that judgement begins in God's own family, His closest ones. Among the righteous? Yes. Christians? Yes. We saw in the preceding pages that believers harbor deep-rooted sin. We used rejection as an example but fear, unbelief, rebellion, greed, pride and others become established as iniquity. Surrender and repentance under God's merciful hand yield peace. Paul warned the Roman Christians that the stubborn set themselves up for wrath:

> ...by your callous stubbornness and impenitence of heart you are storing up wrath and indignation for yourself on the day of wrath and indignation, when God's righteous judgement (just doom) will be revealed.
>
> For those who are self-seeking and self-willed and disobedient to the truth but responsive to wickedness, there will be indignation and wrath.
>
> (And) there will be tribulation and anguish and calamity and constraint for every soul of man who (habitually) does evil, the Jew first and also the Greek (Gentile)" (Romans 2:5-9)

Judgement begins in God's house, first with the Jew (believer). Then the Gentile (unbeliever) will come under judgement.

I am Judge of All, the Lord of Hosts. My Father has given it over to Me to judge. Know that I am your Redeemer, the One who loves you and died for you. Unrepentant men will come under Tribulation Judgement. But those with a shred of remorse and humility before Me will be hounded by My Spirit to repent, to be saved from the Judgement coming upon the whole earth.

Hear Me, My people! Repent on time. Repent before the Judgement comes and get right with God. Repent while mercy still stays My hand. Turn away, completely away, from ties to the world, lest you be judged with the world. For I will judge sin where I see it in the Tribulation Judgement to come. And it will be too late to cry out, "Lord, Lord!" for I will have put on My fierce face of judgement and will not hear. Now is the time to repent and even now the time is very short. Amen! I have spoken and warned you, says the Lord.

Whether we recognize the signs or not, the Lord's day has arrived the way Jesus foresaw, with birth pangs. First, stirrings, then emerging cramps, slowly building strength, regularly increasing their pace. A transition time occurs. Then suddenly hard labor begins with severe and unrelenting contractions, wrenching and pushing—towards birth.

After the birth we forget the labor pains. And birth is what God has in mind. Judgement will cleanse the earth from sin, bringing every high mountain crashing low, filling every valley, consuming all evil with fire. Pangs of tribulation will birth the millennial reign of our Lord, Jesus Christ.

Safe in Hour of Trial

Jesus, in Revelation 3:10, promises the refined Philadelphia church, which "kept My word of patient endurance," that He will keep them safe in the hour of trial to come upon the whole earth, that is, the Tribulation Judgement. His word in the prophecy below repeats that consoling promise:

Know that Judgement begins. Hear this: Judgement begins. Birth pangs, waves are over. The real thing begins. Contractions with great force. Birthing. Birthing something new, something better. Cataclysmic contractions. Wait. Behold. See that My word is true.

But I will hold you, My people, in the palm of My hand and keep you (and yours) under the shadow of the Almighty. Worry not, fret not, for you are cared for and protected.

Anyone who has endured the judgement occurring in the

house of God knows that God is a just judge. No matter how we refuse to look at our own personal sin and continue to cling to it, when God uses circumstances to capture our attention and cause us to confront that sin, we realize He is right. Attitudes and behavior we once fiercely held appear detestable and repugnant. We are relieved that He delivered us from our destructions.

"God shows no partiality (undue favor or unfairness)," according to Romans 2:11, and "we know that the judgement of God falls justly and in accordance with truth..." (Romans 2:2)

That's because the One who judges is Faithful and True.

In the magnificent picture of heaven's pre-Judgement assembly portrayed by John in Revelation 5, the angel thunders "Who is worthy to open the scroll?" No answer comes. Then one of the elders proclaims, "See the Lion of the tribe of Judah has won... He can open the scroll and break its seven seals." Jesus, the Lion of Judah and Victor over sin and death, is worthy to judge. He is the Lord of Hosts who conducts judgement.

The loving face of our gentle Saviour turns into the fierce face of Judge and Absolute Eternal Lord and Master, One who loved us enough to die and is righteous enough to judge. He acts in His role as Lord of Hosts:

> Thus says the Lord, the King of Israel and his Redeemer, the Lord of hosts: I am the First and I am the Last; besides Me there is no God. (Isaiah 44:6)

Revelation 2:8 declares, "These are the words of the First and the Last, Who died and came to life again." Jesus, our Redeemer, died for our sins. How fitting that He is chosen by the Father as Judge.

The entire Book of Revelation illumines Jesus as the Lamb who provided redemption, Him who ever loves us and has once (for all) loosed and freed us from our sins. He will execute judgment and ultimately subdue evil—so His full and final, everlasting and absolute reign can begin.

His love lies behind judgement. Only thunder, mountains crashing to the sea and chaos will get the attention of hardened hearts. He doesn't want to lose a single one. For those judged, both in the church and outside, are His creation, His own beloved children, ones that bear His image.

Regarding judgement in the church, He laments:

The God of Love speaks and says, My love will cover Israel in time of trouble in the church as I tear down pillars of the altar (Amos 9:1) and send them crashing on the heads of the people.

This is the church. My own people! Shall I turn My fierce

face upon them? says the Lord of Hosts. And yet the shaking that topples upon the holy altar of our God—and brings no praise or comfort to Him—is necessary, is vital. So in the very sanctuary you will see it. This church or that will fail, fall apart under the weight of My Judgement, says the Lord. False altars. Eroded pillars. Empty vanity. Hollow. You will watch and see the reward of the wicked. And yet I will save—will not lose one true grain that is Mine in the sieve that I shake. My aim is to restore.

The Lord not only laments, He grieves over the Judgement because He has compassion for the beloved people, His new Israel, who need cleansing.

The God of Love, Peace and Grace, familiar God, loving God, speaks and says, "Woe! Woe is Me. Woe!" Woeful is My heart, a heart of woe for My people Israel. A heart of compassion and sharing with them in their sorrow; an aching, pain-ridden heart is Mine, saith your God. For I love My children and My heart is torn for them. Oh, know Me. Yes! I do suffer for My children for I am locked in relationship with them because of My love, just as you are with your children.

Now know, Israel of God and people of Zion, the God of Love and Peace says, "Judgement falls." And My heart is one of concern and compassion, suffering—with My children. My heart is moved to weeping at what's coming for My children today, in this time period, an appointed time for Judgement.

I weep, Oh, hear Me, I weep for My children today. I weep. Oh, your God, even your God and Lord, weeps.

Jesus, who judges, also grieves because He must unveil before His beloved His fierce face of judgement. How many will He lose when He unmasks His whole Self? Will we continue to love Him when we see the demonstration of His absolute holiness? Can we love the whole God, the One who is overflowing with compassion but also demands righteousness? When the Savior executes justice, damage, destruction and bloodshed will result. Can we accept and love Him in His vengeance against corruption?

He is calling on us not only to understand His Judgement with empathy for Him in our hearts but also to participate with Him in the Judgement. Recognized industries of the corrupt system the Bible calls "Babylon," such as the abortion industry, the pornography network, the drug and tobacco empires will crumble when His people declare their downfall speaking God's word.

He wants all to pray for the restoration He yearns to bring.

The God of Love says, Babylon is fallen! Speak it out after Him: Babylon is fallen. Hear the words of My angel declaring in heaven, Babylon is fallen. Declare it in the earth.

Judgement has fallen on your nation, America. But My people will call forth My mercy in Judgement, urging Me not to destroy but to restore.

It gratifies the heart of God to pour out His blessing as a reward to His own during a time of harsh judgement.

God's heart is a heart of love. He is Love. His Fatherly heart is broken because of judgement. The Savior's heart is ravaged by judgement. The Lord God who is Love and who is a personal God, seeking relationship with His loved ones, needs the consolation of those close to His heart. He promised in Isaiah 61:2 a "day of vengeance and a year of favor from our God." This promise, which we will delve into later, guarantees the simultaneous outpouring of both retribution and glory. The blessing accompanying the glory will create a jubilee of restoration for the fire-refined people who have submitted to pre-Judgement judgement.

The God of Love speaks again saying, Know Me. Know My heart. Know Me today as a God of vengeance, a God of vindication. Know Me in My promise, long ago shown to you, for a day of vengeance, a year of Jubilee redemption and blessing from our God. Know Me now as wrath begins as a God who tenderly blesses His children, His righteous. See Me in My tenderness, as Josephine saw Napoleon, in the quiet moments of the heart together, for I need your solace, beloved, beloved of the Father, beloved of the Bridegroom, beloved and cherished of the Spirit.

I must clothe Myself in zeal because My heart is not a heart of judgement but of love for My children who will go into perdition, whose blood is on My garment. On My garment. (Isaiah 63:2) The ones I loved and made and formed and cherished. Do you see why judgement is delayed? Why I am slow to anger—and justice? Why I say justice comes swiftly? Look at My loss: My own children, the work of My hands.

And yet the time has run out and opportunity for choices, to choose Life, has been given over and over. And now Judgement begins. Stay with Me. Stay at My side, bride of Christ, and see Me through.

Storms and fire have prepared God's people to receive His anointing and to play a powerful role in bringing about the jubilee of restoration He desires to give.

Worshippers Faced Fire First

Refining fire comes in waves. First, the "priests," those who minister and worship before God, went into the crucible that produces pure gold. Then came others in "Zion," which is both the place of worship and the seat of spiritual government, where the spiritual leadership operates. (These Zion rulers may not look like ranking personages from a natural view; they might be little, hidden unnoticed people.) Later "Israel," meaning believers in general, stand in the wind of judgement and in the fire. Finally, all who come under the New Covenant, including people who rarely even think about God, will undergo Judgement fire. The purpose of this battering ram of crisis in their lives is to make them look up, to see Jesus and be changed. God doesn't want one to perish. When the Judgement sickle goes in, it produces harvest. God will have a harvest. He will bring in every person He can, using tough love when that finally becomes necessary.

> Woe to Ariel (Jerusalem)...she shall be to Me like an Ariel (an altar hearth, a hearth of burning, the altar of God). And I will encamp against you round about; and I will hem you in with siege works and I will set up fortifications against you. (Isaiah 29:2-3)

Jerusalem, the spiritual city of God's people, has and will undergo siege works until every high tower and false altar comes down. But the "city" is comprised of individuals. Just as the anointing, blessing and glory set individuals free, so the vengeance against sin affects personal lives.

While natural mountains may tremble and fall into the sea, so spiritual mountains of idolatry in individual lives will crash and fall. While we will see Tribulation signs in the heaven and the earth, much of Judgement's blast will occur largely unseen in individuals' lives.

Great glories will happen while the church is undergoing much suffering. You will see two streams: one a sewer and one the river of life, the pent up stream of My Spirit.

You will see Judgement, great unrelenting siege-works Judgement against even the church. Oh, yes, My own church. You will see and wonder at these siege works. All the baptized are Mine, all who made a youthful decision for Me, no matter how far they've strayed, they are Mine, covenanted to Me in the cross of Jesus, and they are Mine, My church, My people, My Israel. They are not the lost or the heathen. And I will lay siege works against them.

Now I have explained these things to you to give you understanding on a practical level of the things you will see.

I have invited each one separately and uniquely to come to me. All were invited. Some actively turned Me down, rejecting Me in this invitation. Will the whole church have a spiritual feast in the wilderness? No.

So know how to react, how to assess these situations you will see around you, situations of great distress, great tragedy and loss in families (even broken families; they're still families to Me) and know, understand, perceive and recognize that God is a battering ram.

The Kingdom of God is in men's hearts and it is in individual lives where much of the Judgement will take place. Earthquakes, natural disasters, economic ruin will occur, but mainscale Judgement will happen in men's hearts. Only the tip of the iceberg will appear for others to see. So know that God is in control. Rest, despite turmoil and darkness.

Purified to Witness

A witness needs clean hands and a pure heart. Jesus said in giving the Beatitudes, "Blessed are the pure of heart for they shall see God." (Matthew 5:8) God has purified His people because He plans to demonstrate Himself in a new and riveting way. This showing forth will be for us life-changing as was Christ's demonstration at His cross. He wants us to witness this new epiphany of God as Who He Is.

Know beyond knowing, deep in your heart, with bedrock assurance, that I am God. There is no other. What I will do now is unprecedented for I have a people in the earth who have made me their God.

God of Mercy and Love is My name. My mercy will be shown forth in a people appropriate for mercy. My love will be show forth in a people hungry for My love.

As Judgement comes, as Judgement comes, as Judgement comes, the outflowing of My mercy will be unprecedented. I will demonstrate My Self as God, WHO I AM. No one will be left unsure of WHO I AM in this coming hour because I will demonstrate Myself. Jesus at His cross demonstrated My sacrificial, broken love for mankind. He was My demonstration. Now I will once again make a demonstration within the framework of mercy and judgement. Amen. I have spoken.

The Lord has prepared us to witness to I AM.

Witness. I have raised you up and strengthened you for a purpose: to represent Me to a generation, a people.

What is a witness? A representative of Me. What are the 144,000 witnesses in the book of Revelation? (Revelation 11:3) A holy number sent out.

What is their call? To witness to the whole earth. They are virgins. There is no guile in their mouths. They are redeemed of the Lamb and they follow the Lamb wherever He goes. They are like a bell sheep who follows right behind the shepherd and leads the others. Those who know Me deeply and intimately will perform this function.

Now this takes place during the Tribulation. Will not My mercy be greatest during the time of testing to come upon the whole earth? Prepare your heart, for 144,000 of My finest are going out now and soon, equipped to be My witnesses. Study "witness" and see the call to Moses to witness. Know me as my witness. Know Me intimately, then witness to Who I Am. Amen.

Jesus has set the pattern as a Witness, for He witnessed of the Father. Jesus, in His own body, demonstrated the Father's sacrificial love, a humble, giving love that hung naked on a cross. God is saying that His witnesses in the Spirit will evidence Him in a frank, honest way as Jesus did.

I am sure, faithful and true, a Witness of My Father. And the Spirit witnesses of Me, a faithful and true witness. Relax and rely on Me, for I am the Firstborn of the witnesses.

A martyr is a witness to My resurrection, believing so much in My Life that he or she lets go his or her earthly life for Me. A prophet is a witness to the promise made through David, made through Jesus. The two witnesses in the Book of Revelation are the summing up of all My Old Testament and New Testament witnesses, the king and priest figures who testify of Me with signs and wonders following the word.

So go forward knowing that witnesses, 144,000 of them (a figure that signifies a large and perfect number) are going out into the land to speak and witness to Me. Their witness will be honest, real and frank—not a pretty religious picture—but hard-reality, blood-and-guts sacrificial witnessing.

Refined and Prepared

One compelling reason that God refines His people is to prepare them for the coming glory. He wants them so pure that they can withstand His full anointing. Evil falls before the anointing. Sickness flees. Fear melts. Demons retreat. That anointing, that

God-presence, is so holy that presumption can't stand before it. The Old Testament Israelite who reached out to touch the Ark of the Covenant to steady it dropped dead. The anointing is so strong it destroys evil. Ananias and Sapphira who plotted together to knowingly deceive the Apostle Peter died because of the power of the anointing.

God wants us prepared to stand the force of His glory.

So, we undergo judgement and cleansing for two reasons: our eternal good and for the purity to withstand the coming move of holiness.

Know world, know earth, that I am God. I will have ***no*** *false gods before Me. I will judge and topple these idols as the mountains crash into the sea. And know and be convinced, know now beyond a shadow of a doubt, know understand and comprehend that the times are now serious. We're playing hard ball and no shadow, no deviation from holiness is allowed.* ***None****. No sinful indulgence of the flesh is allowed.* ***None****. No demonic control or influence. The times have changed,* ***now*** *and* ***today****. Gears have shifted.*

Be set free by My mighty power over the rule of the flesh, the lusts, wants and demands of the flesh. I command it. Otherwise I must judge it. Amen! My justice demands that I must judge it. Understand now the time for playing with this, vacillating, fence straddling is over!

Who can ascend the mountain of God? Who can stand in His awesome presence? Who can "know" Him? Who can minister love to Him? Who can live in the secret place of the Most High, dwelling with the Holy One, the Ancient of Days, the Lord of Creation in intimacy? The one with clean hands and a pure heart.

A final reason for refiner's fire is to cleanse us so thoroughly that we can stand face to face with Him. He loves us and yearns for heart to heart communion. Our hearts must be pure to relate purely to Him.

When the gold is tested seven times for purity, the refiner's job rests complete. The Lord of Hosts is well pleased. He says to His people, "I have refined you for Myself. And now I give Myself to you as My reward because you have endured My testing with patience and love.

The following words from the Lord are directed to a specific individual. But they demonstrate the refining work God is doing in all His people—and the reward He promises:

I AM. Yes! I AM. I am present in the darkness as well as the light, in the valley as well as the mountaintop, in sorrow as well as joy.

You have walked through the valley of darkness of the shadow of death, you have mourned with the sorrowful—in Me. You have sojourned in darkness, walked in the mist blindly following Me, gloried in Me despite the shame, fought hard to resist the enemy, joyed in a time of sorrow, demonstrated peace in the midst of chaos, loss, fire and ashes. Peace reigned.

I have seen thy ways and found them good. Like Me. Demonstrating My character in you. You have been tested and tried by fire. In patience and forbearance did you deal with your enemies and in humility before Me, not taking things into your own hands.

See, I have worked in you and tested you mightily, with good results, eternal results, all because you were willing. My risk, My great risk, in making man has paid off in you. There is greater value because of the great risk. I stand to lose greatly if My children turn against Me in Judgement. So today, receive your exceeding great reward. That is Me. I am your Reward. More of Me, My life in you.

Receive Me today.

Section Five

The Anointing

Oil flows from its source,
a bounteous olive tree
in the Holy of Holies of God's temple.
It continually fills the golden lamp.
No human hand touches it.

This prophetic picture from Zechariah
illustrates the continual-flow anointing
God's people will experience today.

Consecrated
with the anointing of their Messiah,
God's people have now become
a nation of kings and priests.

Holy and majestic,
Christ our King
now initiates His messianic reign,
through His yielded and perfected people.

Chapter 14

The Anointing of the Messiah

Christ is not the last name of Jesus. Christ is His title. The word *Christos* is Greek (because the New Testament was written in Greek) and is translated "the Anointed One." The name Jesus Christ means Jesus, the *Messiah* (in Hebrew), which means Jesus, the Anointed (in English).

When the Jews asked Jesus if He was "the Christ," they meant, "Are you the long-awaited Anointed One, the Messiah?"

The anointing is God's presence, manifested in power, power that does good. The liberating power of the Anointed One seized the attention of the first century world. The early church ignited with the message of the Anointed and His anointing. Early believers called themselves "the anointeds," or *Christ* ians. (*Webster's New World Dictionary* defines the word "Christian" as a person "professing belief in Jesus as the Christ," or the Anointed One.) Afire with the message of the Anointed, these new anointed ones spread the good news to the ends of their known world.

The message of the Anointed, and the zeal of the early church, began to dwindle from wildfire to a flicker when the Emperor Constantine institutionalized the church in the third century. God's manifest presence, however, continued to rest on individuals throughout history.

But God planned to revive the power of the anointing in the last days. His Old Testament prophets had announced this plan. They foretold a revival of the anointing of David, a "man after God's own heart." They referred to the anointing as the tent, tabernacle or "dwelling place" of David, an Old Testament leader who represents the anointing. God promised:

> In that day will I raise up the fallen tabernacle of David...I will raise up its ruins and I will build it as in the days of old. (Amos 9:11)

Who was David but the anointed of God? Who dwelt in the secret place of the Most High, intimate with God, as David did?

Who "tabernacled" with God in passionate relationship as David did? Who operated in the anointing as did David? Jesus, the Anointed One, is called the son of David because David personified God's anointing.

David was anointed king by Samuel as a youth. He slew Goliath, not with mighty weapons or the armour of Saul, but with a slingshot, a few smooth stones—and the anointing of God. He revered God's anointing so deeply that David refused to touch His enemy Saul when he finally had the chance to kill him because Saul also carried God's anointing.

David's writings express his awe for the anointing. "Touch not My anointed says the Lord." (Psalm 105:15) "I know that the Lord saves His anointed." (Psalm 20:6) "You anoint my head with oil." (Psalm 23:5) "He is the stronghold of salvation to (me) His anointed." (Psalm 28:8) "Great deliverance giveth he to his anointed." (Psalm 18:39, 50)

Chosen as a lad while he served as a shepherd to his father's flocks, David killed a lion and a bear to protect his sheep. God's hand already strengthened young David. As king, David's victories over Israel's enemies were done in God's anointing. His reign culminated in the passage of kingship to his son, Solomon, a type of Christ in His messianic reign. The scriptures call Christ the seed of David and a shoot out of the stock of Jesse, David's father. Jesus was born in the City of David, Bethlehem, as a powerful symbol of the spiritual parallel between the two.

The Last Days Anointing: The Oil of David and Jesus

In latter days, the prophet Amos tells us, God plans to again raise up the tabernacle of David, the anointing.

What kind of anointing does He plan to release? Not an anointing to occasionally flow in His Spirit. He plans a better anointing. This anointing will rest on His people and reside within His people. We will be both endued (from the outside) and imbued (permeated inside) with power from the Holy Spirit. When God says He will build up as in days before the fallen tabernacle of David, He is speaking of this anointing.

David stands as a type and shadow of Christ (the Messiah, the Anointed One). He reveals Jesus, the anointed shepherd-king.

Anointing Empowered Old Testament Kings and Priests

In Old Testament times, kings, priests and prophets received the anointing. The anointing set aside the spiritual leader as a consecrated person. God's strength and power accompany His anointing.

Jesus, King of Kings and Great High Priest, received His anointing at His Jordan baptism through John the Baptist. There "God anointed Him with the Holy Spirit and with power," Acts 10:37-38 affirms.

Jesus, God's Anointed, walked in the power of His anointing. He demonstrated God's manifest presence doing good—healing, delivering, restoring. The Old Testament prophet Isaiah foresaw His anointing:

> The Spirit of the Lord God is upon me, because the Lord has anointed and qualified me to preach the Gospel of good tidings to the meek, the poor and afflicted; He has sent me to bind up and heal the brokenhearted, to proclaim liberty to the (physical and spiritual) captives and the opening of the prison and of the eyes to those who are bound. (Isaiah 61:1)

Jesus demonstrated the Messiah anointing. When John the Baptist sent a message from prison to ask Jesus if He was the Christ, Jesus replied:

> Go and report to John what you hear and see: The blind receive their sight and the lame walk, lepers are cleansed and the deaf hear, the dead are raised up and the poor have the good news preached to them. (Matthew 11:4-5)

Jesus fulfilled Isaiah's prophecy of God's anointing.

He confirmed Himself as the Messiah to His family, friends, neighbors and townsfolk in the Nazareth synagogue soon after His baptism in the Holy Spirit and His testing in the desert. His words identify His prophesied role as God's Anointed. He stood up on the Sabbath day and took the scroll of Isaiah to proclaim:

> The Spirit of the Lord is upon Me, because He has anointed Me (the Anointed One, the Messiah) to preach the Good News (the gospel) to the poor; He has sent Me to announce release to the captives and recovery of sight to the blind, to send forth as delivered those who are oppressed (who are downtrodden, bruised, crushed and broken down by calamity) to proclaim the acceptable year of the Lord (the day when salvation and the free favors of God profusely abound). (Luke 4:18-19)

With every eye fixed on Him, Jesus said, "Today this Scripture is fulfilled in your hearing." (Luke 4:21)

At first the hometown congregation marveled. Then they shook themselves and said, "Is this not Joseph's son?" What they meant was, "Wait a minute here. Who does he think he is? He's not one sent from God. He's one of us."

His own people were enraged. His childhood friends and neighbors drove Him out of town and actually tried to hurl Him over a cliff. The spirit of the antichrist, or translated, anti-Anointed One, raged. No matter. Not even a mob could take Jesus' life. He Himself would lay it down when God's time arrived. He passed through the mob (picture that!) and went on His way.

Imagine the blow to Jesus' faith. He did only what His Father instructed Him to do. He waited for years, then finally received the go-ahead from God the Father to proclaim His role as Messiah to His family and the hometown friends and neighbors of His youth. Their rejection must have been devastating.

Then as now, faith acted as a catalyst for the anointing. Even for Jesus, unbelief blocked the flow of His anointing. In places like Nazareth where the message of His anointing met with rejection He could do no miracles.

He continued to preach the message of His anointing in other towns and God confirmed Jesus' message with miracles. Later, the final confirmation, His resurrection, proved that Jesus was and is the Anointed One, the Messiah. The Apostle John, after recording the resurrection, ended his Gospel by saying, "These are written (recorded) in order that you may believe that Jesus is the Christ, the Anointed One, the Son of God..." (John 21:31)

After Jesus' rising, Peter told the Jews, "God has made Him both Lord and Christ (the Messiah)—this Jesus you crucified."

Zechariah's Picture of Last Days Anointing

An anointing for the church's final-hours appears in a vision the Lord gave His prophet Zechariah (Zechariah 4:1-16) The anointing shown in this vision stands as unique because it flows uninterrupted in a constant well from its source of supply.

At the historical time of the vision, God was restoring Jerusalem after its destruction and the exile of the people to Babylon. The high priest, Joshua, and the civil leader, Zerubbabel, played instrumental roles in rebuilding the ruined temple.

The vision portrayed a solid-gold lamp stand, both a natural and a Biblical symbol for a created thing giving forth light. In this picture, two olive trees flank the lamp stand to supply continual oil through golden pipes. The pipes feed seven lamps mounted on the lamp stand.

The vision seems difficult to understand, but let's read it together now. Later we'll meander through its rich imagery and draw out its symbolic meaning.

> And the angel who talked with me came again...and said to me, What do you see? I said, I see and behold, a lamp stand all of gold, with its bowl (for oil) on the top of it and its seven lamps on it, and (there are) seven pipes to each of the seven lamps which are upon the top of it.
>
> And there are two olive trees by it, one upon the right side of the bowl and the other upon the left side of it (feeding it continuously with oil).
>
> So I asked the angel, who talked with me, What are these, my lord?
>
> Then the angel who talked with me answered me, Do you not know what these are? And I said, No, my lord.
>
> Then he said to me, This (addition of the bowl to the candlestick causing it to yield a ceaseless supply of oil from the olive trees) is the word of the Lord to Zerubbabel saying, Not by might, nor by power, but by My Spirit (of whom the oil is a symbol), says the Lord of hosts.
>
> For who are you, O great mountain (of human obstacles)? Before Zerubbabel (who with Joshua had led the return of the exiles from Babylon and was undertaking the rebuilding of the temple, before him) you shall become a plain (a mere molehill)! And he shall bring forth the finishing gable stone (of the new temple) with loud shoutings of the people, crying Grace, grace to it!
>
> Then I said to him...What are these two olive branches which are beside the two golden tubes or spouts by which the golden oil is emptied out?...
>
> Then said he, These are the two sons of oil (Joshua the high priest and Zerubbabel the prince of Judah, the two anointed ones) who stand before the Lord of the whole earth (as His anointed instruments). (Zechariah 4:1-7, 12-14)

Obviously, the vision addressed a real and immediate moment in time. Joshua, the high priest, and Zerubbabel, the ruler, faced a monumental challenge in transforming a mountain of rubble remaining from Jerusalem's temple mount destruction into a new temple.

But the vision spans the centuries, leaping forward to prophesy of the messianic Priest-King and to symbolize the two anointed ones who appear in the drama of the Book of Revelation's Chapter 11. The vision paints a powerful picture of the anointing and prophesies a last days messianic anointing that will flow from its source, Jesus, without interruption.

Book of Revelation-type imagery abounds:

Seven, a heavenly number signifying completion and perfection, is linked in the vision to the seven-fold Holy Spirit, the Spirit of the I AM, and the Spirit of wisdom, understanding, counsel, might, knowledge and reverential fear of the Lord. (Isaiah 11:2) Feeding the seven lamps is constantly-flowing oil, symbol of the anointing and the Holy Spirit. Zechariah receives understanding that the two olive trees supplying the oil represent the two anointed ones, the king and the priest. Zerubbabel and Joshua stand for temporal and spiritual power. The promise of constant-flow anointing to do a big job of restoration in the earth extends personally to Joshua and Zerubbabel to tackle the rubble of the ruined temple. And the promise also extends to a future leadership of which they are an "omen." (...they are men who are a sign or omen [types of what is to come]—for behold, I will bring forth My servant the Branch). (Zechariah 3:8)

Let's look at the beginning of the passage, taking note of Joshua's new clothes, a rich image.

> Then (the guiding angel) showed me Joshua the high priest standing before the Angel of the Lord, and Satan standing at Joshua's right hand to be his adversary and to accuse him.
>
> And the Lord said to Satan, The Lord rebuke you, O Satan...
>
> Now Joshua was clothed with filthy garments and was standing before the Angel (of the Lord).
>
> And He spoke to those who stood before Him, saying, Take away the filthy garments from him. And He said to (Joshua), Behold, I have caused your iniquity to pass from you, and I will clothe you with rich apparel.
>
> And I (Zechariah) said, Let them put a clean turban on his head. So they put a clean turban on his head and clothed him with (rich) garments. And the Angel of the Lord stood by.
>
> ...Hear now, O Joshua, the high priest, you and your colleagues who (usually) sit before you—for they are men who are a sign or omen (types of what is to come) for behold, I will bring forth My servant the Branch. (Zechariah 3:1-8)

This omen points to the messianic age, for "Branch" is a messianic title for the anointed body of Christ. Jesus is the vine; we are the branches. He made that clear to His disciples and to us by His own words. Yet "Branch" is an Old Testament name for the Messiah. Who is the Branch? Jesus, or His people? We can only conclude that the Branch is the resurrected King and Lord, Jesus, as Head of His body, His people. He is the vine. His life, His resurrected life, flows through His body, the vine branches, giving it victorious life.

Isaiah's prophecy about the Branch supports Zechariah. Isaiah prophesied about the last days church, saying: "In that day the Branch of the Lord shall be beautiful and glorious." (Isaiah 4:3) Jesus, our High Priest and King, is the head of His body, a peculiar people called to be a holy nation of kings and priests, signifying anointing. (1 Peter 2:9)

Going back to the scriptures from Zechariah, we see a priest figure in dirty clothes, a sign of guilt. However, an angel directs that Joshua, representing the priesthood and the intercessor, be given stately robes. Under the condition that he walk in God's ways and keep His charge, Joshua receives the mandate to govern and gains access to the heavenly courts and the throne room of God.

Worshippers, prophetic intercessors, men and women called by God to pray, listen up: God is fulfilling this prophetic vision in our day. What happens in Zechariah's vision is being accomplish in our spiritual lives today. He has given us the stately robes of priesthood and has placed a priestly turban on our heads. Hear what the Holy Spirit has to say about this turban:

Joshua, the high priest, received a new turban. (Zechariah 3) What does that mean? A clean, new turban set upon his head. A new way of thinking and feeling. A new authority. a new power-in-anointing. A new rest.

It was conferred on him, given to him, not earned or strived for. Think about that. A middle-Eastern symbol, the turban.

It's a gift, the new priesthood, given by Me, a share in My anointing of Melchisedek, a new spiritual priesthood, given to My "burnt offerings," My living sacrifices.

I give you the turban of the priest, the crowning. Receive from Me the priesthood of Melchisedek, the conferred priesthood of the Lord Jesus Christ, the Eternal Priest.

Receive! I place it on your head. Your thoughts will be different. Now mediate between a people and their God. Represent Me to them. I make you a priest. I give you the priesthood of Jesus.

O, My people! I would make you kings and priests. Receive the turban; it is the burial cloth of Jesus, His death ***in you****, repeated,* ***in you*** *to make you, the priest, a living burnt offering, a continual sacrifice. Amen! I have spoken.*

(Why has the shroud of Turin re-appeared? Could it be that the Lord wants a powerful reminder of the priestly sacrifice of Jesus? Why has Noah's ark been the subject of recent searches? This also stands as a powerful symbol, speaking in our time of rescue during divine Judgement.)

To show Zechariah his living picture, the Angel had to rouse the dozing prophet, as "a man who is awakened out of his sleep." What a parallel to the sleeping body of Christ which Jesus has shaken from lethargy and unconscious stupor to vitality in Him.

The power that this royal priesthood wields is not by its combined strength or might "but by My Spirit, says the Lord of Hosts." (Zechariah 4:6)

The olive trees, feeding a constant, uninterrupted flow of oil to the lamps, speak reams to us about the flow of the last days anointing. The Lord explains the constant-flow anointing in this prophecy:

Go forth knowing by revelation knowledge that the anointing by the Lord of Hosts in His Spirit in these final days shall flow without ceasing. The anointing will not ***come*** *on you; it will* ***be*** *on you, the glory of God. Know then that all that will be accomplished—mighty things—will be not by might nor by power but by My Spirit, saith the Lord. My Spirit will accomplish these mighty feats by the anointing. So know now as you go forth in Me that the anointing will flow. Trust Me for it. Believe Me for it. I love you and I will supply the anointing to you. Know Me then as God of the Anointing, not you yourself. I am Lord over it.*

The anointing and the release of God's glory brings joy to God's heart. His excellence, manifested through His people, causes celebration in heaven. The whole of spiritual Zion is rejoicing now, celebrating and dancing before the Lord God in joy over the restoration of the anointing. The day has finally come when the messianic promises swell to fulfillment. In the Isaiah scripture that we will refer to several times, we are reminded:

> In that day the Branch of the Lord shall be beautiful and glorious, and the fruit of the land shall be excellent and lovely… (Isaiah 4:2)

Reverence God's Anointing

Despite His exuberant joy, the Lord warns His people to revere His anointing. We must avoid becoming lord over our individual anointing. We must regard it as holy. The anointing is the manifest presence of God flowing through us, performing His good works.

Samson, anointed by the Spirit of Might, succumbed to the temptation to "own" his anointing. He played with it. He treated it as a trinket instead of a hallowed gift, allowing the vessel of the anointing (himself) to sin. He chose a pagan to be his wife. He visited a harlot at Gaza and allowed himself a dalliance with Delilah. His lust-driven choices resulted in a habit of sin, not a once or twice fall. By sinning against his own body, the earthen vessel holding the anointing, he trivialized the anointing. He made himself judge and lord over his anointing.

The anointing is so sacred that we must allow no dalliance with wrongdoing, no fence straddling, no flirting with impurity, no strands connecting us to darkness or bondage, no disobedience. Any opening provides the enemy with an inroad to attack. The whole world has witnessed what greed, pornography and a "Delilah" did to some prominent TV evangelists. They played with holy fire. Many more visible figures lie in the rubble heap of those who received God's anointing and failed both to hold it in awe and to guard its sacredness.

None of us is perfect. We will sin and repent. But habitual sin, hidden sin, combines poorly with God's anointing.

Our humanness, on the other hand, is no drawback at all. Our imperfection is an asset, for God declares that His power is made perfect in weakness. (2 Corinthians 12:9) His glory will pour through imperfect vessels. We have this treasure, God's holy presence and anointing, in earthen vessels. To resist God's anointing on the basis of our inadequacy would be a mistake.

The anointing is the oil in our lamps. Jesus told a story of ten virgins who waited for the bridegroom. (Remember, all ten were "virgins," qualified to attend the wedding feast.) When the wait stretched into the night, all ten fell asleep. (Remember Zechariah had to be roused to see the end-time anointing vision?) When the bridegroom's shout came, five had their lamps full of oil, trimmed and ready—but his arrival caught five unprepared. The door shut behind the wedding party and left them in the darkness.

Maintaining the anointing, that is, replenishing its oil with time in God's word, time in His presence listening to Him and time spent praying in the Spirit, will keep the lamp full, trimmed and ready. (We can also "watch" in the Spirit. Using the gift of our prayer language, we can keep watch in spiritual dimensions, wide awake and observant, as we await the coming of the Bridegroom, Jesus Christ.)

Also important to maintaining the lamp is to keep the oil fresh. Hoarding the anointing, refusing to allow it to flow at every opportunity and to meet every authentic need presented, will make the oil stagnant. Taking offense and refusing forgiveness will clog the golden pipes. Slavery to demands of mind or body will damp the wick and quench the light.

On the upside, keeping our lamps full will yield the confidence of standing fully prepared. We can rest assured we will be ready by the Spirit of God.

Lo! I come quickly, surely, irrevocably. Oh yes, I come to judge, but I also come to My people, to save and restore "bringing My reward, My recompense with Me." Oh yes! I am coming soon, saith the Lord, and quickly, or unexpectedly, at a time that you think not. Think not.

But yes, you can watch in the Spirit. Watch, therefore, and be ye ready, prepared in that way, fully prepared and fully ready for My coming. The Spirit will not fail you if you watch. And yes, the oil is in your lamp, the oil is there in your hearts, an ever-ready flow, deposited inside you: the anointing. So be ye ready by and in the Spirit!

Yes! You will be able to carry out My (Jesus') command to be ready and you will do it by My Spirit!

We can trust in the Spirit to do all that is necessary while we relax and abide in Christ (the Anointed and His anointing).

As we reverence and maintain the anointing, the anointing continues to maintain us. The anointing teaches us what is true and false:

> As for you, the anointing you received from him abides in you; and you do not need anyone to teach you. But his anointing teaches you about all things and as that anointing is real and not counterfeit—just as it has taught you, remain in him. (1 John 2:27-28 NIV)

How does the anointing teach us? When we abide in God, our hearts beat to His rhythm. He stirs our spirits. He speaks truth deep into our spirits. This establishes the truth in our hearts. Sometimes it takes only one phrase or sentence from an anointed man or woman of God to make our spirits leap and our minds to say, "That's true!" The anointing in us has taught us the truth.

Glory Accompanies God's Presence, or Anointing

The anointing and the glory that has come and is coming on God's purified people will be so obvious that everyone will observe it. The prophet Isaiah saw this day when he said, "The glory of the Lord shall be revealed, and all flesh shall see it together." (Isaiah 40:5 RSV)

Jesus endured the shame of the cross for the joy that was set before Him. (Hebrews 12:2) He looked across the centuries to this time in the Spirit and saw the fullness of His anointing on His people. That is why He said, "Greater things than these (miracles) will you do." He has formed a people for Himself who will walk in the fullness of His anointing and will exhibit it fearlessly, boldly.

Jesus said that Abraham had rejoiced "to see My day." (John 8:56) Well, that day has come! Days the saints and prophets of old would have died to witness are coming now upon the people of God. Every eye will behold the glory of God.

All flesh shall see the glory of God. In you. In My people. The glory is coming. Prepare your heart for it will be strong like the wind of judgement. Strong. Your heart has got to be right to withstand the glory. No deviation from holiness. Bombard those demonic thoughts right away when they come. Don't harbor anything that's not of Me. Resist impurity. Don't play or toy with idols at all. Allow no unholy thing, no work of the flesh. Stay highly alert to those things that the glory might not destroy you.

The anointing will grow so strong that people will seek out God's anointed ones and lay power and money and lives at their feet. We must have prepared hearts to withstand the seduction of such power. The words of God's anointed will become like liquid fire, liquid love, filled with light. We must be chastened to avoid misuse of the power of our spoken words, practicing now to "touch no dead thing" with the power of our tongue. We must speak no thoughtless words. Comments such as "Well, I guess Johnny will be sick all winter; he always is" are negatively charged in the spirit realm. We are playing with holy fire when we fail to reverence our role, speaking as anointed kings and priests.

Power will swell, growing stronger and stronger. We must take care not to let it sweep us away in pride or presumption. We maintain our awe of it, for it belongs not to us but to God. Overwhelming, irresistible anointing will flow from God's anointed. The temptation to respond in the flesh to power seekers, hangers on and flatterers will pressure God's people.

Another caution emerges from our human tendency to put our own expectations on God's work. The Pharisees, scripture-trained, missed the Messiah because of their expectation that He would come as a King, not a common carpenter out of hated Nazareth. In our expectations of the glory accompanying the anointing, we may miss God's best.

Zechariah's vision came as those who labored to restore the temple gazed dejectedly at a mountain of debris, the ruins of their glorious former temple. When the river of God flows into flood stage, its glorious streams will bless many. Its flooding will moisten barren ground where the seed of God's word, planted over many dry seasons, will sprout and take root.

But the river of Holy Spirit life will also churn like the Mississippi flooding. For some, it will uproot, overturn and sweep away. This upheaval must occur because it precedes restoration. The continual-flow anointing will be there to bring salvation:

My Spirit will pour forth across this nation as a swift river bubbling, churning, stirring up, moving things out of its way like a river, cutting through the land, doing a great and mighty work.

My anointing will be heavy upon you in these, the last days, and with this anointing you will go around stirring up, stirring up things inside people. Things that are dormant, waiting to be stirred up. Watering the seeds that have already been planted.

You will be like fertilizer making them grow rapidly. They will grow fast because the time is short and there is much to do. Everything will escalate and happen at a much faster pace. My work will be done quickly in people, in a concentrated time. Many times it will call for drastic measures. But the job will get done, for I am the author and finisher of your faith.

Receive the anointing for this time, My children. It will come like a river. Anointing will be on you and in you, for the Lord Jesus Christ, the Anointed One lives within you exuberantly, alive, dynamic. You will see more than you ask for or imagine.

Wait and I will loose the anointing.

When we honor and reverence the anointing, we regard it as a sacred and holy life-love-light surge flowing up from the I AM presence within. It is not ours; it is His, in us. The holy oil flows through our refined golden pipe to bring light, to heal, deliver and restore.

Cyrus: Anointed To Free the Captives

God has given us Biblical pictures of this anointing on His last days church. He has anointed us to triumph.

The first picture appears in Isaiah's oracle about Cyrus, a restoration figure, whom the scripture calls "the Lord's anointed." "Anointed" in Old Testament tradition was a title originally reserved for Israel's kings and later used as a title for the Messiah. Here, this sacred title was conferred upon a Gentile. God chooses whom to anoint, perhaps those we least expect.

Let's take a look at how God's presence-in-power enabled Cyrus. It will help us to understand both the restoration anointing of Jesus and our own anointing to restore.

God called and anointed Cyrus for a huge task: to restore God's exiled people back to Israel's soil. Isaiah's prophetic poem about the anointing of Cyrus echoes the prophet's later description of the anointing of Jesus. (Isaiah 61) God says of Cyrus:

> He will let my captives go. ...I will go before you and level the mountains (to make the crooked places straight); I will cut asunder the bars of iron. (Isaiah 45:13, 8)

With His way made level and straight by John the Baptist, Jesus Himself came with the anointing to open prison doors and set captives free.

This anointing always comes to restore. Isaiah's Cyrus oracle (Isaiah 45:8) portrays the earth springing forth salvation and heaven raining down righteousness. When the Holy Spirit inspires writers to use this language, He has restoration on His mind. They repeat other restoration passages such as Psalm 85 which speaks of messianic restoration and blessing using similar words: "Truth shall spring up from the earth, and righteousness shall look down from heaven."

Cyrus personifies the last days church, a triumphant people, anointed to set the enemy's captives free. Isaiah 45:23 declares "every knee shall bow, every tongue shall swear allegiance." The Holy Spirit has moved on the people of God today to subdue the enemy (Romams 14:11, Philippians 2:10, Hebrews 6:13), declaring to hell's horde, "Our God reigns!"

"I will give you the treasures of darkness and the hidden riches of secret places, that you may know that I am God." (Isaiah 45:3) Similarly, God reveals Himself to His intimates today with the message "Know Me: I AM." He enables us to take back the treasures that powers of darkness have stolen from us for generations. The God of restoration anoints us as He anointed Jesus. In turn, Christ, the Anointed, will use us to help Him bring about the "complete restoration" promised in Acts 3:21.

> I will raise Cyrus up in righteousness (willing in ev-

> ery way that which is right and proper) and I will direct all his ways; he will build My city, and he will let My captives go, not for hire or for a bribe, says the Lord of Hosts. (Isaiah 45:13)

This same anointing will flow down over Jesus' triumphant church. The anointing is described similarly in Isaiah 61:

> They shall rebuild the ruined cities, the devastations of many generations...The glory (once that of your captors) shall be yours...The Lord will cause righteousness and justice to spring forth before all the nations. (Isaiah 61:4, 6, 11)

Make no mistake: God has an anointed, holy people fitted out to accomplish the restoration He intends. A newly-purified people seeks the Lord for guidance in every decision. This people serves from a heart of love, not payment. This people comprises what Peter called "lively stones," building on new foundations of righteousness. And who directs the work of calling together, transforming and equipping this people? The Lord of Hosts, who has refined His own body with fire, the Lord of judgement and restoration, who is Jesus.

Anointed To Triumph

A second picture of the church triumphant at the end of the age appears in Psalm 68. This magnificent song capsules the whole history of Old Testament Israel, touching on the exodus, Sinai, victories under Israel's judges, Elijah's chariots, battles won by Israel's kings, the death of treacherous Ahab and Jezebel and tribute from nations such as Egypt and Ethiopia. David's triumphant psalm also prophesies the victory over evil that Jesus accomplished at the cross. The power outflowing from His cross earns this final end-time victory.

In words Paul later repeated in Ephesians 4:8 referring to Christ, David prophesies about the Anointed One:

> You have ascended on high. You have led away captive a train of vanquished foes; you have received gifts of men, yes, of the rebellious also, that the Lord God might dwell there with them. (Psalm 68:18)

David was celebrating saving the ark of the covenant, which, after a great victory, was carried in triumph to Zion. But he sees it as symbolic of God's kingdom. In ever-widening circles he touches on the triumph of Jesus in His cross and rising. The blood that Jesus, the Anointed Messiah, shed on Calvary will be finally and ultimately vindicated in a people who demonstrate the full victory of His cross.

That blood-bought victory insures a final triumph in the church of Jesus Christ. When David describes the triumphal procession of the King into the sanctuary, his prophetic words highlight the power of praise and rejoicing in this move of God. David also prophesies the role of today's youth generation:

> They have seen thy goings, O God; even the goings of my God, my King, in the sanctuary.
>
> The singers went before, the players on instruments followed after; among them were the damsels playing with timbrels.
>
> Bless ye God in the congregation, even the Lord, from the fountain of Israel.
>
> There is little Benjamin with their ruler, the princes of Judah and their council, the princes of Zebulon, and the princes of Naphtali.
>
> Thy God hath commanded thy strength; strengthen, O God, that which thou hast wrought for us.
>
> O God, thou are terrible out of thy holy places; the God of Israel is he that giveth strength and power unto his people. Blessed be God. (Psalm 68:24-28 KJV)

Note that "little Benjamin" takes the lead. God's prophets, both those of today and those centuries ago, have called for a mighty move of God among the youth of this generation. The prophet Joel promised that, after repentance and cleansing, God planned to "pour out His spirit" on our sons and our daughters. Mario Marillo, author and youth worker, prophesies an anointing of today's youth that will carry fire to the ends of the earth. The Lord showed us His pattern in the book of Joshua, where the sons of those who wandered in the desert went in to take the land. (Joshua 5:2-7) Now the Lord is asking His intercessors to loose power for that on-fire youth generation.

Triumph and Glory

The author received this prophetic word after a study of this triumphal psalm:

Psalm 68 presents a picture of the last days church, of Zion, My church in triumph. Psalm 68 mentions Jesus' triumph. "He made a show of His enemies, triumphing over them," a historical reference to the triumphal parade which displayed captured ene-

mies. Psalm 68 is for today and it is what I want for you.

Strength is mentioned over and over. "The Lord has commanded strength in endurance, impenetrable hardness to temptation." This is what I want for My youth generation, this kind of strength. "Corn to make the young men strong" is promised in Joel and other prophecy. Pray for this strength. Now go your way knowing that this strength, this triumph over enemies, this joyous celebration of Jesus Christ's victory is what I want seen today in My church, Zion. You've heard about the Church Triumphant. This is it!

My Spirit expressly speaks and says, Know this son of man, know this child of the kingdom, know this anointed of the Most High, know this men of the world and children of darkness, know this one and all, great and small, mighty and lowly, and all those inbetween, listening to what I am saying:

Behold My glory. Behold My glory now to be seen in the earth in unprecedented power, light and revelation of glory. All flesh shall see the glory of God outpoured now. All flesh. Every man, woman and child. My mercy at its pinnacle in time of judgement. So know, earth, you have been visited by your God. Do not miss the time of your visitation. And know, peoples of the earth, masses, oceans of people, that your God has great and mighty plans for you. Amen!

Pray in the Glory

When we hear the will of God expressed through prophetic word and backed up by Biblical prophecy, then we must act. We must pray in God's will. He wants our cooperation. The whole body needs to labor joyfully in prayer.

"God does everything through prayer and nothing without it" has become a maxim—and it's true. The prophet Isaiah, to whom God poured out abounding revelation, said about the intercessors, "Keep not silence and give God no rest until Jerusalem is fully restored." (Isaiah 62:6-7) We are co-laborers with Christ, especially in prayer. God has given Jesus the high honor to be chief intercessor. He "ever intercedes" before the throne of God for us. (Hebrews 7:25) He honors us by allowing us to share Jesus' role as intercessor.

God urges His people to pray for His anointing of strength upon this youth generation. Psalm 68 says "Ascribe to the Lord strength. It is He who gives strength to His people." He wants us to praise Him for His strength and ask Him to strengthen our sons and daughters to carry out His anointed mission.

The God of Love and Peace and Rest speaks to you saying, Yes! I am that I AM! I am all you need. I am available to you. Rejoice therefore in the Lord your God who IS, sufficient and available. I wish to be I AM to My people Israel. Now go forward knowing that I AM is sufficient unto thee, will be sufficient in the future for what comes now and all that is coming upon the earth. My anointing in you and others will be sufficient to accomplish all in My plan. Pray! Continue to pray. Beseech Me and intercede and I will give. Oh, how I will give to you in a time of an open heaven.

Daniel, one man praying, turned a whole nation around, for the timing, the appointed time, was right. The timing is right today! For restoration. For change for the better. For mighty moves of God to unfold. And you're here, in position, to pray! Think about it! For all eternity you (and I) will rejoice over this: you are here in position to pray. Amen! Alleluia!

We pray and then we expect glory! But beware of expectations of the conventional. God will always surprise us.

I am no respecter of persons. I reward those who diligently seek Me. I am the God of Israel, My people, a holy nation, a kingdom of priests (finally!) and I am wrapping this thing up in glory. Glory!

Expect glory. On your sons and your daughters, the young. On servants, humble, unseen, less visible people. On kings, yes, but on the lowly and even the outcasts will My glory be seen. So know beyond a shadow of a doubt that My glory is coming down in an unprecedented fashion and know that the whole earth will see My glory. Pray for My glory to come down.

God will pour His holy anointing into vessels so lowly, ungainly, sinful-looking, deformed and possibly offensive that we might be repulsed by them and miss out on His glory. His glory will also occur in circumstances and situations that appear entirely ungodly—chaos, sin-infested, twisted, bondage-held situations. That's where God will manifest His excellence.

Behold My glory. Open your eyes and see My glory in the spiritual world. It's there. Behold My glory. Read Ephesians and behold My glory there. Read about the resurrection with an eye to beholding My glory. See My glory in the birth of Christ.

I want to prepare your heart in this way to truly receive and participate in the glory of God when it is manifested fully.

See that My glory will appear in raw human circumstances—no pomp or majesty or even "properness." See that My glory appears despite sin, in fact amid a high level of sin activity. See My glory in simple people, the simplest, in fact. Not intelligent or high placed or "proper" individuals but even thieves and crooks like Pilate who don't know they're being used by the Almighty One.

So look and see My glory. Note how it operates that you might not be dismayed by false expectations when it arrives. Prepare your heart!

Think of Mary, a young teenage girl embarrassed by a pregnancy outside wedlock. God works in strange (not proper) ways. Feelings, lack of convention, unusualness (like laughter sweeping the church) mean nothing to God. So expect the unexpected. I will move in ways strange to you. Don't resist because of conventional thinking.

Glory in Sin-infested Places

We need to open our minds. God's glory may not arrive in a vaulted cathedral with beams of light shafting through magnificent stained glass windows. He may use the mentally retarded and the schizophrenic to preach sermons. He may manifest His glory in a drunk tank or gay bar. He is already pouring out His Spirit in the darkest places, our prisons.

Now know, child of Mine, that My ways are not your ways. In ignominy and sin and humiliation did I raise up My own son. In sin did I raise Him up. The glory of God in a dung heap born. An angelic pageant staged for ignorant shepherds. The sacrifice that saved the world at the hands of demonically-driven "priests." Resurrection of a dirty, untended, bruised and battered and bloody body. Nothing right or glorious here.

See now that I will pour out My glory in human circumstances, even the worst, most ugly and brutal, lack-ridden, sin-infested, demonically driven and humiliating human circumstances. Open your eyes and see. I will go out into the hedgerows and gather the refuse of society. I will use the ignorant and illiterate. I will choose and favor whom I will choose and favor.

Behold, I AM God. See that you do not fall into disbelief or disparage or undervalue or fail to reverence My anointing when it comes to rock the conventional church. Be prepared for sinners and outcasts and people repugnant to you to be vessels of My glory, vessels of the anointing. They won't look good or be politically correct. If fact, they might appear to be sinful like Mary did or appear to be unqualified like Jesus did to the Pharisees because they thought he was born in hateful Nazareth.

Oh yes! The credentials will be missing. I will glorify the humble. So watch out for worldly, conventional thinking when I pour out My glory. Every one will have a disfiguring quality based on appearances but will be a pure and spotless vessel chosen by Me. Each will have a "limp"—a humiliating past mistake that people will remember, but oh! they will be men and women after My own heart, like David, a king with a sordid past.

So rejoice that I will use you and those like you, and those even less conventional, and **open your eyes**. *Open the sense gates, Jerusalem, and let the King of Glory come in! He may be riding on a broken-down donkey instead of a white charger. Don't look for me amid the trappings of men. I won't be there. Look for Me in the refuse heap. I will be there!*

The Fullness of the Anointing: Life, Love and Light

Jesus predicted that the anointing on His body would be greater than His own anointing. The five-fold ministry of the apostle, prophet, evangelist, pastor and teacher will soon mature into fullness. God has raised up and restored these giftings in tremendous ways.

We have already seen the early fruit of the maturing five-fold anointing in the teaching ministry. A flood of spiritual teaching has washed over the body of Christ in the last two decades. Audio tapes, videos, television teaching programs, books, magazines, newspapers, newsletters all pour forth to soak every dry place with spiritual truth. Gifted spiritual teachers arise to explain and illuminate the word of God. New revelation comes so quickly that we can barely absorb each fresh insight.

The full anointing in the teaching ministry has brought light in a time when light is desperately needed. Our society operates in deep darkness. But the God who Himself is Light has promised to overcome that darkness. God is Life, Love, Light. His anointing in its fullness will abound in life, love, light.

"Thy Light has come." (Isaiah 60:1) The Light of the Nations has risen upon thee, even the glory of the Father: the Son.

Lo, He is risen! The resurrection glory of our Lord Jesus Christ has "risen upon thee." So arise! Shine with that glory, My people, My church, and walk in the awareness of it and the full authority of the anointing. And what is that anointing? To set the captives free, to break every yoke in intercession and prayer is ministry from the body, the body of Christ.

So go forth with a new anointing of light today. Yes, I have anointed My people with life and with love. Now with light. And that full anointing will fully break and destroy the yoke. For the darkness will submit to it, succumb to it, fail to comprehend it, be overcome by it.

Rejoice! This is the fullness of the anointing that was on Christ Jesus.

What is the anointing of life, love, light? It is God Himself. He is Life, Love, Light, fully present and operational in us. God has waited for this day and He rejoices that His people are ready to walk in the fullness of His manifest presence.

Fullness Marks Harvest Time

We live in the season of God's harvest. At harvest time, fruits and vegetables reach maturity with a rosy ripeness, a fatness, a sweet scent that pleasures the soul. We experience an earthly sensual joy in the fullness and rich color, the fragrance and peak flavor, the height of perfection and the abundance of the harvest yield. God delights in the fullness and fatness of His harvest in people's hearts. The supernatural harvest is ripe.

I have made My people fit for My service, to worship Me, and I rejoice. I rejoice! I am thrilled, delighted, happy. So shall you be. Now child, know Me as your One God, your only God, your all in all. Know Me in My ***fullness****, replete-and-fat-and-ripe-and-bursting-with-goodness God. A harvest time God. A replenishing God. A mighty God and strong to save (including those in distress that you pray for). Know My fullness, My fatness, My goodness, My bounty, for I will bless you.*

Yes, I will BLESS you! I am well pleased with you because of your yieldedness to My Spirit and the work My Spirit has done in you and a Father's heart is one of generous reward. It is joy to the Father to reward. What joy!

Prepare for reward. Yes, remember from whence you came. Stay humble. Stay needy. Stay in thanksgiving and praise. Stay blessed! It's an attitude of rejoicing and thanksgiving. So I say, stay blessed!

I Myself am the fullness, the fatness, the all in all sufficiency. The fullness is Me, a person, rich and ready and available in fullness.

Full Harvest Anointing

It's harvest time in the Spirit. And Jesus is Lord of the Harvest. His abundance, His lavish economy, His expansiveness will flood the hearts of His people. Freely we have received;

freely we will give, lavishing upon the needy the abundant, rich, full blessings of God. Healing, financial miracles, provision, protection, shielding, shepherding, all these and more we will give in the bounty of harvest blessing.

We need to adjust our expectations and expand our consciousness. We need to upgrade our spiritual quality standards. We need to expect not just the good but the excellent. We need to believe for not just some, but superabundance. We need to settle for nothing less than God's best—because that's what He wants to give. He needs us to raise our faith level so He can accomplish restoration through us.

You are ripe and fertile, like ripe round melons, rich with the word and seed, like a ripe canteloupe, full of seed. It is the fatness of the anointing. This is just the beginning. You're going to feel this wonderful fullness and fatness, pregnant with the word. You're going to be full and satisfied—a wonderful thing—and bring forth much fruit in the Spirit, like a seed pod that's ripe and ready to burst and throw forth the seed.

Just as seed has let go to be carried to many places, I want you to have a light hold on people, things and circumstances so your seed can be spread.

The anointing in its fullness, though rich, replete and wonderful to enjoy, is poured out upon us for more than our delight. The natural fruits, vegetables and grain of harvest, though satisfying to stack up and look at, must be used as food, to sustain and energize the people. Those in charge must rush the food to need areas and use it at its peak of freshness and nutrition. The anointing must not be stored up. Like the harvest bounty, it must flow quickly to meet needs.

I have provided for you. Provision. Jehovah Jireh provision. Now go forth and use it to My benefit, sharing what you have with others in need by sacrificial love. This is "flow." I will reward it. The Kingdom is a flow, a river of life, flowing, moving continually, never a cistern, always a spring.

Faith and Power-in-Love

It's important to know three things about the anointing:

The anointing functions by faith. The anointing energizes and enables those walking in God's authority. This authority, by virtue of sonship, relies on the word of God, the name of Jesus Christ and the power of the sacrificial blood of Jesus to make things happen in the spiritual and natural realm.

Intimacy is our power source. The anointing is rooted and grounded in love. God has fused His I AM life into us. The I AM in us flows as the anointing. We will experience I AM available to us in fullness. He **is** the power, residing in us. The power originates in our love relationship with Him. He abides in us in love and that is the source of power.

The anointing, raised up again in this generation, precedes God's next great move: initiating the reign of the Messiah. The anointing, as in ancient Israel, enables us to operate as kings and priests. We are called to reign with Christ and His Day has come. Called and anointed, filled to fullness, God's I AM life will burst out in all directions as we step into the first days of an eternal reign with Jesus.

Jesus read the first part of Isaiah's prophecy about His anointing to the synagogue at Nazareth. But He stopped reading at verse 2. Why? Because the fullness of the anointing awaits the last days. God will fulfill the remaining verses of Isaiah in our day, through us.

Just as when He did His first miracle at Cana, He has saved the best wine for the last. In and through His anointed people, He can now fulfill the final part of Isaiah's prophetic word about the anointing of the Lord Jesus Christ:

> To comfort all who mourn, and to provide for those who grieve in Zion—to bestow on them a crown of beauty instead of ashes, the oil of gladness instead of mourning, and a garment of praise instead of a spirit of despair.
>
> They will be called oaks of righteousness, the planting of the Lord for the display of his splendor.
>
> They will rebuild the ancient ruins and restore the places long devastated; they will renew the ruined cities that have been devastated for generations.
>
> ...You will be called priests of the Lord, you will be named ministers of our God. You will feed on the wealth of nations, and in their riches you will boast.
>
> Instead of their shame my people will receive a double portion, and instead of disgrace they will rejoice in their inheritance; and so they will inherit a double portion in their land and everlasting joy will be theirs.
>
> ...Their descendants will be known among the nations and their offspring among the peoples. All who see them will acknowledge that they are a people the Lord has blessed. (Isaiah 61:2-4; 6-7; 9 NIV)

These words from Jesus sum up the anointing:

I am Lord of the Anointing. It is Mine to give and I give it freely today, to those who believe in Who I AM, to those who know Me. And yes! It's for a hurting world.

The anointing is made to FLOW, FLOW, FLOW. Flow like a river into the desert, bringing life! The anointing is Me, My presence at work. It's the God-touch on things. It's Me moving into the see-able material realm.

"The desert will blossom as the rose," Isaiah, My prophet, said. The anointing of Life, Light, Love will bring it to bloom. For that is Me, as I have told you. I AM Life, Light, Love. The anointing carries My presence as life, light, love. The anointing brings life and healing, light and revelation, love and freedom. Oh yes, My people, I am Life, Light, Love and you'll see all this, all of Me, in My anointing.

The same Spirit that raised Christ from the dead dwells in you and He will quicken your physical bodies. Life!

The light that burst Jesus out of the tomb will explode in your minds, driving out darkness, giving you bursts of spiritual (and earthly) understanding.

And My love will spread like oil poured out, like anointing oil, spreading, covering, balming, soothing and uniting all in Me. It's love, an anointing of love, the anointing to love, that will bind up the broken body of Christ into one vibrant, bonded and connected whole, every joint supple and working perfectly.

Oh, yes! Oh, yes! I AM says this with joy! Now My new people, fresh from the womb of the morning, a new Day has dawned. This is the morning of the Day of the Lord. And you thought of that Day with fear and trembling. But remember: perfect love casts out fear. There is **no** *condemnation in Christ Jesus. Even for the world, My attention-getting wrath will release many, many millions, into the kingdom of God. The boat will rock to get their attention. But Jesus is in their boat too, ready and available to minister salvation to them.*

And you'll be there also, ready and available with the anointing. Anointed words will pierce them to the heart. Anointed actions will demonstrate the power of God to them. Though the boat rocks and quakes in the storm, your peace will be perfect, your assurance and composure great. Because you know your God! He is in charge and He is trustworthy.

So know now, children of Mine, that your God is in control And His anointing will flow in the strangest places, under the most unusual circumstances. Remember My laughter which swept the church? It was to prepare you for the ridiculous and the out-

rageous, the ludicrous and the silly.

For Jesus to be born in a stable, the filthiest place of its time, is outrageous. And yet I did it that way. For glory to come through the brutality and humiliation of the cross, at the hands of a crook like Pilate and brigands like the Pharisees, is ludicrous. Yet I did it that way. So prepare for the glory—the anointing—to flow in infested, dark and sinful places, in messy, chaotic, turbulent situations, in all the wrong places for something holy.

I came anointed to say to the prisoners, "Come out!" And if it takes My presence in the jail cell or the prison pit or the foul grave, I will go there, in you. Amen!

Chapter 15

Holy Nation Called

God has achieved the dream of His heart. He has created an anointed nation, a people set apart for Him. Millions of believers have drawn close to Him and surrendered their lives to worship Him. Do we, as His children, know and understand the reality of this? Do we, His own family and household, we who know His heart, understand His joy?

God has always wanted an anointed people, a people He could bless and send out to change the whole world. From the beginning when God brought Israel out of slavery in Egypt, He desired a holy nation, a people set apart to worship Him and to minister His salvation to the nations. He expressed His purpose to Moses during a holy appointment on Mount Sinai. These words reveal the dream of God's heart:

> ...if you will obey My voice in truth and keep My covenant, then you shall be My own peculiar possession and treasure, from among and above all peoples; for all the earth is Mine.
>
> And you shall be to Me a kingdom of priests, a holy nation (consecrated, set apart to the worship of God). (Exodus 19:3-6)

Roughly 45 centuries have passed since God declared His desire to Israel to make them His treasure, to choose them and to set them among and above all peoples. God honored the nation of Israel with His choice and made this favored people to be a natural, physical demonstration of His "holy nation" dream.

What God called Israel to witness in the natural arena, He called the church of the Lord Jesus Christ to represent in the spiritual realm. Neither has truly lived up to its high calling as a nation of kings and priests set apart to worship God.

But God isn't finished.

Can the Lord God form a nation "in a single day?" (Isaiah 66:8) He has gathered a dispersed natural Israel from the nations and on June 6, 1967 restored her seat of government, Jerusalem.

During this same time period, God has carried out a concurrent feat in spiritual Israel, the church. His Holy Spirit has called millions of people from around the globe to come close to Him, to worship Him in spirit and in truth and to take up their authority position in Zion, the spiritual seat of government. A holy nation now truly exists.

This massive work has been accomplished by the member of the Godhead who carries out God's large-scale operations, the Lord of Hosts, who is Jesus.

Imagine the delight of Father God that today His Son, the Lord of Hosts, has formed a spiritual Israel, a nation "in a single day," His Day, the Day of the Lord of Hosts. Through the Son, the vision of the Father's heart, His dream, has come true. Soon Jesus will present this people, and the earth they have subdued to the Father.

We are witnessing in natural and spiritual Israel today two parallel works of Jesus, the Lord of Hosts. Natural Israel is restored in our generation and spiritual Israel has come alive.

God purposed to bond spiritual Israel to Himself not only in traditional covenant loyalty and unity but in tender love, the kind of experiential knowing and loving found in the marriage relationship. His holy nation, made up of individuals on fire for Him, responds willingly as one people, with self-giving, loving trust, abandonment and deep affection. This is a nation in love with its God.

This people is the church, but **not the whole church,** only those who have spent time in the wilderness and really met God there. They have died to their own wants, goals, needs, their very life, making Jesus Christ king in their personal lives.

His surrendered spiritual nation in no way diminishes God's love for and faithful commitment to natural Israel. The status of one does not negate or replace the other.

In fact, He will one day bring the two together. Like a grape vine, the two will be grafted together and the new plant will flourish with its combined vitality. Varying interpretations have arisen over the image of a woman clothed with the sun, a tiara of twelve stars on her head who is pictured in Revelation 12:1. Could it be that this woman, who looks like natural Israel—but also looks like the Lamb's own wife, the church, the new Israel—is the last days union of the two? When Yahweh fulfills His word about the ingrafting of the old and the new Israel, His heart will be satisfied. Then the Lord, who says, "Hear, O Israel, the Lord your God is one God," will be worshipped as one God. That worship will be accompanied by great joy.

For now, however, He deals with the two as a loving parent

individualizes treatment of two children.

The Lord of Hosts has gathered together His spiritual Israel and formed its people into a holy nation, the spiritual counterpart of a physical Israel that He called centuries ago.

Jesus Is Delighted

The Lord of Hosts, who is the Lord Jesus, rejoices over this people. Here is His expression of delight:

Today I say that My people are a nation, a holy nation, a called Israel, a holy people formed unto Myself. Never in history have I had a nation such as this, of one heart and one love in Me.

Do you know what I will do with this nation? Spread the word of the Gospel to the ends of the earth as I always intended. It gives me great delight to say this and to see that My purposes will be accomplished. Rejoice with Me.

God rejoices over this people as a husband rejoices over his bride. He foretold it long ago through the prophet Hosea:

> In that coming day, says the Lord, she will call me "My Husband," instead of "My Master." O Israel, I will cause you to forget your idols and their names will not be spoken anymore.
>
> At that time...you will lie down in peace and safety, unafraid; and I will bind you to me forever with chains of righteousness and justice and love and mercy. I will betroth you to me in faithfulness and love, and you will really know me then as you have never before.
>
> In that day, says the Lord, I will answer the pleading of the sky for clouds, to pour down water on the earth in answer to its cry for rain. Then the earth can answer the parched cry of the grain, the grapes and the olive trees for moisture and for dew; the whole grand chorus shall sing together that God sows! He has given all.
>
> At that time I will sow a crop of Israelites and raise them for myself!...I will say...You are my people and they will reply, You are our God. (Hosea 2:16-23 LB)

Both marriage and harvest appear as themes in Hosea's prophecy. "I will betroth you to me in faithfulness and...you will know me as never before" signifies the intimate love relationship between this people and their God. The outpouring of rain for a harvest of grain, grapes and olive oil reminds us of harvest time.

The spiritual harvest will yield strength (grain), joy (wine) and the anointing (oil). God has also grown up a harvest of men and women, a "crop of Israelites," smitten with their Savior.

The intimate union of the people with their God, and God's presence with them, on them and in them, empowers them to do His work in the earth. When the ancient Israelites returned from sin and exile in Babylon to their homeland, they rebuilt Jerusalem's temple. Then the glory of God returned to the temple's sanctuary, the Holy of Holies. Today's spiritual Israel, restored to relationship with God and faithful to Him, becomes an abiding place for His presence. Our bodies are a temple for His presence, the anointing. For them, His manifest presence—His excellence, His anointing, His glory—show forth. A new temple...a new level of glory.

God has long awaited the Day of the Lord. In that day, which is today, He witnesses the fulfillment of His words to Zechariah, "I shall say, 'These are My people,' and they will say, 'The Lord is My God.'" (Zechariah 13:9)

Throughout human history, the Father has kept this dream in His heart. He created Adam to enjoy relationship with Him and to father a vibrant, happy, holy human family. He placed His own life in Adam, creating Adam in His image. God's life and presence was both on and in Adam. God's anointing or presence on Adam clothed Adam, so he had no need of other covering. God's life and presence in Adam permeated him. He actually shone with God's glory because the presence of God within radiated through.

He lost Adam, but Father God still planned to have a consecrated people. He has achieved that plan in us. Though still unseen, the light covering does clothe those who walk in God's presence today. We have the glory of God both on us and in us. Today the people of God are fulfilling the Colossians 1:27 promise of "Christ in you, the hope of glory."

An angel who appeared to the exiled prophet Daniel in Babylon promised him a special generation, a purified people in "the time of the end."

> Many shall purify themselves and make themselves white and be tried, smelted and refined. (Daniel 12:10)

God Rejoices Over His People

God is calling on His people to share His joy, His unbridled delight, His exuberance over this unique moment in history. God Himself has jumped to His feet, twirling and dancing in joy. He wants His people to not miss an instant of this festive moment.

I AM, I AM, I AM. Know that I AM today, essence of life and life itself. And that life is in you! I have put My life in you. Know that you are a little less than Elohim, bearing His very life, a copy in flesh of Him. Hidden in Christ was the Godhead, the Most High God. Hidden in you is Christ the Anointed One. Hallelujah!

Realize, recognize this and live!

We put this treasure in earthen vessels to confound the wise! And now the fullness is coming out. All that we placed in man is being manifested in the spiritual world. Remember how Adam walked with God? The Adam-walk is being walked by men today. The intimacy is restored between Me and My people—the original intent—because My people have realized who they are in Me.

Yes, I am excited about this, My plan through all the ages fulfilled! Now go and bear fruit from that life, bear fruit. Go forth and multiply, as I told Adam. Go forth! Multiply! And make My earth a garden for Me once again, saith the Lord.

Never before in history has God had such a people.

Wait—hasn't God created a holy nation before? What about Israel under Solomon? The early church?

Natural Israel did reach a peak of unity and love under David and early in Solomon's reign. Yet the nation quickly fell away, as King Solomon himself did during his adult years. The people of Pentecost, the early church, certainly demonstrated consecration to God and the zeal of Christ's anointing. Signs and wonders confirmed the gospel words they spoke.

Yet the Bible promises more. The prophet Joel forecast both an early (to mature the spring wheat harvest) and a latter (to mature the fall olive and grape harvest) rain of the Holy Spirit. The early rain corresponds to the time of Pentecost. The latter rain corresponds to the Spirit's outpouring in our time, the time of full harvest.

Harvest Time Glory

Pentecost celebrating spring harvest, and the Feast of Tabernacles, celebrating Israel's full harvest, portrayed in the natural realm what the church acts out in the spiritual realm. The Book of Acts Pentecost outpouring constituted a spiritual early harvest. The spiritual harvest promised by the prophets will come now at the end-time.

> All this happened to them as a warning and it was written down to be a lesson for us who are living it at the end of the age. (I Corinthians 10:11 JB)

In Old Testament days, God poured out the latter rains on His obedient people to prepare the land for harvest. The annual harvest rains of ancient Israel predicted the reality of the messianic or anointed age, the outpouring of the Spirit on all flesh.

We now stand at the brink of the Great Harvest. Jesus clarified it: "The harvest is the close and the consummation of the age." (Matthew 13:39)

God's word guarantees that the last days will demonstrate His glory in its full excellence and power. He promised a messianic age (not the millennium but a precursor to it) that will happen before the second coming of Christ.

> In the last days, God says, I will pour out My Spirit on all people...before the coming of the great and glorious day of the Lord. (Acts 2:17, 20 NIV)

As the darkness characteristic of the Day of the Lord descends upon the world, God is pouring out His glory.

> For behold darkness shall cover the earth, and dense darkness (all) peoples, but the Lord shall arise upon you...and His glory shall be seen on you. (Isaiah 60:2)

The angels will reap the wicked, Jesus said, "then the righteous will shine like the sun in the kingdom of their Father. (Matthew 13:43) The angel told Daniel, "...those who are wise shall shine like the brightness of the firmament..."

A righteous remnant, reduced in number and purified like the finest 24-carat gold, has become a powerful anointed nation. Zion, the purified people, is the "mother of nations" pictured in Psalm 87. From Zion the glory and the anointing will spread to all of spiritual Israel and then to the nations of the earth.

Isaiah's promise, that God would visit this messianic people with His glory, will appear in various chapters because it so aptly describes God's work in our times. Remember that the Branch refers to God's people as we hear it again:

> In that day the Branch of the Lord shall be beautiful and glorious, and the fruit of the land shall be excellent and lovely to those of Israel who have escaped.
>
> And he who is left in Zion and remains in Jerusalem will be called holy, everyone who is recorded for life in Jerusalem and for eternal life.

> After the Lord has washed away the (moral) filth of the daughters of Zion (pride, vanity, haughtiness) and has purged the bloodstains of Jerusalem from the midst of it by the spirit and blast of judgement and the spirit and blast of burning and sifting,
>
> And the Lord will create over the whole site, over every dwelling place of Mount Zion and over her assemblies, a cloud and smoke by day and the shining of a flaming fire by night; for over all the glory shall be a canopy (a defense of divine love and protection). (Isaiah 4:2-5)

A Purified Remnant

God has always preserved some of His people, a remnant, even in the midst of judgement, to continue His nation. In ancient Israel, the remnant survived despite enemy invasion, torture, slavery, mass extermination and exile to foreign lands. In natural Israel today, a remnant has survived many centuries of exile. A people scattered among the nations, the Jews are now restored to the ancient land. This restoration creates a clear parallel to what God is doing in the Spirit.

More prevalent and indestructible as the dandelion in spring is God's thriving promise that He will preserve His remnant. Among the many Biblical guarantees about this survivor people, God promised the prophet Zechariah:

> And in all the land, says the Lord, two-thirds shall be cut off and perish, but one-third shall be left alive.
>
> And I will bring the third part through the fire, and will refine them as silver is refined and will test them as gold is tested. They will call on My name and I will hear and answer them. I will say, It is My people: and they will say, The Lord is my God. (Zechariah 13:9)

God has a spiritual remnant today, a surviving people, brought through cleansing fire. "So too at the present time there is a remnant (a small believing minority) selected (chosen) by grace..." (Romans 11:5) The role of the remnant, the purified, cleansed survivors, is to multiply and fill the earth. The remnant reproduces, birthing many into spiritual Israel.

Be aware: high activity is occurring in the spirit realm. As waves of returnees have poured into the land of Israel, so millions have poured into spiritual Israel. They throng to their spiritual capitol in Zion.

The Lord of Hosts doesn't want us to miss the pageantry of

this spiritual event. It is truly happening in the spiritual realm. Of course, we will marvel at it when we arrive in heaven. But the Lord wants us to marvel at it now.

The holy nation that the Lord of Hosts has assembled will bring other nations into His wonderful kingdom. God has called Zion His fruitful spouse and the mother of nations. Paul wrote, "But the Jerusalem above (the Messianic kingdom of Christ) is free, and she is our mother." (Galatians 4:26)

We find difficulty in making God's prophetic vision real for ourselves. We don't absorb and interiorize His prophetic word as we do, for example, a practical promise for healing of our bodies such as "By His wounds, you have been healed." (1 Peter 2:24) However, the Holy Spirit has supplied us with a psalm that gives a vivid description of the forming, organizing and assigning of authority in God's holy nation which is happening right now. Psalm 87 is hard to understand, but let's take at look at it.

> On the holy hills stand the city (of Jerusalem and the temple) God founded.
>
> The Lord loves the gates of Zion (through which the crowds of pilgrims enter from all nations) more than all the dwellings of Jacob (Israel).
>
> Glorious things are spoken of you, O city of God. Selah (pause and calmly realize what that means)!
>
> I will make mention of Rahab (the poetic name for Egypt) and Babylon as among those who know (the city of God)—behold, Philistia and Tyre, with Ethiopia (Cush)—(saying), This man was born there.
>
> Yes, of Zion it shall be said, This man and that man were born in her, for the Most High Himself will establish her.
>
> The Lord shall count, when He registers the peoples, that this man was born there. Selah.
>
> The singers as well as the players on instruments shall say, All my springs (my sources of life and joy) are in you (city of God).

In Psalm 87, the various nations say of Zion "This one was born in Zion." (Jesus told Nicodemus that even a religious person like himself needed to be born again to enter the kingdom). "Indeed of Zion it will be said, This one and that one were born in her and the Most High himself will establish her." People from the pagan neighbors of Israel are adopted by Zion in Psalm 87. God records each person for life when He registers the citizens of

Zion. God rejoices as He Himself completes the task of an official census for a new holy nation.

"The Lord shall count, when He registers the peoples, that this man was born there." (Psalm 87:6)

Streams of new Christians are pouring into underground churches in China and other repressed nations. The fat nations of the world will also yield their spiritual harvest when divine "hot weather" ripens the harvest.

Psalm 87 prophesies the joyous work of the Lord of Hosts. He assigns all the tasks that Zion must perform in bringing about the Lord's reign. Here is what He spoke to the author:

God is registering, counting up, testing the people of Zion. He is calling together battalions, corps, bastions, defenses. With joy He is writing up the peoples of Zion, the ethnic groups, people, "nations," and preparing their assignments, joyously listing, arranging, scheduling, timing, with great energy and joy.

What is the meaning for us? One answer leaps out of these words: if God is calling us to complete an assignment for Him, we'd better do it now or forever miss the opportunity. Now is a peak time in His plan. But we need to stay close enough to hear His heartbeat, for it all happens in the spirit.

Today is a day of all days, a day of destiny in Christ Jesus, a day of segmentation and leave taking, just as when Israel gathered into family groups to travel into the land. They were all mixed together but traveled as family groups.

Now I am knitting you into a family group, the family of God, separate from all the families of the earth. And the family of God will have ascendency in the land, the new land. This family, appointed and assigned, shall make up the ruling class of the land. The scepter shall not depart from Judah.

A ruling class of kings and priests is set up and fully operating, destining what is happening in the land. And should the word fail? No. It is the Law. Enforce it.

Now go forward knowing that the godly class of Psalm 87 is established for all eternity. Know this now. It is important. The rulers over many are already established. To reign with Christ implies authority and it is given already. Already established and laid down. No go forward in it, believing in it and acting upon it.

Take up thy scepter and reign, Christ Jesus, **in your people**. *Proclaim it. Witness to it, My children.*

Old Testament prophets declared that the pagan nations will pour into Jerusalem because of the glory. This is not the natural city of Jerusalem but the spiritual Jerusalem, the seat of holy government. This is the heavenly Jerusalem that Paul mentions in Hebrews 12, a holy city founded on the holy mountain, Zion, is the capitol of a holy nation that rules and reigns. The city is wedded to the Lord Jesus Christ.

Zion, the spouse of the Great I Am is in birth pangs, giving birth to a new world that Jesus will govern in righteousness. Jesus predicted that the end of the age would come with birth pangs. Surely we see tribulation being birthed with contractions even in our planet—ever increasing earthquakes. A parallel birthing is happening in the Spirit. On January 17, 1995, the day of the massive earthquake in Kobe, Japan, God spoke this word about the birth of a holy nation that He is raising up.

Yes, It has begun. Birth pangs have turned into hard labor, just as Jesus said, to bring to birth a new world, a new world order, what the new agers have counterfeited from My plan. Yes, these are birth pangs. The chaos that follows can distract from the truth that there is ***birth*** *going on.*

Hear Me. Hard labor has begun. The earth itself mirrors what is going on in the spiritual realm. God will give birth to a mighty nation of kings and priests, bigger than Zion, the seat of authority: Israel, the nation of our God, born out of chaos and birth pangs, a people to populate heaven, a people taken from darkness into His wonderful light, a people taken from slavery and sin into glory. Go thy way knowing that our God is in control. Our God reigns.

Birth Pangs, Pain and Sorrow

The Father's heart is grieved and saddened in this hour of judgement. But from the hard labor of judgement He will bring to birth many children who would not be His children without the birth pangs.

Because He is so grieved, God (yes, even God) needs His people's love and encouragement. The praise that God most wants to hear in this hour and that His people most need to give is "Hallelujah! Our God reigns!"

God is bringing about a new era. The transition from the former age has already begun. God is moving toward the fullness of Christ's reign.

What is the ultimate role God intends for this nation of kings and priests? To reign with Christ Jesus, our King. But before Solomon could reign, God required a David. He beat back every foe, quelled every insurrection and wrested the land from its enemies, establishing peace. Before the reign of peace, divine order, abundance and blessing, warfare must take place to cleanse the land of its enemies and usher in the prerequisite unity.

Today, spiritual warfare is a prime concern of the church. Instruction on strategies of warring in the Spirit spill from bookstore shelves and magazine pages. They occupy speakers' time in conferences as well as TV and radio teaching programs. The body of Christ has learned how to bind satanic forces and squelch demonic attacks. This warfare has won many skirmishes and battles holding back the enemy's onslaught.

High Level Warfare

But a higher and more effective level of warfare exists.

The Holy Spirit wants to teach us how the anointing of David, the warrior king, operates. David was a worshipper. He brought the ark of God's presence to Zion and worshipped there. David, God's intimate, "inquired of and required" the Lord. David sat at the feet of his Lord. He ministered unto the Lord, in reverent companionship and worship. He went out from the presence of the Lord to fight for Israel.

We are a nation of Davids, anointed for worship and battle. This chapter's title is Holy Nation Called. We've seen that God's own people, formed into a worshipping nation, have truly become a spiritual Zion. We need to realize something important: our highest warfare is accomplished **in Zion**, the place of worship. It is in worship that we battle best. Rejoicing subdues the enemy. Praise opens heaven's door. It was praise, a rising song of praise from a prison cell at midnight, the darkest hour, that broke the chains of Paul and Silas. Another surprising way we undermine the enemy is holy silence. In silence, worshipful stillness before the Holy One of Israel, our enemies are simply overcome.

Because we embrace and believe what God says about His presence in us, we can rejoice, no matter what challenge we face. Because we accept and interiorize what God did for us in Jesus at the cross and resurrection, we identify with Christ (the Anointed and His anointing). We see ourselves raised to new glorious life in Him seated with Him in heavenly places.

Because we actually believe this, we express it. We rejoice before our God in praise and gladness. We speak His word as law and as judgement on the enemy to bind and destroy his works and power.

Two Psalms Teach Battle

Psalm 149. Here's how the Holy Spirit wants us to do warfare. We do it according to Psalm 149, by exercising our victory. Before Solomon's reign of peace and prosperity, God had to have a David to destroy Israel's enemies. We must use the authority of our anointed words in faith to perform these two vital roles. We chain powers of darkness and build God a dwelling place. In doing so, we participate in creating the reality God has promised. We **speak** judgement on the enemy; we **speak** life and restoration.

> Let the saints be joyful in glory, let them sing aloud on their beds.
>
> Let the high praises of God be in their mouths and a two-edged sword in their hand,
>
> To execute vengeance upon the heathen and punishments on the people,
>
> To bind their kings with chains, and their nobles with fetters of iron,
>
> To execute upon them the judgement written: this honor have all His saints. Praise ye the Lord! (Psalm 149:5-9 KJV)

Joy, high praise and the word of God (the two-edged sword) are the weapons this jubilant people use to bind evil powers. They execute upon powerful enemies of Zion the judgement written, that is, the word of God regarding the enemy bondage of God's people or the theft of their goods. Micah 4:2 says, "The law goes forth out of Zion."

Yes, it does. Out of our mouths. We declare and promulgate the law, God's written word. We execute the judgement written in the scriptures by our faith-filled spoken words. In praise and rejoicing this triumphant people puts the clamps on evil. We prophesy the promises.

Our greatest offensive weapon and our best defense strategy lies in worship. The center of battle lies in the center of worship. In worship we see the enemy fall before us. In worship, all anxiety, fear and unrest melt in the radiance of God's presence. Fear can't stand before Him. Nor can any negativity. Joy, which is our strength, swells in His presence. In His sanctuary we see our victory; it is Him.

In worship we go into the secret place of the Most High, the hidden place of His heart, the protected dwelling place. He becomes our hiding place, safe and secret, far from any penetration of enemy forces.

Psalm 76. This teaching psalm points out three relationship levels on which God's people operate. The psalm also links worship and warfare.

Its three rankings, based on relationship, are: believers (Israel); praise people (Judah); and worshippers (Zion).

> In Judah is God known, his name is great in Israel. In Salem also in his tabernacle and his dwelling place in Zion. There break he the arrows of the bow, the shield, the sword and the battle. (Psalm 76:1-3 KJV)

Paraphrasing the psalm, it says:

> God's **name is great** in Israel (believers)
> God is **known** in Judah (praisers)
> God **dwells** in Zion (worshippers).

What the Holy Spirit is saying here is that Israel (believers) know God's name. Like the Israelites in the desert, they have seen His mighty acts and He has revealed His name to them. They have called upon His name for salvation. But these people didn't ascend Sinai with Moses who "knew" God. Moses knew God's ways and had an intimate relationship with the Almighty. Because they don't really know God and trust His character, these believers may abandon faith in a crisis--and lose their battles.

In Judah God is known. These praise people recognize His attributes. They declare His mighty works and see His glory. Praise brings down the strongest walls—and did so, at ancient Jericho.

But Zion is the place of worship. The people of Zion minister in love and self-sacrifice, of yielding all before a holy God. They are a continually-burning altar hearth, themselves a burnt offering. Like their Lord, they are both priest and sacrifice.

In Zion, the citadel in the city of peace, is God's tabernacle and His dwelling place. Salem or Jerusalem, city of peace, represents the seat of government and rule. Zion, within Jerusalem, is the temple mount and the mountain of worship. There God dwells.

In the spiritual realm, living our lives in God's presence is "the secret place of the Most High" of Psalm 91:1. When we stay in close, intimate relationship with God, we reside "under the shadow of the Almighty." Then we tabernacle with Him. We're in the war room, the shielded place where orders go out and information comes in, the spiritual control center.

Again, the center of worship is the center of battle. Psalm 76 identifies Zion as the place of victory: "There (**in Zion**) he broke the flashing arrows, the shield, the sword, and the weapons of war." (verse 3, boldface mine)

The psalm's historic reference is to the threat from Assyria in 2 Kings 19:9-35. Sennacherib, the Assyrian king, brought his huge and ruthless army to the gates of Jerusalem. He sent a demand for surrender to Israel's king Hezekiah. Hezekiah took the letter to the temple on Mount Zion and spread it out before the Lord, praying and worshipping.

> O Lord, God of Israel, enthroned between the cherubim...you alone are God over all the kingdoms of the earth. You have made heaven and earth...deliver us from his hand, so that all the kingdoms on earth may know that you alone, O Lord, are God. (2 Kings 19:15, 19 NIV)

Hezekiah's answer to prayer and worship came quickly. The Angel of the Lord slew 185,000 in the Assyrian camp; Israel never fought. Worship had brought the enemy to destruction.

Sennacherib escaped to Ninevah, only to suffer death at the hands of his own sons as he worshiped Nisroch, his god.

After that victory, the Lord made a promise about a future remnant destined to go forth out of Zion:

> And the remnant that has survived of the house of Judah shall again make root downward and bear fruit upward,
>
> For out of Jerusalem shall go forth a remnant and a band of survivors out of Mount Zion. The zeal of the Lord of Hosts shall perform this. (2 Kings 19:30-31)

Today's band of survivors out of Mount Zion not only walks in God's glory, but this remnant inhabits His holy war room, the place of worship. Zion, God's citadel, is coming into excellence.

Seat of Government

Zion, the city of God, is coming into its fullness. I want you to know about it. I will teach you about Zion, mother of the nations, fruitful spouse of Yahweh, the citadel and place of worship and dwelling of God Most High, where the nation of priests before Yahweh resides. There I will break the bow and slaughter the enemy, all done in the secret place (dwelling place) of the Most High, the war room and seat of government in Zion. Behold: it will be done this way. Alleluia.

We abide in our God, I AM. He is Alive Forevermore. He is Faithful and True. He is the Alpha and the Omega, the Beginning and the End. We dwell with the One who is transcendent and glorious, resurrected and glorified in the glory of His Father, the Holy One, the All-knowing One, the Omnipotent Almighty God, El Shaddai. We are the people of God, Elohim, the Most High God, the God of all the earth, the One who comes in glory.

This is the God whose glory we walk in. We are covered with the glory of God as surely as Adam, who wore glory as a light-garment. Our glory clothes are unseen; our garment is a spiritual covering. But it is more real than earthly clothing. It's time we realize that we're clothed in royal garments, as the king and priest dressed in the garments of their high office. The fullness of the reign of the Lord Jesus Christ is come in His people. We need to put on the garment of praise regarding this achievement because in God's eyes the work is finished.

The God of Love speaks and says, ***rejoice!*** *Rejoice, My people! Rejoice, for our God reigns. Rejoice for the fullness of the reign of our Lord Jesus Christ is coming and has come in His own people. It has happened in the Spirit; now let it happen in the flesh (or material world). So be it! says the Lord. Amen! shouts the chorus of heaven.* ***Amen!***

The reign of our Lord Jesus Christ has come. And all that happens now related to that reign is joy, pure joy. Heaven was made for such a time as this: to rejoice in pure joy. Fulfillment of all My plan, My righteous work, is now. Hallelujah!

Rejoice with Me, Oh, church of the Lord Jesus Christ. Rejoice and praise! For this mighty work is done. Let the earth rejoice as heaven is rejoicing in this hour, this day. It is finished! The God of Love has spoken.

When God speaks, it's done. The instant He says it, the work is complete. When He said, "Let there be light," light was. The work is done in the Spirit, irrevocably done. Our role is to declare it into the natural world. God has spoken it. It's done and we believe it. We put faith-pressure on His promise by our praise. Let us rejoice in the fulfillment of His plan.

His plan will manifest:

> For in Him the whole fullness of Deity (the Godhead) continues to dwell in bodily form (giving complete expression of the divine nature).
>
> And you are in Him, made full and having come to the fullness of life (in Christ, you too are filled with the Godhead—the Father, Son and Holy Spirit and reach

full spiritual stature). (Colossians 2:9-10)

God's holy nation will rule and reign with Him forever. We exert the King's authority over the enemy today, when we execute judgement, or decree justice, peace, righteousness and truth. The rule is both preparation for, and the beginning of, our heavenly reign with Christ.

If we begin now to rule and reign with Him, we will continue that activity in heavenly realms. If we refuse the king-priest authority, failing to step into that role here on earth, we may not exercise that same authority in eternity.

The anointing to rule and reign is not coming. It is here, within us and we are beginning to realize the awesome presence of the Almighty within. Though our new life is "hidden with Christ in God" (Colossians 3:3), it is nevertheless vital and real.

We are not controlled by the kingdom of darkness that surrounds us. Jesus said that the kingdom of God is within us. When we live from the inside out, not the outside in, we control the darkness with the power, light and word of God and the name of Jesus. We have dominion, authority and control. We must choose to use it.

We will reign with Christ forever. That reign has begun here and now.

Chapter 16

Rule and Reign

> ...they shall be ministers of God and of Christ (the Messiah) and they shall rule along with Him a thousand years. (Revelation 20:6)

God Almighty has planned from the beginning to set up a final kingdom of righteousness, justice, truth and peace. This kingdom will supersede the world's empires, which have all corrupted and failed. This kingdom will crush a final antichrist kingdom not yet manifest. (antichrist translated, we saw earlier, literally means anti-the Anointed One and His anointing.)

The exiled prophet Daniel, living under the rule of the Babylonian Empire, interpreted king Nebuchadnezzar's dream of successive world empires. He finished his explanation by saying:

> And in the days of these (final ten) kings shall the God of heaven set up a kingdom which shall never be destroyed, nor shall its sovereignty be left to another people; but it shall break and crush and consume all these kingdoms and it shall stand forever. (Daniel 2:44)

The word "forever" reappears in prophecies about Christ's kingdom. Isaiah said:

> Of the increase of His government there shall be no end...to establish it and to uphold it with justice and righteousness from the (latter) time forth, even forevermore. (Isaiah 9:7)

The eternal king of this sovereign reign is the Lord Jesus Christ. The angel announcing His birth told his mother, Mary:

> He will be great...the Son of the Most High and the Lord God will give to Him the throne of His forefather David, And He will reign over the house of Jacob throughout the ages; and of His reign there shall be no end. (Luke 1:32-33)

The seventh angel of Revelation blows his trumpet to announce this reign as heavenly voices shout:

> The dominion (kingdom, sovereignty, rule) of the world has now come into the possession and become the kingdom of Our Lord and of His Christ (the Messiah) and He shall reign for ever and ever. (Revelation 11:15)

The co-reign of His people with the Messiah will also last forever.

> ...they shall reign (as kings) forever and ever (through the eternities of the eternities). (Revelation 22:5)

Rule In Love

Love drives this kingdom. His dominion begins in the hearts of bondservants who freely pledge to serve out of love. It begins in the hearts of kings and elders who cast their crowns before Him. The King of Kings reigns over, in and through these people. "Your people will offer themselves willingly in the day of your power." (Psalm 110:3)

The kingdom increases by love. When we love the Lord enough to surrender all to Him, He takes first place and He becomes king in our hearts. We ourselves move out of the number one spot and put Him on the inner throne. We enter into a close love relationship with Him.

Rejoice! Rejoice, for the Lord our God, the Almighty reigns, reigns like never before, reigns in the people He has made for Himself.

He reigns.

Rejoice, oh, rejoice, earth. Oh, peoples, rejoice.

Rejoice, Almighty One, for thy work in a people is done and is good, very good. Rejoice, man. Rejoice, earth. Rejoice, nations.

Let the whole earth rejoice now for the Lord our God cometh. He comes to rule the land! With justice and peace will he rule, and fairness and righteousness—through His people! It will begin now: dominion and reign, just as Adam was supposed to do and to continue into eternity. Let the earth rejoice! Let the heavens be glad, for our God, the Almighty reigns.

It is finished!

This ever-increasing reign will conquer more and more hearts. Though very real, this kingdom is unseen. Jesus reminded us, "The kingdom of God does not come with visible display... the kingdom of God is within you." (Luke 17:20-21)

Psalm 91, the psalm for the '90s and beyond, promises, "I will set him on high because he knows and understands My name (has a personal knowledge of My mercy, love and kindness)." God has promised to give authority to those who have gained an intimate knowledge of Him.

God is no respecter of persons. Any believer can press in to Him and mature into the calling of king and priest (although the candidate must willingly undergo refining fire). But just as God has ranked the angels, placing archangels in the highest echelon, so He has established rank in His heavenly kingdom. (We already know that the position of elder exists and that the 12 Apostles occupy an honored position. Their names appear on the 12 foundation stones of the heavenly city, the New Jerusalem.) As the Lord registers the peoples in Psalm 87, He puts a check mark by the names of those born in Zion. Though God loves each of us equally (with the same quality of love He has for His son, Jesus) those worshippers intimate with Him have special status with God. They are, in spiritual terms, the people of Zion, not only Israel (believers) but Zion (operating in the seat of government).

Those who dwell with Him "in the secret place of the Most High" (Psalm 91) have entered the rule and reign stage. They rule and reign with Him in prayer, intercession and spiritual warfare.

I AM. Know Me as I AM, not all My facets but the essential core Me. Know Me as I AM: I AM. Now know that I am a respecter of persons, in certain cases. It is true what I will do for one I will do for another, if they seek Me and ask. But I have made a line of kings and priests, male and female, who are special before Me. When they ask, I listen. When they speak, I perform it. They are My people and I am assuredly their God. They have great sway with Me.

Why do I tell you this? You need to know the great power of concerted group prayer. And also, I love you, so I want you to know these things. Now go forward convinced, assured, recognizing that your corporate prayer is highly effective.

Reign Flows From Surrender

Jesus will rule through His perfected people. He already has a remnant people who have yielded their lives as sacrifice on a burning altar. His people have and will lay their lives at His feet to serve Him. They have and will leave behind all their personal dreams, hopes, visions.

The Lord has revealed by His Spirit that His praying people are repeating a single, unified cry in the Spirit. It is a prophetic call for Christ's kingship. His people cry out to the anointed messianic King, "Come!" They declare, "He reigns!" In doing so, they establish His kingship in the earth.

Psalm 110 defines Jesus' reign as High Priest and Heavenly King, seated at the right hand of the Father. And the scepter, His scepter of rule, will go forth out of **Zion.** He will rule and reign through His perfected people, beginning now, here on earth—and for all eternity. This plan, culminated in Christ Jesus, the Vine, is carried out in Israel, the branches.

Jesus, the Messiah, combines and consummates the role of King and Priest. He also harmonizes the kingship and priesthood roles in His own body, the body of Christ. He is the head of His body, the people of God, called to be a nation of kings and priests.

> Here is a man whose name is Branch (the Messiah) and he will branch out from his place and build the temple of the Lord...and he will be a priest on his throne. And there will be harmony between the two. (Zechariah 6:12-13 NIV)

The Living Bible phrases it:

> ...the Branch...will build the temple of the Lord...He will rule both as King and as Priest, with perfect harmony between the two!

Let's take a look at the kingship of Jesus Christ revealed in Psalm 110. This prophetic song was written by David, the king who prefigured Jesus, the Eternal King. David's gracious God allowed him to hear a conversation between the Father and the Son. (What an awesome thing!)

> The Lord said unto My Lord, Sit thou at my right hand, until I make thine enemies thy footstool.
>
> The Lord shall send the rod of thy strength out of Zion; rule thou in the midst of thine enemies.
>
> Thy people shall be willing in the day of thy power, in the beauties of holiness from the womb of the morning: thou hast the dew of thy youth.
>
> The Lord hath sworn, and will not repent, Thou are a priest for ever after the order of Melchizedek.
>
> The Lord at thy right hand shall strike through kings

> in the day of his wrath.
>
> He shall judge among the heathen, he shall fill the places with the dead bodies; he shall wound the heads over many countries. He shall drink of the brook in the way: therefore shall he lift up the head. (Psalm 110 KJV)

The breathtaking kingship of Jesus, in all its holiness, integrity, power and victory shines through David's song. Also evident is the role the people of Zion play in this rule. The conversation between the Father and the Son makes clear that Jesus, who sits at the Father's right hand, reigns over an earthly kingdom. Rule occurs "in the midst of thine enemies." God has no enemies in heaven; no evil exists there. This reign exerts justice on God's enemies in our world. The kingdom is here and now.

Where will Psalm 110's rod of justice come from? Out of Zion!

Let's pause in our look at Psalm 110 for a moment to expand our idea of Zion. We talked about Zion as a place of worship and a seat of government. We saw a purified remnant people coming forth out of Zion. We viewed its role in spiritual warfare.

What else is Zion?

Zion, A Place of Kings and Priests

Zion, a physical mountain in Jerusalem, appears in Genesis 14:18 as a place of priesthood. The patriarch Abraham visited Melchisedek, King of Jerusalem and "the priest of the Most High" there. This mysterious king and priest ruled over Jerusalem, where Mount Zion is located. Later, in Genesis 22:2, Moriah, the Mount of the Lord, is established as the place of worship where Abraham went to offer the sacrifice of his son, Isaac (a foreshadowing of God's son sacrificed there later).

We discover that Mount Moriah and Mount Zion are one and the same place. In 2 Chronicles 3:1, Solomon began to build the Jerusalem temple (known to be on Zion) "on Mount Moriah."

Under Zion became a place of rest and festal gathering. As Israel celebrated the Feast of Tabernacles on Zion, God entered the dwelling place Solomon had built, the new holy temple. Psalm 132 describes Zion, God's resting place:

> Arise, O Lord, and come to your resting place, you and the ark of your might.
>
> For the Lord has chosen Zion, he has desired it for his dwelling. This is my resting place for ever and ever; here I will sit enthroned, for I have desired it.

> Here I will make a horn grow for David and set up a lamp for my anointed one. I will clothe his enemies with shame, but the crown on his head will be resplendent. (Psalm 132:13, 17)

David re-established Zion as a place of kings. In 2 Samuel David conquered the stronghold of Zion, establishing it as the seat of Israel's kingdom. Zion became known as the Citadel or "City of David" in 1 Kings 8:1. (David, we suggested earlier, represents a man operating under the anointing.)

The Psalms offer more clarity about Zion. In Psalm 2, God declares: "I have anointed My King on My holy hill of Zion." Psalm 9:11 praises the Lord who dwells in Zion. Psalm 14 proclaims that salvation comes out of Zion. The law goes forth out of Zion, according to Isaiah 2:3. Psalm 48, 146 and 147 establish Zion as a place of high praise to the King who reigns forever. Zion is a stronghold (2 Samuel 5:7), a fortress, a God-protected city whose rule shatters earthly kings. (Psalm 110:2) Zion fulfills a role as mother of nations (Psalm 87) and fruitful spouse of God (Isaiah 66:7-9)

So, the scriptures identify Zion as:

- a holy mountain of kings and priests
- a sanctuary of worship where God dwells
- the city of David, a man who did his mighty acts in God's anointing
- a wellspring of both salvation and justice from God's word or law
- a stronghold against the enemy where praise builds fortress walls
- a resting place

Clearly, spiritual Zion is a holy place. In Zion reside anointing, worship, kingship and priesthood, reign and overcoming praise. We suggested earlier that a worshipping people, intimate with God, are the people of Zion. Zion is the spiritual dwelling place of the anointed people of God. In rest, joy and festal gathering, the people of God celebrate on Mount Zion, according to Hebrews 12:22.

With more understanding of Zion, let's return to Psalm 110.

The psalm's poetic description of the Anointed King's reign prophesies: "The Lord shall send the rod of thy strength out of Zion; rule there in the midst of thine enemies."

The rod of Christ's strength will come out of Zion, not only the mount, but the city of the great king. What is that city but a spiritual seat of government, the residence of a kingdom of priests, a people anointed, consecrated and set apart?

This is how God sees us! The rod of Christ's strength will come out of us, His spiritual Zion. The splendor of His reign takes place in us.

A description of this people follows immediately in verse 3: "Your people will offer themselves willingly in the day of your power, in the beauties of holiness and in holy array out of the womb of the morning." This willing people, flowing in God's continual anointing, dwells in His presence, full of worship and praise. This holy nation performs the role of king and priest that Almighty God originally intended for His people Israel.

During the Israelites' desert journey, we saw earlier, God announced His intention: "And you shall be to Me a kingdom of priests, a holy nation (consecrated) set apart to the worship of God." (Exodus 19:6)

This people, instead of being God's faithless, wandering wife (as pictured in Hosea), becomes His loyal, fruitful spouse. Zion's womb nurtures a nation.

Important things are coming. Import-things. The scripture says, "A great sign appeared in the heavens." Where did that sign appear? In the earth, that is, in a physical way? No! In the heavens, in the spiritual realm. Lift up your eyes to see the woman clothed with the sun. Behold her, My bride, dazzling in her light-beauty, Mother Zion, giving birth to Christ in us, our hope of glory, giving birth, so to speak, to the reigning messianic king and His reign.

So rejoice, My children, for there is a great sign in the spiritual world and that sign is the bride of Christ, formed and ready, the valiant bride of Song of Solomon 6:7 "coming like a troop with banners." Know that the bride will be jealously and fiercely protected as she fulfills her remaining mission on earth. No weapon formed against her will prosper, as Revelation 12 clearly depicts. The whole history of salvation and the victory is pictured because she is the culmination of it all. Rejoice! for this picture is true and amen, says the Lord of Hosts.

"From the Womb of the Morning"

Now Zion, bride of Christ, already praised in God's word as mother of nations (Psalm 87) and fruitful spouse of the I AM (Isaiah 54:5) births "from the womb of the morning" a new people and a new era of Christ's reign. Clothed like a bride in the beauty of holiness and "in holy array" Zion goes forth, multiplies and fills the earth with sons of God. *The Amplified Bible* says,

"To you (will spring forth) your young men who are as the dew."

Psalm 110 goes on to say, "Thou are a priest forever after the order of Melchizedek." Jesus is the holy high priest of Zion, according to the book of Hebrews. He heads a nation of priests. In Revelation, Jesus receives praise as the slain Lamb who purchased men for God from every tribe and language and people and nation.

"And you have made them a kingdom (royal race) and priests to our God, and they shall reign (as kings) over the earth!" (Revelation 5:10) Defining the priestly anointing, Isaiah 61:6 declares "But you shall be called priests of the Lord; people will speak of you as the ministers of our God."

Zion, a refined remnant now, a fruitful spouse, will give birth to an ever-increasing nation of kings and priests to fill the earth and have dominion in Christ. "In the womb of the morning" alludes not only to birth but also to the dawning of a new age. Satan has attempted to grab God's idea and create his own "new age." But God's era of justice, peace and righteousness will be no fake. It will be the real thing. We will rejoice in it, though a much-prophesied time of shaking will precede it.

The Feast Will Take Place As the Earth Shakes

The ancient prophets agree on a time of shaking, when trembling and earthquakes will drive men into caves. The prophet Isaiah said:

"For there shall be a day of the Lord of hosts against all who are proud and haughty...when He rises to shake mightily and terribly the earth." (Isaiah 2:12, 21)

Ezekiel prophesied the same "great shaking":

> All the men that are upon the face of the earth shall tremble and shake at My presence: and the mountains shall be thrown down and the steep places shall fall and every wall (natural or artificial) shall fall to the ground. (Ezekiel 38:20)

"I will shake the heavens and the earth," Haggai 2:21 affirms. The prophet Joel adds the presence of a host of conquerors to the equation:

> a mighty people, set in battle array...The earth quakes before them; the heavens tremble. The sun and the moon are darkened and the stars withdraw their shining. (Joel 2:5, 10)

Don't think that the shaking signifies a world out of control. God Himself controls the quake, rattle and roll!

The Lord of Hosts speaks, the Holy One of Israel: Yes, I am holy. Ruler, Lord and King of all. And to those who recognize it, the firstborn (Psalm 87, Hebrews 12) I come as King and Lord, Lord of their lives. I rule and reign over their lives and nothing shall in any way harm them because I rule in righteousness, in peace, love and mercy.

My reign over all the earth shall begin with the shaking, (Hebrews 12:26-27) the trembling (Ezekiel 37:7), the rattling, the earth moving and shaking. Everything that can be shaken will be shaken. Heaven and earth, believe Me, will shake. And I am Lord over the shaking, Lord of Hosts, I AM.

Know now as the shaking begins, you who have sought Me for wisdom on "the "calamity" to come, that I control the shaking to come upon the whole earth and the trembling and I will cause you to rejoice as things shaken flow into the kingdom. Amen!

When the earth begins to shake and mountains tumble and crash down, we need to know that our God is in control. The angel who showed the prophet Daniel the end times and the anti-christ (who himself is on a tight leash held by God) told Daniel: "that which is determined (by God) shall be done." God is in control.

A New Day

As sure as the shaking is the promise of a glorious new day for God's people.

Dawn or morning is the symbolic time of salvation and favor. In speaking of the city of God, Psalm 46:5 promises, "God will help her right early" (at the dawn of the morning). When Sennacherib's Assyrian army positioned itself to attack Jerusalem, salvation from God came at dawn. The Sun of Righteousness will rise with healing in His rays (Malachi 4:2) Jesus arose on the morning of the third day. God's salvation and favor come in the morning, at the beginning of a new "day."

Jesus Christ's reign described in Psalm 110 ends with a curious comment: "He shall drink of the brook in the way: therefore he shall lift up the head." (One translation adds "triumphantly.") The Lord has revealed to His praying people that He wants and needs our praise support during this grievous time of wrath. The brook the Lord drinks from to refresh Himself is the living water that flows from us, His people, in praise, honor, reverence and worship of Him that is highly specific to His majestic cleansing work in this hour.

Those judged will, as the result of the Messiah's intervention, "reverently fear the name of the Lord from the west and His glory from the rising of the sun." Rule and reign, with its necessary judgement of evil, releases people groups from the enemy's grip. Triumph and victory result.

"Therefore shall He lift up the head!"

Is this all the realm of far-off fancy, visions and dreams? No. It is happening in the spirit—right now.

The Book of Revelation is happening now. The thunder chorus of praise is rising before Me now. Jesus is taking up the iron scepter to rule over the nations NOW. A scepter shall come forth out of Zion now because of the prayer movement among His people. (The worldwide October prayer for the 10-40 window countries is an example.) So rejoice that all that is prophesied is coming true and the end is near.

Whether or not we are aware of it, heaven has erupted in wild jubilation at the events now unfolding in the earth. This joy has resulted from the massive, global work of the Lord of Hosts, Jesus Christ, in assembling a true people of God, a people to usher in His reign.

The God of Love speaks and says, Rejoice now, O earth! Rejoice now, My people. Let the earth rejoice; let the people be glad for our God reigns! For the millennial reign of the Lord and King, Jesus Christ, has begun in the spirit with a holy nation, a people set apart for His rulership. Yes! It is completed! A mighty, mighty work.

Shall a nation be formed in a single day? Yes! In this Day of the Lord God Almighty. And so, a people has been formed for My purposes, one people, one nation under God, of kings and priests in the land. A ***holy*** *nation. A people set apart in holiness. Rejoice in Me this day, O people of the nation of God, that I might loose a mighty rejoicing celebration in the earth.*

There is coming a time of turmoil and triumph of our God. For many will come to Me. As soon as the shaking begins, they will return, sobered and shaken, to the God of their childhood, for they have a foundation in Me.

Why did they have to wait for the shaking when I was present and waiting all the time? But they are My children, errant children, but My children, and I will always welcome them back with love. Harder shaking will release harder hearts. And so be it, until the hardest are tested and remain in their hardness. But not one grain of wheat will be lost in this harvest shaking. Not one heart with a softness toward Me will be allowed to be lost. This is My mercy at work, for the eyes of the Lord go to and fro across the face of the earth looking for the ones who have something in their heart for Me. I will use anything as a basis to save them from what is to come.

So, expect turmoil. You will see it and will be tempted to distress, but know and understand that our God reigns. It is in My hand and it is causing eternal good. So be not distressed but offer comfort from our God with a sense of peace.

The shaking that characterizes the Day of the Lord is rearranging and realigning earthly authority for the full reign of the Lord Jesus Christ. The Almighty will shatter kings. The song of Zion, Psalm 48, pictures the joyous city of the great King and praises it as a refuge and a stronghold. Then it shows thc kings who march against it. "They were stricken with terror and took to flight. Trembling took hold of them there, and pain as of a woman in childbirth." (Psalm 48:5-6) The power of men, be it in individuals or institutions, will succumb to waves of judgement. Expect some leaders to topple from their positions.

Birth pangs, Jesus predicted, would accompany His day. Zion births the millennial reign of the Lord Jesus Christ and the natural earth quakes, birthing judgement on its inhabitants. Mountains must be reduced to rubble; authority, institutions and power structures must fall. Unholy alliances will break apart. The authority of the King will prevail.

The contractions may surprise us. When we see church authority disintegrate and the church take on a new form, we might conclude that all hell is breaking loose. We need to remember that the Holy Spirit's organizational structure may be quite different than our own. The Spirit likes a supple structure that can bend, an open structure that He can flow into, a structure held so gently by human hands that it can change, rearrange, expand or branch out in a new direction at a moment's notice.

Social order will disintegrate also, resulting in apparent chaos. Man's rigidity and order do not enhance the flow of the river of life. Some huge spiritual dams and barricades may need to be demolished to allow the river to flow.

Prepare

Prepare to see My glory, the shekinah-presence glory of your God. I will come and demonstrate My glory.

All things work together for good in My plan and I do not falter or fail. See the big picture now, the vast picture of My plan for the earth: the coming millennium-reign of the Lord Jesus Christ and all that has to happen to usher it in.

The time is up for man and man's reign. Now comes God's reign (and rain!) and it is good! What happens prior is shaking and tumult and disaster in men's eyes—but not in Mine. Yahweh Sabbaoth (the Lord of Hosts) is in control. And shaking is rearranging, realigning, planing (the valleys come up, the mountains come down) to prepare for the coming Kingdom. So look up! Your salvation is nigh! saith the Lord.

Prepare. Prepare now. I have everything in place, I have moved My people to (and from) where I want them to be and I am ready. Heaven stands ready now. An arsenal of our God is prepared to shake mightily the earth, indeed the heaven and the earth. So stand firm, prepared and ready for the shaking that is to come. I have planted your feet firmly on the Rock. Remember: first comes the shaking and then "the desired of nations shall come."

So rejoice with Me at the outcome. I need your rejoicing. Hear, O Israel: rejoice in the Lord your God. He needs your rejoicing now.

"Prepare" is the word the Lord speaks now to His people. Prepare your heart. The unprepared will miss the totality of this heaven-and-earth work. How can we prepare? One way is to shift our perspective and view the shaking and judgement from heaven's viewpoint, not our own. Heaven anticipates the restored earth with peace and happiness. Heaven sees tearing down as vital for restoration to righteousness.

Another way to prepare our hearts is by rejoicing. Embrace it by praise and joy. God's uprooting and restoration are too big to understand completely, but we can prepare our hearts to witness the unlimited power and energy of Jesus Christ in this all-encompassing work.

He is accomplishing a massive, large-scale revolution, destined to subject all things to His reign of righteousness. God wants us to witness His work with the trust of Moses who did not tremble in fear of His glory as the Israelites did. Instead Moses climbed a black, rumbling, cloud-swathed Mount Sinai in confidence to behold His God.

When the Lord Jesus brings everything into submission to Himself, He will in turn submit the whole to the Father.

I wish to speak to you of exciting things, good things. Know now that millennial things are happening. Reign is beginning. Worldwide submission of all things to Jesus. ***All things****. This is* *beginning now.*

Has it not happened in your life and the lives of many of My people? Will it not spread and multiply by the work of My Holy Spirit? Yes!

So know and recognize signs of the millennium reign of the Lord Jesus Christ. Hallelujah! Nations, whole nations, shall submit themselves to Me, as in Psalm 66. By the greatness of My power, I will rend the heavens and come down. Wide scale, mighty blessing-acts of God. What joy!

Know that in the time coming you will see "veracity and judgement" works of God, according to Psalm 111. My works will become very obvious to the children of men. They will not fail to notice and see that it is Me acting (on their behalf) in judgement and in truth. So know when you see it that it is My hand.

I believe, know and have faith for My people. They will respond to My mighty acts. They will turn back to Me when I pour out My wrath. I will get their attention. They will respond because of that "something good" deep inside them. The word of a mother or teacher. The guiding love of a father. So know now that rocking and shaking are not in vain. They will produce results. And Satan will be dismayed.

Again, a gut-wrenching change of gears becomes necessary on our part. Faith asks us to regard reality from God's surprisingly fresh stance. For example, faith demands we look at death, a final and hideous reality, in the hope of Christ's resurrection. Today, in these last hours, faith demands that we rise above fear of the prophesied Day of the Lord and the Great Tribulation and see these earth-shaking events as God sees them—productive contractions designed to birth salvation for multiplied millions. The shaking will bring heaven-on-earth restoration and the golden age of Christ's reign.

The New Jerusalem, the dream city of His dominion, is no fairy tale. That heavenly city is arising now.

Rejoice! Rejoice with Me. Rejoice, O native of Zion! Rejoice beloved of the Father. Rejoice with Me and all the angels and saints in joyous festival gathering in Zion, for the city of our God has formed. The New Jerusalem created and made in Me, Jesus Christ, is formed and taken shape and built and ready. Rejoice, O rejoice, My beloved, for herein you will dwell for all eternity. Your city, My city, is debuted, inaugurated, dedicated. A ceremony will take place in heaven and I want you to be part of it!

Oh, Lord, our Lord, how majestic is thy name in all the

earth! Now city of majesty arise and take thy place as seat of government for the millennial reign of the Lord Jesus Christ.

See? It is in place! Such joy in heaven. Let there be joy now in the earth, for we are one, one church, one body, one unit in the faith. Oh, God, your God, is excited about this. The culmination of all things prophesied is happening now. Heaven has been busy, but now the results are appearing. Oh yes, rejoice!

Jerusalem. The name means city of peace. He means to permeate His holy city of the spirit with peace.

The Lord our God is One God, worshipped in spirit and in truth by His people, a holy nation. This is what I hoped for in Israel and achieved briefly during Solomon and David's reign because of the fickleness of the people and their kings.

But now I have a people who are not warped or twisted, tested many times in fire like gold, prepared and ready, like David's provision for building the temple.

Do you see what I see? The time for Solomon's reign of peace is ready, the time for Solomon's fulfillment (he was a type) has come, the reign of peace with the building of a glorious temple to our God.

Could I be happier? In My great love now I can bless My people. Could I be more delighted? (Yes, when My people come home to Me out of the world's darkness and pain.)

Now the God of Love, your beloved God, says, I am pleased with My people. I will draw them out of the world and world system, establish them in peace and mightily bless them. I am the Lord and I can and will do it. Strife and suffering will be going on around them, but they themselves will be blessed.

How did the Israelites operate when the plagues hit Egypt? With compassion and concern, caring but not suffering themselves except in empathy. So be it for My people, says the Lord. Touch others lives as much as you can with the anointing. Use the anointing with compassion. Don't hide in your churches (they won't be the same) but mix with the world to assuage their pain.

Citizens of Zion

Zion will accomplish God's purposes in the earth in this hour. He will use us to execute His word in the earth. He will ask us to demonstrate His mercy. As each of us participates in this mighty work, God plans to enrich and bless us. We are registered as citizens of a holy city that Paul describes:

> ...you have come to Mount Zion, even to the city of

> the living God, the heavenly Jerusalem, and to countless multitudes of angels in festal gathering,
>
> And to the church (assembly) of the Firstborn who are registered (as citizens) in heaven, and to the God Who is Judge of all, and to the spirits of the righteous (the redeemed in heaven) who have been made perfect,
>
> And to Jesus, the Mediator (Go-between, Agent) of a new covenant, and to the sprinkled blood which speaks (of mercy), a better and nobler and more gracious message than the blood of Abel (which cried out for vengeance.)
>
> So see to it that you do not reject Him or refuse to listen to and heed Him...
>
> Then (at Mount Sinai) His voice shook the earth, but now He has given a promise: Yet once more I will shake and make tremble not only the earth but also the (starry) heavens.
>
> Now this expression, Yet once more, indicates the final removal and transformation of all (that can be) shaken—that is, of that which has been created—in order that what cannot be shaken may remain and continue.
>
> Let us therefore, receiving a kingdom that is firm and stable and cannot be shaken, offer to God pleasing service and acceptable worship, with modesty and pious care and godly fear and awe;
>
> For our God (is indeed) a consuming fire. (Hebrews 12:22-29)

The foundation Jesus builds His kingdom upon cannot be shaken. It is built upon Himself, the Rock of our salvation. The Lord is tearing down people's lives to their foundations and is rebuilding these foundations on Himself. Isaiah 54:11 prophesies:

> O you afflicted (city), storm-tossed and not comforted, behold I will set your stones in fair colors and lay your foundations with sapphires.

The description echoes that of the new Jerusalem of Revelation 21, with its foundations of precious stones. The individual lives represented in the body of Christ will make up the New Jerusalem.

Through His anointed people, the Anointed One will finish the prophecy of Isaiah about Himself. Earlier we looked at this glorious prediction of the Messiah, the one that Jesus began reading in the Nazareth synagogue but did not finish—at that time. We mentioned that Jesus put down the book after the first two verses, prophecy words that referred to phase one of His ministry. Let's look at this passage again:

> The Spirit of the Lord God is upon me, because the Lord has anointed and qualified me to preach the Gospel of good tidings...sent me to bind up and heal the broken hearted...

He will now complete the mission for which His Father anointed Him. The mission will be fulfilled--in us. Notice once more how Jesus' language switches from "me" to "they:"

> They shall rebuild the ancient ruins; they shall raise up the former desolations and renew the ruined cities, the devastations of many generations...But you shall be called the priests of the Lord; people will speak of you as the ministers of our God. You shall eat the wealth of the nations and the glory (once of your captors) shall be yours. (Isaiah 61:4, 6)

The prince of this world has blinded God's people to the basic truth of Christ's message: the message of the anointing. Now God has ripped the blinders from the eyes of His people. The truth of the anointing is unleashed. God told His prophets He would accomplish this. He told the prophet Isaiah 25 centuries ago. God promised that on this mountain (Zion) He would remove the veil, shroud or covering cast upon the people, the veil of wretchedness and take away their rebuke or reproach. He will show them the power of I AM in them and their anointing in Christ Jesus. It happens on Zion.

I will speak to you about My Word in Isaiah 25: what I am saying here is that I rejoice over My people Israel gathered on Mount Zion, that I prepare a feast for them in the presence of their enemies, that I am their God and they are My people. I am saying that the cloud or veil has been ripped from their eyes. I have done it supernaturally and sovereignly. They now see what they did not see before. They see My plan, My reign, My hand working like never before. They participate in prayer like never before. The prince of this world who blinded them is thrown down.

Hallelujah! Blind no more! (Will not physical healings of blindness follow? Yes!) The blinders are pulled off. The confusion is gone and doublemindedness. My people see clearly Who I AM and what I am doing in the earth. They are rising into the new-

Adam position.

Oh glory! I have longed to see this day and now it is fulfilled. What joy fills My heart over this. Rejoice with Me!

So know ye, My child and all My children, that I am God and no more shall the heathen and the Moab-fleshly have supremacy or dominion, but My people Zion shall take dominion and have rule over the land, ***their*** *land. Rejoice! Dominion and rule are the words I now give you. Dominion and rule.*

The law goes forth out of Zion, the city-seat of government, out of the mouths of My people to exact obedience from the nations and the peoples of the earth. Their knee will bow now as I raise My people to high position in the kingdom and My people take up the seat of government and ***My people*** *rule and reign in Christ Jesus, in the Anointed Jesus, in His anointing, saith the Lord. Oh rejoice with Me!*

Oh rejoice, My people, that this thing is finally done and this is to prepare you to continue this rule and reign eternally. Oh, hallelujah! The Spirit of God rejoices and labors in joy, giving birth to this nation, this people in JOY, JOY, JOY.

Rejoice, O Zion, with your God. Rejoice. Rejoice! Your God is laboring in joy. Shall I give birth to a nation in a single day? Yes! The Day of the Lord, day of darkness and light, and the light shall overcome the darkness. I say it in great, great joy.

God views the great Day of the Lord as a parallel work of blessing and judgement. And, because of His goodness, even the wrath will produce good results. We who are with Him must embrace His vision of this Day.

The Father Will Be All in All

We have the honor to participate in the great work the Apostle Paul describes:

> The end will come when he hands over the kingdom to God the Father after he has destroyed all dominion, power and authority. For he must reign until he has put all his enemies under his feet...When he has done this, then the son himself will be made subject to him who put everything underneath him, so that God may be all in all. (1 Corinthians 15:24, 25, 28 NIV)

Come into the heavenly plan of My Father. Let it be revealed, revealed as you walk it out in the Spirit, revealed now and made plain as on tablets, written, known and made public to those who need to know.

Let His heavenly plan be known: it is the restoration of all things in Christ Jesus. It is bringing everything under His feet—and that means everything. He reigns. He will reign over all with a rod of iron, a rod of justice and integrity.

"He reigns!" And this prayer now is the taking of the Kingdom. A worldwide, mightily-orchestrated major effort in military terms. All the hosts of heaven are involved. All these on earth who are purified, equipped and ready are called up and involved.

Know this mighty plan and participate in it for you are called of Christ Jesus, the mighty King and head of all the hosts. ***Everything*** *will be brought under His feet and you are part of the mighty battle to do it. This is not battle in the traditional sense of battle. It is a mighty move of the Spirit of Conquering. Know what is going on in the Spirit. This is it.*

When Jesus subdues every earthly power structure, He will submit the whole dominion to the Father. The King of Kings yields in love to the Father. The same is true for us. Just as Christian leaders discover that true leadership equals servanthood, so we discover that reign equals submission. Rule and reign in God's kingdom is not a power thing. "Kings and priests in the land" are not glittering luminaries. They have the quality of littleness. Rule and reign come out of surrender and yieldedness. We consent in love to the Master, Jesus, and He uses us to accomplish His rule—sometimes in strange ways. It is yieldedness, listening and obedience that qualify a worshipper to serve as king and priest. We continually cast our crowns before Him in praise. Any accolade we may receive goes directly to Him as praise. We know our victories occurred not in our power but in the anointing, the God-presence of I AM in and on us.

Before God's work manifests in the natural world, He accomplishes it in the spiritual world. The reign of the Lord Jesus Christ has come in the hearts of men, women and children. It will soon appear in natural events.

My kingdom is not of this world and comes not by observation but reigns in men's hearts. What does this mean? It means that I am Judge and Lord in the hearts of My people. It means that the fourth kingdom in Daniel is fulfilled and that My reign has come.

Prophecy fulfilled and the world has not seen it! The Book of Revelation is happening now. Believe Me, it is. I am overjoyed at My kingdom come. I am delighted at the finishing of your faith and that of others at the finalization of My kingdom. The battle has gone on and I will stop it with the breath of My mouth, the sword of My mouth, when the time is up. Understand, the big battle is going on in the Spirit now and judgement is coming into the hands of the saints.

The world does not see this. The church does not see this. Believe Me: this is true, though outrageous to the thoughts of men. It all happens in the spiritual, in men's hearts. Know and understand this truth. Begin to see My glory demonstrated now as earthly kingdoms fail and My dominion and rule arise in My people. Yes, the devil will raise up a final kingdom in his people, but it will be destroyed utterly. The time for rule and reign is here, My children, but it is not of this world. Though not observable by human eyes or even human understanding, all things are coming to a close now in the Spirit.

God anointed Cyrus to restore His people Israel to their inheritance. He anointed David to squelch the enemy, unite the kingdom, organize the temple construction, and prepare the people for a reign of peace, righteousness and abundance. He anointed Jesus to set the captives free, to heal, deliver, bring salvation and to overcome death, finally and irrevocably.

God promised to send Christ, the Anointed, the Messiah, "Even Jesus, whom heaven must receive (and retain) until the time for the complete restoration..." (Acts 3:20-21)

The Anointed One, through the people of the anointing, will accomplish the restoration of everything lost to Adam and everything promised in the word of God. He will reign.

The time is coming when all things draw to a close. I will protect thee in time of trouble and bless thee in time of darkness, for I am with thee, My people Israel. Look up! Your salvation is nigh, even at the door, your beloved Jesus. Rejoice, My people, at such a time as this, the time of the end, when all things draw to a close in Christ Jesus, in the Anointed Jesus. He is anointed as King and Priest and we will now see the fulfillment, the fullness of that anointing.

Reign, O Holy King! Sanctify thy people, O Holy High Priest, who is their Atonement! Oh yes, do all that was prophesied, O Lord of Hosts, for now the time has come!

The Anointed Jesus and His anointed will do the job.

Section Six

Refreshing

God promised
through His ancient prophets
an incredible time of future restoration.

Then, through the Apostle Peter,
He foretold fulfillment
of every Bible restoration promise
prophesied throughout the ages.

God planned
that His heart's-dream reparation
be accomplished
in a person,
the Anointed One, the Messiah.

This consummation,
held back till the time just before Jesus' return,
has now begun.
His "days of heaven on earth" will make us ask,
"Is this real?--or am I dreaming?"

Chapter 17

"When I Bring Back the Captivity of Jacob"

When Old Testament prophets promised restoration to a sinful Israel overrun by its enemies, they often lifted their eyes to a far-off time of full restoration. While they prophesied return to a people being dragged off to slavery, they also envisioned a time of heart-expanding, beyond-all-hope, full divine restoration.

When the prophets looked centuries ahead, they foresaw a final restoration that would make the wilderness blossom as the rose. Justice and righteousness, peace, quietness and trust would spring up from barren land. Later, a New Testament prophet, Peter, revealed that all the promises of the ancient prophets would see fulfillment in a person, Christ Jesus, the Anointed, who would finally achieve "the restoration of all things."

In this chapter, we'll work to raise our awareness of the stunning scope of God's restoration plan to be accomplished in this messianic moment.

Jeremiah

When God pledged to restore the Jews after exile, He added promises of future end-time restoration. Before the deportation to Babylon that followed centuries of warnings to Israel from its prophets, the people received a promise. Through Jeremiah, Israel learned that in 70 years God would restore the exiles to their land. (Jeremiah 29:10)

The subject of Jeremiah's prophecy moves from a message for an Israel threatened by cruel invaders to a promise of a new covenant. Jeremiah foresaw a time when God's law would be written on men's hearts. (Jeremiah 31:31-34) God promised the heavy-hearted people a righteous Branch, who would be their Messiah. "And He shall execute justice and righteousness in the land." He gave the sin-hardened people a new name to call Him, "The Lord is Our Righteousness." He promised:

> I will cause the captivity of...Israel to be reversed and will rebuild them as they were at first.

> (Jerusalem) shall be to Me a name of joy, a praise and a glory before all the nations of the earth, that hear of all the good I do for it, and they shall fear and tremble because of all the good and all the peace, prosperity, security and stability I provide for it.
>
> For I will cause the captivity of the land to be reversed and return to be as it was at first, says the Lord. (Jeremiah 33:7, 9, 11)

God used Jeremiah, and prophets such as the psalming sons of Korah, as well as Joel, Amos, Isaiah and the apostle Peter, to promise a far-off time of restoration for the church, God's spiritual Israel. These prophets caught God's vision of a messianic, or "anointed," age to occur here on earth. Their promises will shape our concept of the heaven-on-earth restoration God plans to bring. The apostle Peter will point us to a person who **is** both the promise and its fulfillment, the alpha and the omega, Christ Jesus.

The scriptures we will weave into this tapestry of God's vision are:

Jeremiah 33:7-11
Psalm 85:1-13
Joel 2:21-32
Amos 9:11-15
Isaiah 32:15-20
Acts 3:19-21

Harvest Images Portray Restoration

The six prophets whom this chapter will consider described messianic restoration by using harvest images. For example, spiritual rain to bring the end-time harvest to fruition will be a deluge, according to the prophet Joel, who foretold early (spring) and latter (autumn) rains in the same month. God will restore a harvest of "corn, the wine and the oil," representing strength, joy and anointing, to a drought-destroyed land. (Joel 2:18) Psalm 85, the poem of restoration, declares, "The land shall see her increase." Everything barren and unfruitful "shall overflow with spiritual blessing," Amos 9:13 pledges.

Psalm 85

Psalm 85 emphasizes spiritual fruit, a rich harvest of mercy and truth, righteousness and peace. The psalm pictures a back and forth flow between heaven and earth, a spiritual harmony. It describes the climate of the messianic, or anointing time, restoration.

> Lord, thou hast have been favorable unto thy land; thou hast brought back the captivity of Jacob...
> Mercy and truth are met together; righteousness and peace have kissed each other.
> Truth shall spring out of the earth, and righteousness shall look down from heaven.
> Yea, the Lord shall give that which is good, and our land shall see her increase. (Psalm 85:1, 10-12 KJV)

Most of the prophets prefaced God's promise of restoration with these words, "When I bring back the captivity of Jacob." They use this intriguing language to pinpoint the time of restoration. Returned from sin-bondage, a people cleansed by fire come back into the land. Only a remnant, or part of the people, are able to stand in Judgement and make it into the restoration blessing time. This prophesied remnant became a reality in Old Testament Israel. The remnant returned from Babylon after the prophesied 70 years of slavery. The remnant has returned to natural Israel in this century. And the church, paralleling natural Israel's return to the land, has undergone cleansing by fire and returned to Zion, the place of worship.

"The captivity of Jacob." The name Jacob points to the Genesis story of Jacob, a supplanter and a manipulator who wrestled with God and obtained a new name, and a new identity—Israel. Jacob must undergo punishment for sin, but Israel, with a new holy identity, returns to the land.

"The captivity of Jacob" refers to the slavery and sin-bondage the people brought upon themselves because of idolatry.

The psalm's rich language expresses a harmony in the spiritual realm and a bonding between heaven and earth. Mercy and truth meet. Righteousness and peace kiss. Truth rises from the earth and righteousness reaches down from heaven. In the following prophetic word, the Lord God rejoices in the praise rising from the earth and promises an outpouring from heaven.

I AM God; there IS no other. Rejoice, O earth, for the Lord comes to rule the land. His people have gathered in praise, true praise. They have worshipped in spirit and in truth. Now the Lord comes to save.

I AM God; there is no other. See what I will do in the lives of those who worship Me. I am your God alone and now I will do and fulfill all that I have promised. Recompense and reward in this earth now. Realize it and proclaim it, for it is truth, hidden truth, ready to be brought out now. The God of Recompense will recompense in this hour. Prepare for heaven on earth reward. Joy unspeakable and full of glory. Soundness, health, wholeness. Freedom from bondages. Love. Happiness Peace. Wells filled and overflowing. Vats full. Barns bulging. Good to excess, so there is waste because it overflows. Press down, shaken together, overflowing, abundant life. Restored life and wholeness.

Oh, you say, it sounds like a dream, too good to be true. But I say, Eye has not seen, nor ear heard, nor has it entered into the heart of man to imagine what the Lord will do for those who love Him. Amen. I have spoken.

The Prophet of Restoration

Joel

In Joel's day, the destroyer sent locusts to devour Israel's crops. A litany of destruction, describing wave after wave of stripping and gnawing locusts, gives Joel's readers a blow by blow account of the devastation. Then, abruptly, God gives a heart-stirring restoration promise through Joel. It goes beyond the immediate to a full-scale spiritual restoration for spiritual Israel.

> And I will restore or replace for you the years the locust has eaten—the cankerworm, and the caterpillar, and the palmerworm...
>
> And you shall eat in plenty and be satisfied and praise the name of the Lord, your God, Who has dealt wondrously with you. And My people shall never be put to shame.
>
> And afterwards I will pour out My Spirit upon all flesh; and your sons and your daughters shall prophesy, your old men shall dream dreams, your young men shall see visions. (Joel 2:25-28)

Time Speeded Up

Amos

The spiritual harvest will "overflow," according to Amos, and accelerate in a speeded-up spiritual pace. "The plowman shall overtake the reaper and the treader of grapes him who sows the seed." (Amos 9:13) Isaiah adds his prophetic voice to this timing promise, "I am the Lord; in its time I will hasten it." (Isaiah 60:22 NIV)

We are experiencing the reality of this promise today; time is compressed. Events have accelerated. We stand on the brink of the greatest spiritual harvest the world has ever seen.

Spiritual and Material Prosperity

Amos 9:14 promises both earthly, material fruit and spiritual prosperity.

> I will bring again the captivity of My people of Israel, and they shall build the waste cities and inhabit them; and they shall plant vineyards and drink the wine thereof; they shall also make gardens, and eat the fruit of them. (Amos 9:14 KJV)

Isaiah

Isaiah 32 deals with the 600 BC Assyrian invasion, a judgement on faithless Israel. But it moves to a messianic level with words such as, "Behold, a King will reign in righteousness and princes will rule with justice."

Isaiah merges the idea of the natural fruitfulness of the "land" with its spiritual prosperity. Isaiah says that during the time of the anointing a king will reign in righteousness. (v1) The prophet laments the loss of pleasant fields and vines to invasive thorns and briers, "until the spirit is poured upon us from on high, and the wilderness becomes a fruitful field." (v15)

> Then justice will dwell in the wilderness and righteousness (moral and spiritual rectitude in every area and relation) will abide in the fruitful field. And the effect of righteousness will be peace and the result of righteousness will be quietness and confident trust forever. (Isaiah 32:16-17)

With restoration comes rest. "My people shall dwell in a peaceable habitation, in safe dwellings and in quiet resting places." (v18)

This restoration, this messianic age, has begun.

The God of love and peace and joy says to you that I am bringing back the captivity of Jacob, My chosen. I am quietly doing this work behind the scenes for all to be amazed at when it is manifested. It will come to a head like a tidal wave cresting. Now it is like the energy wave running across the ocean floor, but when it hits the beach, watch out! It will be big, noticeable and obvious.

For as surely as sin led ancient Israel into captivity by for-

eign nations, so sin today leads to spiritual servitude and bondage. Know that your freedom from your former tyrant master is complete and that full restoration has begun.

Blow the trumpet in the time of the new moon! Make known the restoration message to all who will hear! Let it be said of our God, He is a great God of restoration and rejoicing! He has comforted His people, Israel, His chosen, Jacob, and will not relent until the blessing is full and fulfilled! Amen!

Repentance Brings Restoration

In the last chapter we looked at God's discipline—storm, fire and judgement. Sin causes slavery and exile. Repentance paves the way for restoration. Restoration and outpouring of the Spirit flows only after repentance. Though the passage from Isaiah 32 quoted earlier soars in its promise of restoration peace, it also admonishes, "Gird sackcloth upon your loins." (v11) Storm, fire and judgement shake us into looking at our own sin.

God will not be thwarted in His plan to bless and restore His chosen. Amos speaks of the shaking beforehand.

> For behold, I will command, and I will sift the house of Israel among all nations and cause it to move to and from as grain is sifted in a sieve, yet shall not the least kernel fall upon the earth and be lost. (Amos 9:9)

Remember what Jesus said to Peter just before the crucifixion? "Satan has asked to sift you as wheat. But I have prayed for you, Simon, that your faith may not fail." Sifting implies the work of the enemy. Be aware that God has the enemy on a tight chain and is using him to accomplish His purposes. He is in firm control. "Not a single grain shall be lost."

After the sifting, which is part of the refining process, comes blessing, both material and spiritual. Amos describes rich rewards from our physical and spiritual work. We will build and inhabit homes; plant vineyards and drink the wine they yield; work gardens and eat their produce. (In contrast, Old Testament punishment for sin involved building houses that others would inhabit and tending vineyards and gardens for others to drink and eat.)

A remnant of refined purified people returns to the spiritual land and enjoys its fruit: mercy, peace, truth and righteousness. (Psalm 85) This people builds and plants—and reaps a spiritual harvest overflowing with prosperity. (Amos 9)

Repentance Brings Anointing and Glory

The message of repentance always precedes the anointing and restoration. Isaiah 32 says, "Gird sackcloth upon your loins (in grief)...they shall beat upon their breasts..." (v11-12) Acts 3:19 stresses repentance first. "Repent ye therefore and be converted that your sins may be blotted out." The prophet Joel also promised that God would restore the years the destroyer has consumed. But first, he said, we must gather in sacred assemblies to repent. (This gathering in sacred assemblies has begun. Promise Keepers, Intercessors for America and others have gathered praying people to repent. More and larger assemblies will come.)

Return to Me with all your heart and with fasting and with weeping and with mourning. Rend your heart and not your garments and turn unto the Lord your God. (Joel 2:12-13)

This heart rending results in the blessing of Joel 2:23, "Be glad then, ye children of Zion, and rejoice in the Lord your God for He has given you the rain...(Rain signifies the outpouring of the Holy Spirit, the anointing.) Rain brings fruitfulness and restoration. "And I will restore to you the years that the locust has eaten..."And ye shall know that I AM...the Lord your God." (Joel 2:25, 27)

Restoration stirs rejoicing among the people of God. David prophesied it in Psalm 14, saying "Oh, that the salvation of Israel were come out of Zion! When the Lord brings back the captivity of his people, Jacob shall rejoice and Israel shall be glad."

Crossing Over the Jordan

For ancient Israel, returning to the land meant crossing the Jordan. The return to the spiritual land also involves a crossing of the Jordan river, a symbol of crossing to life. Israel of the Exodus crossed the Jordan to enter their promised land. Jesus Himself received His baptism at the Jordan, modeling new life to us, and at the Jordan received the Holy Spirit, the Spirit of Life.

God's spiritual Israel, a nation of kings and priests, also needed to complete this symbolic crossing—as a nation. God has told his prophets, including well-known pastor and speaker Dutch Sheets of Colorado Springs, that His spiritual Israel has crossed over.

In the Spirit, the people of God have crossed over the Jordan and entered their "land" to now defeat all their enemies. Miraculous victories, soon to become commonplace, will take place in the name of I AM. In the Spirit, the people of God have completed a major event in their salvation history. They have crossed the Jordan.

The following words came from the Lord in the mid-1990s, when He said the crossing over event occurred:

Know Me in My mighty acts upon the earth, before the children of men. My people shall be willing in the day of My power! Exciting! Through and in My people, accomplished via My people, I will do a mighty thing comparable to crossing the Jordan.

For this people, brought out of captivity, parallel My ancient, physical Israel. They will go in to take the land, overcome all of their enemies (Jebusites, Hittites, Hivites and the rest) to conquer in Christ Jesus, the Anointed Jesus. Jesus in them, their victory. Jesus in them their hope of glory. So know that a mighty time in the Spirit, a mighty event period is coming up, a crossing over for the purified people of God coming out of the desert, coming up with the ark of the covenant, the expressed presence or glory of God, to cross over as Jesus provided in the cross, to cross over into a new phase of occupying the land and victory over enemies.

And before this faith people **in the Spirit** *(not physically) the enemies shall fall, just* ***fall****. I have spoken it, says the Lord. Believe and act on it.*

Some months later, the Lord spoke again:

Yes, the captivity, the exile of My people is over. Waves, waves have come back to Israel, to take over and inhabit the fruitful land. And now, you who are poised to cross over the Jordan, go in, go in to the land of plenty, the land flowing with milk and honey and abundance. Take over houses you did not build, wells you did not dig, vineyards you did not plant. Know then, My children, that all my abundance awaits you. Cross over in faith into this abundance.

It is a spiritual crossing over. Put the shoes of good news on your feet and cross dry-shod. I will hold back the raging waters as you purpose in your heart to cross. I invite you now, with My word "Come!" that I spoke to Peter. "Come!"

Finally, the Lord said:

I am so glad, so merry, so full of rejoicing, so joyous at an event in the earth, an appointed time event. Rejoicing! Delight! Joy! All heaven sharing it! I will let you know so you can share in My joy. I will tell you: the river crossing is complete. The crossing over the Jordan of this people is complete. Heaven rejoices. Rejoice. What a time, what a "moad" (appointed) *time! Oh earth, rejoice. Oh lands, delight and exult. Oh people, rejoice with Me!*

The Lord God has shown us a model in the Book of Joshua and confirmed by His Spirit that our enemies will bend their knee to us now. Now is the time to go forward in prayer, fasting and intercession to accomplish victory over all the enemies that beset us. Wherever the enemy has come in to steal, kill and destroy is the place to now wage battle against him. The victory is assured. It is ours. We simply need to do it.

Prayer Unleashes Restoration

God has ordained that every major move and every tiny detail of the restoration work be accomplished in prayer. Remember the words of Isaiah to the intercessors:

> Upon your walls, O Jerusalem, I have set watchmen; all the day and all the night they shall never be silent...-until he establishes Jerusalem and makes it a praise in the earth. (Isaiah 62:6-7 RSV)

Conquering our enemies and opening the windows of heaven for restoration are accomplished, already-spoken God-works that we release in prayer. God has ordained this end-time restoration to happen through prayer. Prayer always births the major moves of God. This is the way God works.

Daniel, a servant in Babylon, prayed in God's purposes upon completion of the prophesied 70-year exile to Babylon. He fasted, repented for his nation and prayed three weeks for the fulfillment of God's promise. Today, God has raised up a mighty army of intercessors to pray in every aspect of His planned restoration.

The God of Love speaks saying: I am He who brought you out of the land of Egypt, out of slavery and self-induced bondage, out of "the captivity of Jacob." And now is the time to restore. All My promises on "when I bring back the captivity of Jacob" will be fulfilled. I am the God of Restoration. It is Me, Jesus, who is mentioned in Acts 3:19-21. So know Me, Jesus, now as the God of Restoration, for times of refreshing are coming from the Lord. Know that it is My desire, My heartfelt desire, to do this work of restoration.

Through Isaiah, God calls women to intercession and repentance. "Rise up you women who are at ease!" In one of our key passages, Isaiah 32:9-14, the women listen, pray, tremble, grieve "until the Spirit is poured out among us..." In the old

Testament story, both Deborah and Jael played key roles in delivering Israel from enemy hands. It was Jael, an ordinary tent wife, who drove the spike through the enemy leader, Sisero's, head.

God has called women today to repent and intercede. Many worldwide ministries which focus on prayer, such as Women's Aglow Fellowship, Intercessors International and End-Time Handmaidens, are spearheaded by women.

The true prophetic intercessors are declaring the judgements written and speaking restoration into the earth. The power of their words spoken in faith and directed by the Holy Spirit is causing God's will to spring forth in the earth.

God has a mighty purpose for His intercessors to birth:

I will gather all nations unto Me. I will send out "survivors" from My "remnant" who are "brought back from captivity," brought out of slavery and bondage to strange gods and restored to Me. I will make them witnesses to My glory. Glory is a key word here. Witnesses to My ***glory****.*

(The next paragraph the prophecy below may confuse readers. The Lord refers to "girding Himself alone." This comes from Isaiah 63 which describes God carrying out judgement alone. He did so "because there was no one to help; I was appalled that no one gave support." (No one interceded in prayer.) The people a few decades ago were either in a spiritual slumber or too sin-bound to cooperate with Him. He was forced to carry out the first wave of judgement, which took place in the house of the Lord, alone.)

Now know ye that I will accomplish these My purposes on the earth and prayer will bring it about. How have I girded Myself alone "with no intercessor" for judgement? Because "no one" (not enough) was praying when I launched that judgement and the pray-ers (at that point) didn't know Me well enough to pray (en masse) to accomplish that part of My will. So I launched that recompense against My enemies alone. (Isaiah 63) But now I have a prayer army, a mighty warring nation of pray-ers who can declare and decree and accomplish My will in the earth by their spoken word, which was My plan for man all along. Godly government.

So now go forth with understanding of My purposes on the earth and pray for those sent 1.) to go and 2.) to accomplish all My purposes in the earth by My word and the message of My anointing/My glory. "O Lord, how excellent is thy name in all the earth! Oh, yes, praise Me for the excellence (glory) of My name in all the earth. It shall be done. Amen!

Only a mature intercessor can pray judgment. Most pray-ers would plead for judgement to be averted, but God knows His timetable. It calls for a prophesied holy shaking that will jar His errant children into seeking His will instead of their own.

Judgement in God's own house has already awakened, shaken and stirred up the hearts of His people. With this prepared people He has formed a mighty army of intercessors who will pray in every detail of two concurrent moves of God—the judgement of sin and evil and the glory of God, demonstrated in healing, miracles, deliverance and joyous blessing.

God had to bring His people into conformance with His will so they could pray His will. Instead of pleading with Him against judgement they understand His heart. He has waited but now the time has come. This people realize that mercy and love lie behind judgement. They know His desire and purpose. He will tear down only to rebuild. God's judgement will bring good; we will often find it refreshing! He will shake the earth only as a last resort to get the world's attention. His intercessors support Him with worship, no matter what the circumstances around them. They undergird Him with praise for righteous judgment and pray for salvation for those in whom evil is judged. They shout a mighty chorus of praise, thundering "Our God Reigns!" And they participate in that reign.

Like all of God's promises, restoration becomes material reality through faith. And faith's highest verbal expression is praise. Praise will usher in God's planned abundance. If Almighty God plans something, we might ask, why does He need our praise or our prayer to accomplish it?

Because He purposed that we acquire His promises by faith and by using His word to give expression to that faith. To usher in the blessings of God's long-prophesied restoration, He challenges us to pray—and praise. We must use His word to create faith-filled prayers that get results.

We put crucial faith-pressure on God's promises when we proclaim them, praise Him for them and rejoice.

Know Me. Know My heart. I would not lead you astray. I am the good Shepherd. I would not promise and fail to give. I am called Faithful and True. Hope and trust in the person of the God of blessing. Don't trust in the blessing. Trust in Me.

Appropriate it by praise. Know Me as the God of your Blessing and praise Me as such. I reveal My ***Name*** *to you. Praise My name, the God of Your Blessing, and all it stands for to ap-*

propriate your blessing today. Know My name, the God of Blessing

God's heart for His ancient people Israel was to reveal Himself and His name to them, to bless them and then make them a witness to the pagan nations. So today God will take His "Israel," brought back from bondage to strange gods, and send them as messengers of His glory. Prayer will open the door.

The Anointing for Restoration

God is raising up the anointing of Old Testament king David for this day of restoration. God is ushering in the final kingdom, a final world empire, the reign of the Lord Jesus Christ. David, who was anointed as a boy to be Israel's king, did all his exploits under the power of God's anointing. He was anointed to crush Israel's enemies and regain its territory, to establish a kingdom. Jesus will not take up His reign today until His enemies feel our foot upon their necks. This is part of the restoration process. Once finished Jesus will take up His Solomon scepter for a messianic reign of prosperity and peace.

The anointing is the manifestation of God's presence. David slew Goliath under the anointing, that is, with the manifest presence and accompanying power of God. He refused Saul's offer of armor and sword but instead went armorless, using smooth stones and a slingshot. (Don't you love teenagers?) He did not forget that as a shepherd boy he slew a lion and a bear who ravaged the sheep—not by his own strength as a teenage boy but with the power and presence of the anointing.

God plans to raise David's tabernacle. What does that mean?

> In that day I will raise up the tabernacle of David that is fallen, and close up the breaches thereof; and I will raise up his ruins, and I will build it as in the days of old; that they may possess the remnant of Edom and of all the heathen, which are called by my name, saith the Lord that doeth this. (Amos 9:11-12 KJV)

As outlined in Section Five, the tabernacle was where the manifest presence of God rested. The express presence of God, His *shekinah* glory resided there. God's manifest presence, evidenced by a pillar of cloud and a pillar of fire, had accompanied the Israelites as they left Egypt and traveled through the desert. Later, after God commanded that the tabernacle be built, His glory dwelt there.

The anointing that God placed on David prefigured the

anointing of the Messiah, Jesus. The last section explored that anointing. Here, we will look at the anointing of God's presence-in-power as the key to the long-promised end-time restoration.

The "fallen tabernacle of David," we said, is the truth about God's anointing, the same anointing of power that Jesus operated in. Jesus, who in His humanity relied on the anointing, operated in God's power only after He received the infilling of the Holy Spirit at His Jordan River baptism. In this, He was dependent, like us. His anointing had a purpose: to restore. We, His anointeds, have the same anointing of restoration that God gave Jesus.

> *The message of the anointing, the fallen tabernacle of David must be restored. And My sent ones, a handful of them, are preaching that now, restoring that message of Jesus upon the earth. Jesus was* ***anointed****—and so are you. The power of God was on Him and in Him. He did no mighty works before His baptism in the Holy Spirit. No, He was a man like you. But the anointing did the work, broke the yoke, and set the sin-captives free.*

God's presence or anointing dwells in us. We are tabernacles of His presence. The same anointing that enabled David to subdue Israel's foes and the same anointing that enabled Jesus to deliver and heal resides in us.

The anointing of David and the greater anointing of Jesus achieved restoration. David unified the kingdom and ushered in a reign of peace through Solomon. Jesus anointed to bring men salvation and to usher in the everlasting reign of God's own Son. The raised-up tabernacle of David, prophesied by Amos, is the anointing to usher in the messianic reign of the Lord Jesus Christ.

The anointing will set our world afire, as it did in the era of the apostles. They acted in the power promised by the prophet Amos and repeated here in Acts 15:

> After this I will come back, and will rebuild the house of David, which has fallen; I will rebuild its (very) ruins, and I will set it up again. So that the rest of men may seek the Lord, and all the Gentiles upon whom My name has been invoked, says the Lord, Who has been making these things known from the beginning of the world. (Acts 15:16-17)

Today God's people who have passed through judgement and fire recognize the truth of the awesome presence of I AM within. They have been stripped of reliance on their own strength and have yielded themselves to His power working in them.

The Apostle Peter, inspired by the Holy Spirit, points out in Acts 3:21 that this restoration has been "spoken by the mouth of all His holy prophets since the world began." Surely the witness of the great prophets we've examined here—Jeremiah, Isaiah, Joel, Amos, Peter and others—is an emphatic statement of God's resolve to accomplish an unprecedented last days restoration.

Restoration Is A Person

Acts 3

God's promise of end-time restoration is affirmed in the New Testament. This time, however, the promise includes the last days era of the Anointed One and His anointing—our present moment. The promised leaps to a true messianic level, a vow to restore every single thing pledged by God through His prophets.

Peter preached to the Jews after Pentecost and restated the promise, the restitution of all things prophesied:

> So repent...that your sins may be blotted out, when the times of refreshing shall come from the presence of the Lord; And he shall send Jesus Christ (the Anointed) which before was preached unto you Whom the heaven must receive until the times of restitution of all things, which God hath spoken by the mouth of all his holy prophets since the world began. (Acts 3:19-21)

Jesus Himself is the restoration. He is restoration in a person. We will be restored **in Christ,** in Jesus, the Anointed One and in His anointing. He came to bring life, and life more abundant. He is the Lord of Hosts to whom the prophet Isaiah cried, "Restore us, O Lord of Hosts." Jesus is the God of Our Blessing.

*For I am a great God, a mighty God, called El Shaddai. And My moment, My Day, is coming when I do great and mighty works. One of them is the **full** restoration of My people Israel.*

*And I will use My son, Jesus, to do this work of blessing. Acts 3:19 refers to Jesus, the Anointed Jesus, Christ Jesus, "whom heaven must hold until the restoration of all things." Yes, because Jesus is full to the point of bursting with blessing, pregnant with blessing and heaven must **hold** Him till all things be accomplished.*

*So know now that this anointing, this **anointing of Christ Jesus,** will do the full work of restoration in the earth today. Watch and see. Oh, watch and see!*

Jesus declared that He came that we might have life and have that life in abundance. He will accomplish His goal fully and completely. When we savor this fullness of life, we will relish its richness, like feasting in heaven on earth.

Yes, I AM God and the world will see soon I AM WHO AM, Everlasting One and Alive One. I mean to restore all things in Christ Jesus.

Life! and life in abundance. Heaven on earth life. Life, life, life! Rejoice, O daughter of Jerusalem, in the life you now see in the spirit for it is coming in the natural.

Holy Laughter, A Sign of Restoration

The laughter that has swept the church is a refreshing wave of restoration. The recent laughter resembles that of ancient Israel, when laughter marked the return from captivity.

> When the Lord turned again the captivity of Zion, we were like them that dream.
>
> Then was our mouth filled with laughter, and our tongue with singing; then said they among the heathen, The Lord hath done great things for them.
>
> The Lord hath done great things for us...we are glad. (Psalm 126:1-3 KJV)

Other scriptures elaborate on holy laughter, pointing to how God and His people will laugh when the Day of the Lord arrives:

> The wicked plotteth against the just and gnasheth upon him with his teeth. The Lord shall laugh at him for He seeth that his day is coming. (Psalm 37:12-13 KJV)
>
> He that sitteth in the heavens shall laugh: the Lord shall have them in derision. (Psalm 2:5 KJV)
>
> The joy of the Lord is your strength. (Nehemiah 8:10 RSV)
>
> They that sow in tears shall reap in joy. (Psalm 126:5)

The time for laughter has come! The Lord God is laughing at His enemies (Psalm 2:4) and His people on earth are laughing in the Spirit. The release from bondage has been accomplished. And "we are like people dreaming." In laughter He shows us the victory over the enemy. Victory is ours! And we see it while transported in holy laughter, "drunk" in the Spirit.

God is laughing at His enemies *through us* and that laughter is heard in the earth *through us*. This enhances the higher level warfare, which is not waging war but waging victory in worship, praise and joy.

I have called you to positions of leadership. But when you call for hosts of angels you do not call like generals for men to go in and die. My battlefield and My leadership are different. You are called to lead, to go in and win—and be happy. You send in angels to do victory.

Just praise Me and be joyful in your service to Me. Go in and hold that high ground in joy. You sit at the top of Zion. Praise Me and laugh and be filled with joy and praise. My battle is to win. The war you carry out is a blessing, not a curse like the world's war. My battle is a blessing.

Did I not say in My word that you will laugh at the sword, laugh at famine, laugh at darkness? You have authority over these and you pull them down. You shackle them with praise. Shackle them down with laughter.

We can go to the battle in joy, laughing at the enemy, without fear. We are singing, rejoicing, laughing, celebrating, giddy on the way to battle. Unlike the world's kind of battle, it's going out to do victory.

The following is a word from the Lord on victorious laughter:

I am ***strengthening*** *My people for the day of battle. They shall go forth in strength and joy. They shall go forth in praise as Hezekiah's strange troops who sent the praisers out first. Remember that the cantors, not the foot soldiers, led off.*

So shall the battle be. The enemy will be wasted before My refined people who will be ***willing*** *in the day of My power. Not as the warriors of Ephraim who turned back in the day of battle, though they were armed and prepared. No! My people shall be ready* ***and*** *willing.*

Submit to My strengthening process, My refining process. For the Lord of Hosts will sit as a refiner of fine gold and silver in these last days. (Malachi 3:1ff) I am in charge. I am in control. Fear not. What is happening is in My hands and it is a process you undergo to refine and strengthen you. Pure gold is tough as steel and is lustrous, enduring for all eternity in beauty and value.

Now reach out. Reach out to others around you who are undergoing the fire and comfort them with the news that ***I am in control.*** *I will not take my hand off their lives. I will not abandon them or leave them destitute. I am always with them, for I love them with a tenderhearted love, even a brokenhearted love.*

The result of this refining work is great joy in heaven. For the Lord of Hosts, Jesus, your Redeemer, has refined His people so beautifully, so perfectly, that no attack of the enemy against them will prosper. There is no inroad left for the enemy. No crack or "fault" for the enemy to use as entry. No blemish or flaw or imperfection to give the enemy territory to camp on. No dark areas to block the light shining through. The gold is strengthened, solidified, so that no onslaught of the enemy will penetrate.

No weapon formed against you can prosper! Rejoice, for I have made you strong in the refiner's fire. There is no chink in your armor for the enemy to see and strike. There is no flaw in your solid ability to endure.

And now we can laugh! Heaven and earth can join in laughing at our enemies. "When the Lord restored the captivity of Zion we were like people dreaming." (Psalm 126:1) We were giddy, light-headed, transported on gales of laughter. Laughter!

So don't sneer at or put down the holy laughter you see around you. This laughter over our enemies expresses our confidence and joy in the knowledge of victory. It's full assurance in the face of attack.

The Father catches the contagion of His children's laughter. He sees the purity and joy of their hearts. He rejoices, finally, in His people. "The Father will dance, as on a day of joy. He will rejoice over you and renew you with His love." (Zephaniah 3:17)

The Age of the Father's Love

Jesus has shared with us His anointing for restoration so that we can participate in bringing it about. What a delight this restoration is to us! Yet there is someone even more satisfied. This restoration of Jesus is not so much about us as it is about Father God, whom Jesus has the joy of delighting with His restoration. Think of the Father, who created His earth for Adam with such deep love, fashioned its beauty for all of us in love, and who will now see that beautiful gift to us restored. Father God is elated.

Notice the scripture just above, the one quoted in the prophecy. "And the Father will dance, as on a day of joy. He will rejoice over you and renew you with His love." People of God, prepare for the Age of the Father's Love. Let us prepare our hearts for a new thing. Sing to the Lord a new song, for the outpouring of love that the Father of Love will soon release.

Get ready to be renewed with the Father's love! When He brings back the captivity of Jacob, ***He will restore.*** *Get ready for* *restoration.*

You will drink the new wine. It will make you drunk in the Spirit. It will rouse you as a mighty man full of wine. It will gladden your hearts. It will be as the days of heaven on earth. Such Joy! Such Peace! Such delight!

For I have given you the desires of your heart because you have delighted in Me. (Psalm 37:4) Delight shall be yours, all you who have delighted in Me. Know Me now as a God of delight, joy and recompense. I will give you back double for all that you have lost.

"When the Lord brought us back to Zion, we were like people dreaming." The laughter, the confoundedness, the strangeness all will be repeated and magnified. Laughter and song will be on the lips of My people who are like dreamers as the times of refreshing come, as My kingdom comes into fruition. Get ready for that "Pinch me. Is this really happening?" kind of joy because it's coming on the people of God. Amen!

The giddy and light-headed, those who walked around transported by the joy of God's presence, those dissolved in the recent laughter could all say, "Praise the God of my restoration, Jesus, the Lord of Hosts!"

The God of Love and Restoration, Jesus, speaks and says: I am restoring the fortunes of My people Israel, them and their children. I am the God of Restoration. Restoration is what's going on now.

And "when God brought us back from Babylon, we were like people dreaming." The laughter, the confoundedness, the strangeness—all will be repeated and magnified. Laughter and song will be on the lips of My people who are like dreamers as the times of refreshing come, as My Kingdom comes into fruition.

Am I a God of wrath? No! I am a God of Blessing, and I will show forth the full extent of My blessing in a time of wrath to demonstrate just that. Know that times of refreshment are coming for the people of God, that their troubles and warfare are over, that judgement on the church is over, that restoration is coming.

Look for more revelation in coming days regarding the Age of the Father's Love.

Rest

The Lord of Restoration, who is also the Living Word of the Most High God, loves words. He loves laughter. He loves humor. Here, the Lord plays with the word "rest:"

There yet remains a rest for the people of God. (Hebrews 4) Look at the word "restoration." It begins with "rest." Full ***restoration****. In the restoration will come times of refreshment. Rest and restoration. Times of refreshing.*

Yes, there remains a sabbath rest for the people of God, one they have not yet entered. It is a seven-year rest, during the time of tribulation, the Great Tribulation. This is the rest I have ordained for the people of God, My sabbath rest, when all their striving is over and I do all the "rest."

It's time for restoration. It's time for rest. It's time for restitution. It's time for vindication. It's time for the people of God to rise up in the full anointing. The fullness: it means all My people pulling together. For "My yoke is easy and My burden is light." My anointing will be shared, spread out over the whole body, running down like oil from Aaron's beard over his body. (Psalm 133) The work is shared by all. No one is a star, responsible and heavy-burdened. No. All are pulling their share of the load, yoked to Jesus Christ, their anointing. And so the burden is light, so light. So light that it is rest. You'll go from working hard to hardly working—and get more, lots more, done.

Enter into that Hebrew rest. Take a deep breath and relax in Me. For the times of refreshing, true refreshing and delight, not as the world gives, are come.

But know that delight takes strange manifestations. Were the disciples drunk on Pentecost morning? Yes! Drunk in My Spirit!

Have I not told you to laugh at your enemies? Yes, laugh! Heaven is laughing at the enemy right now, laughing in derision as in Psalm 2, laughing hilariously as in 126. Be drunk in the Spirit as the disciples on the day of Pentecost when 3,000 came to Me from the words and testimony of Peter, a "drunken" man.

Being drunk in the Spirit can be hilarious. But the serious note is that this laughter results from exposing the weakness of the enemy. His power, compared to the absolute authority and splendid glory of the Lord Jesus Christ soon to be fully revealed, is like that of a buffoon. He has all the dignity of a cockroach scuttling before the feet of a majestic king. The whole situation begins to look ludicrous.

"The Lord laughs at (the wicked) for He sees that their own day (of defeat) is coming." (Psalm 37:13) "He who sits in the heavens laughs; the Lord has them in derision." (Psalm 2:4) Job was comforted in his trial with the words: "He will yet fill your mouth with laughter (Job) and your lips with joyful shouting." (Job 8:21)

As God's people laugh, the enemy, though numerous and

well-armed, will fall before us.

And they will fall, like the Assyrians did before Hezekiah's praising people (Isaiah 37:36) when the Angel of the Lord slew 185,000 of the enemy's best. It will be like that. No more skirmishes, repeated attacks, guerilla warfare, failure-and-success. No! Wholesale victories, amazing defeat of the enemy with God's glory upon you and in you. Like the Gulf War, the victory will be swift and sure, a concert of many "nations" of one people, one committed people coming together from every walk of life to meet and do victory. Hallelujah!

After Israel's ancient king Hezekiah prayed and received assurance of victory from the prophet Isaiah, he sent his army out to meet the Assyrians. Who led the military procession? The praise and worship team, singing and rejoicing in God! No fear there. Absolute trust in God, their Victory, and in His assurance through Isaiah. They came to the Assyrian camp and found 185,000 strong men lying dead. They retrieved the Assyrian valuables and returned, still rejoicing, to announce God's victory. They were giddy with victory, drunk with amazement at God's mighty power.

They didn't have to fight! That's the way our spiritual battles will be won. As this people goes in to take the land, they will overcome all the demonic power bases and take back their rightful territory.

Not only our enemies but the mounting pressures of modern life will melt before us when we covenant to enter the rest. Life's pressure won't diminish. The change will be in us. True rest is calm during the storm.

There is a rest for the people of God on this earth. It will come in a time of darkness and chaos. It will be rest in a storm. My people will be unflappable, their "hearts established, trusting in the Lord." Speak My word over your life and family that it would be established in you.

Rest! What is rest but ceasing from labor? And yet more. Rest is enjoyment of the ceasing of labor and Sabbath rest is holy rest, with the time dedicated and consecrated to God for worship and fellowship and joy. It is heaven on earth. It is tabernacling with the Most High. It is an attitude, a life attitude. It is a heavenly thing.

I AM your God. You have no other. Rest, abide in Me in a Psalm 91 rest, a tabernacling rest, a Sabbath rest.

Though the world has begun to spin like an unstoppable

merry-go-round, we can relax and rejoice, serenely unruffled by the world's dizzying chaos.

Behold, I am doing a new thing. I am providing you rest. Rest in Me now, as the world begins spinning wildly out of control, in chaos. Take your rest in Me, for I am Lord of the Sabbath Rest. There remains a rest for the people of God to enter into. An active entering in, a "striving" to seek that rest, a Godly decision, yes, even a covenant meal, will form or constitute entry into that rest.

Can you rest amid the pressures of this crazy world? Yes. In Me you can find your rest. Those who have crossed the Jordan and entered into the land will now achieve and receive their Sabbath rest.

For I mean to spread peace everywhere, says the Lord, peace in your homes, your castles, and peace on the streets where you walk. Peace in the marketplace when you enter. Rest and peace.

Go forward into the land I have given you to enjoy as I bring all things—all My spiritual themes throughout the history of My natural and spiritual people—to culmination and close. Rejoice that you live in this hour, entering in to the "seventh day."

The proclamation of this rest is our job as representatives of the king. His prophets and leaders, using His authority, declare His will and promulgate His law. Just as surely as we must shout to the heavens that Babylon is fallen, we must also affirm and establish His rest.

And what is this passing over the Jordan (as in Joshua 3)? What is this following the ark in "a way you have not passed through before?" What is this following the glory-presence of our God into rest-oration? How will it happen in the spiritual history of My people?

It is a symbolic act. You have covenanted with Me to enter in to the rest. And Hebrews says, though the people entered into the land they did not have the rest and there remains yet a rest for the people of God. They must put their foot confidently in the raging, spring-flood waters, which is like the rush and danger of modern life, step boldly and follow God into the land of rest. The leaders must prophecy the rest, in the time of spiritual harvest.

God has given us pictures of restoration. The Old Testament leader, Nehemiah, persuaded King Artaxerxes to allow him to return from exile to Jerusalem. He galvanized a group to rebuild the shambles of the destroyed city wall. Under Nehemiah's unswerving direction, despite taunts and threats, the 12-foot thick wall was rebuilt in an astounding 52 days. Evil was constrained.

After repentance among the people, full-scale restoration began. Revival of scripture teaching, public reading of God's word and renewed celebration of Israel's ancient feasts took place. Then, a key event occurred: the Jerusalem temple was rebuilt.

The Spiritual Temple Restored

Today God has launched the rebuilding of the spiritual temple—His dwelling as I AM in His people.

Behold I do a new thing. Yes! A new thing. Behold as I build My body, My temple. Behold as I bring it together, as in Solomon's time, all the rich provision and the hard-won unity David arranged coming together in a beautiful, resplendent temple built by Solomon, the man of peace, the type of the Prince of Peace.

So show Me, show Me your eyes that I might fix your gaze on this as I build. I build with great joy the **new** *temple of Jerusalem. Its beauty is much, much greater than the former, because it is eternal. It is spirit and truth.*

Go forth knowing that this joyful work is in process and your God has the joy you desire and you shall see it in the earth, says the Lord God of Hosts, who is building.

See people come together in Me. Unity. Love. Peace the mortar. Joy the gavel and the tools. Hand of God the overseer. And who will do the work? My people with My own Spirit activating them, motivating them.

See? The Book of Revelation is happening now. See it and believe. But it is all in the spirit. Great storms and battles are taking place, but it is in the spirit which is more real than the natural.

So know that this is going on and rejoice, for this is the Day that the Lord has made. We will rejoice and be glad in it. Heaven and earth will rejoice. My people will join Me in My joy. Amen.

After shaking, stripping and judgement comes restoration to holiness. After restoration comes glory.

> After the Lord has washed away the (moral) filth of the daughters of Zion (pride, vanity, haughtiness) and has purged the bloodstains of Jerusalem from the midst of it by the spirit and blast of judgement and the spirit and blast of burning and sifting.
>
> And the Lord will create over the whole site, over every dwelling place of Mount Zion and over her as-

> semblies, a cloud and smoke by day and the shining of a flaming fire by night; for over all the glory shall be a canopy (a defense of divine love and protection). (Isaiah 4:4-5)

The shekinah, evidenced by cloud, smoke and fire, will mark every "dwelling place." I AM dwells in us. His presence, or anointing, will overshadow us. His glory will cover us.

When Solomon dedicated the Jerusalem temple with great praise during the Feast of Tabernacles, God's shekinah glory filled the holy place. Is there a parallel for today?

My glory fills the temple as you praise Me. As the assembly of the firstborn (Psalm 87, 1 Kings 8) gathers in unity on Zion at the time of the Great Feast, My glory fills the temple. Oh, yes. this is true, My children. Celebrate with Me. Come celebrate the joy of the feast, the culminating feast-party with Me.

Oh, yes, I am coming in glory to fill My temple. The glory will be on each one of you, My tabernacle. A tent of meeting is your body, a shelter for the Holy of Holies. Yes, believe Me, I AM in you.

Know and believe that in these days and in these times you will see the glory of God. For I have formed a people to Myself and to them I will show forth My glory. My glory! I have waited for this moment in time for all eternity. I have patterned it in physical Israel thousands of years ago in Solomon's time. And now I do it in the most real arena, that of the spirit. Oh yes. How I rejoice! says the Lord, your God, your own God, that My people are a fit place for My dwelling. Oh, yes!

We have long awaited the coming of His glory. What a magnificent, majestic and holy coming it will be. But let's consider the first coming of the King of Glory and observe its pattern. He came as a servant, a lowly man of Nazareth. He rode as a king entering Jerusalem astride a donkey. Many, including the Pharisees, missed His coming because they failed to recognize Him. They expected someone far more splendid.

When the glory of God fills the spiritual temple, let's not miss it.

People will seek Me and find Me, in a time of judgement.

So rejoice! Your Savior is nigh. He will save the world from sin and death, freely, finally and completely fulfilling His mission.

Christ will come again to fulfill completely His role as Savior, as Messiah.

How will this be? Not as men see it, the glorious reappearing. Christ will come again in His people, His glory. He will! It has been misinterpreted. I give you the interpretation: He will come again in glory in His people.

It will be done according to My word. Seek it out in My word. This is the glory of God, man fully alive (in Yahweh, I AM) and flowing in the anointing of Messiah, Son of God and sons of God, looking like Him and manifesting His glory as in Hebrews 1. This is what Adam was supposed to do and this is what My people will do. Now!

The life and power of I AM living in His people will not be hidden. Just as when God's glory filled Solomon's temple, His manifest presence and power will be seen and felt. "And the glory (majesty and splendor) of the Lord shall be revealed, and all flesh shall see it together." (Isaiah 40:5)

Now I am and there is no other.
Sovereign.
Lord.
My absolute power will be demonstrated in and by My people. It will be ***in Christ, in you****.*
Be aware and know and understand that Christ will come in His people. His appearing will be in them, the body of Christ. He will indwell His temple and oh! it will be glorious.

The glory of God, Yahweh told Moses, is His goodness. Remember when Moses asked to see God's glory? Yahweh replied, I will let My goodness pass before you. Now, today, the goodness of God, His glory, shall be seen.

That we encase, in our flesh, a holy of holies where I AM resides is almost too much for our minds to absorb. Our spirits know it and rejoice. Our minds fail to realize the treasure we have among us.

The Tent of Meeting and Tabernacle testified to it, gave an example and demonstrated it—the Treasure you have in your midst. Now it will be seen and demonstrated once again in the earth, in the midst of My people.

Oh, praise Him! Alleluia! Oh, rejoice, earth! Let the very land rejoice for the coming of the King in glory.

Let us expect it. Let us declare it. Let us praise Him for it and watch Him "inhabit the praises of His people.

By His Holy Spirit, Almighty God has gotten us into a position where He can bless us. His heart overflows blessing, and our cleansing as a people has prepared us to receive. Our suffering in refiner's fire has paid off. God's promise to comfort the misery of His repentant betrothed has come true, "I...will make the Valley of Achor (troubling) be be for her a door of hope and expectation." (Hosea 2:15)

Now we will see that hope realized.

Your blessing God is ready to bless. You have read of Judgement. Now read of blessing! Seek out My promises for they will all be fulfilled! What joy! What wonder! What beauty! What purpose in Almighty God to bless His children, His own, in a time of darkness upon the whole earth. Oh, rejoice, people of God, for the blessing time, your blessing and recompense, is coming.

The next section, called The Blessing Feast, details just how the restoration blessing will take place. The invitations to the feast have gone out, but there is still a little more time to get on the guest list. Hear what the Spirit is saying:

Things are coming to a close. See what I will do! Witness it!

Just as a child wants mommy and daddy to watch something special, so I want My loved ones, those important to Me, to watch as I unfold My wonders upon the earth. Oh, hallelujah to the Lord for the great and mighty plans He has for the earth and the peoples of the earth to bless them. Oh, how His Spirit has wooed, calling them in to the blessing feast, encouraging, explaining its delights, pulling them from the grip and hold of the world to come in. Strong has been His invitation and magnetic has been His wooing of their hearts. Yet many have not come. He is still wooing, though the time is short. Let not one be left out who is invited to the feast. The King's feast.

Remember Ahasuerus in Suza? (Esther 1) What a royal feast! Will this not be like it? (Even better.) A feast hosted by the King Himself. Think of it, My children! A royal feast! No earthly king of olden days (or even a mid- eastern potentate today) could give a feast like this one. Oh, rejoice that you are invited. Your name is on a tablet of gold, inscribed by the hand of your Master Himself. He has planned for you to be there and delighted in your presence. So be it!

Section Seven

The Blessing Feast

Moad in Hebrew is an appointment.
God ordained that the feasts He instituted
for ancient Israel begin at a set
month, day and hour,
their moad.

Each Old Testament feast has a spiritual
celebration in the New Testament.
Passover saw its fulfillment at the cross.

Now arrives the moad for the spiritual
fulfillment of the ancient Feast of Tabernacles.
The Lord of Hosts plans a rich harvest feast
against a backdrop of darkness,
a glorious feast in the wilderness.

God's glory filled the tabernacle
of Solomon's temple during
the Feast of Tabernacles.

His glory will fill the tabernacle
of a new temple,
one not made by human hands,
during the celebration of this
God-ordained heaven-on-earth feast.

Chapter 18

The Feast of Tabernacles

God is giving a party, a big party, and we are invited. It's a party in the Spirit, a festival. It's patterned after Israel's week-long Feast of Tabernacles celebration. In fact, it will fulfill that Biblical feast, just as the cross spiritually fulfilled the Feast of Passover.

So come! The Spirit and the bride say, "Come!" Come to a party hosted by the Lord of Hosts. Come celebrate with God His joy that He now fully tabernacles and dwells with His people.

Rejoice! Come eat of the abundance of the Lord God, the Lord of the Harvest. Eat His choicest harvest fruits and drink His new wine. Rest in His presence and celebrate, for the time has finally arrived for a promised "feast in the wilderness," a feast in the presence of our enemies, a banquet from our God.

God introduced the Israelites to His plan for this feast while they journeyed in the desert. (See Numbers 29:12 and Deuteronomy 16:13-15.) He told the people that when they came into the promised land that their feast would celebrate abundance from the harvest field and the memory of God's sheltering love during their exodus tent-dwelling days.

Let's look at the ancient Feast of Tabernacles to see what the Lord has prepared for us today.

The Biblical Feast of Tabernacles

Rest...Praise...Celebration. All these characterize the Feast of Tabernacles, the joy-feast of ancient Israel. Instituted by God as a harvest feast, Tabernacles called for praise, rejoicing, leisure, and banqueting amid the backdrop of nature's bounty. At feast time, harvest grapes heaped up in baskets and olive oil filled vats. Ripe fruits and vegetables overflowed bins. God's provision blessed the gathering.

The Feast of Tabernacles originated when God commanded Israel to celebrate a seven day festival during the seventh month. (In God's word, the number seven signifies fullness and perfection.) To insure that the people remembered their miraculous escape from slavery in Egypt, God instructed the Israelites to dwell for seven days in temporary shelters (tents, booths, huts) as they had in the desert.

Jewish people today still celebrate their ancient feast. Jerusalem becomes the scene of great festival every autumn. Believers from many nations gather to join God's natural chosen people in the pageantry of Tabernacles.

When the Israelites left Ramses in Egypt under Moses' leadership, a place named Succoth was their first camp. Succoth marked the people's transition from slavery to freedom. Still used as an alternate title for the Feast of Tabernacles, Succoth got its name when Israel's forefather Jacob built livestock shelters on the desert site. The place retained the Hebrew name for "booth," succoth. (Genesis 33:17)

God's command, "Rejoice!" captures the spirit of this celebration. "You must rejoice at your feast," God told the people. "The Lord God will bless the harvest and you will be filled with joy." (Deuteronomy 16:15)

The Israelites gathered fragrant citron and choice fruits, leafy palm and myrtle boughs and willow branches to festoon their shelters. The whole family moved into their outdoor tabernacle, set up in their own home's courtyard, atop the home's flat roof or in a public space cleared for the celebration. After the festive construction of their shelter, families began the feast with a day of complete rest.

For seven days the people celebrated as the priests prepared meal and drink offerings and burnt sacrifice. They prayed and praised. They sent food to those who had none prepared. Freewill giving, each in proportion to his blessing, played a vital part in the festal gaiety. They enjoyed music and conversation and told stories of faith-heroes to their children. Pilgrims poured through the gates of Jerusalem to celebrate and family reunions with country relatives added to the gaiety. Household customs emphasized God's provision, protection and promises.

The people staged a great banquet on the last day of the feast. Dancing and singing under torchlight, colorful processions and festal gatherings took place. This culminated a gala celebration of what all Israel called "The Great Feast."

Finally, they dismantled the tents for the eighth day, the Feast of Ingathering. People had celebrated half holidays, doing only necessary work. Now a second day of full rest allowed all to attend a sacred assembly and prayer for the latter (autumn) rain.

The Hebrew word for feast, *moad*, means "appointed time." Even today Israelis use the word to refer to determined, set times, such as a medical appointment. God established the seven feasts of ancient Israel as definite set times, each one scheduled by dates and times recorded in the Old Testament books of Leviticus, Deuteronomy and Numbers.

Israel's Feasts Foreshadowed Spiritual Realities

Israel demonstrated in the natural what God foreshadowed for the church to fulfill in the spiritual realm. The feasts, ordained as "types and shadows" by God, have almost all seen fulfillment in the spiritual life of the New Testament church. Their almost literal fulfillment serves as an eye-opener for God's people today.

We saw earlier that Pentecost, for example, reached its full spiritual expression in the outpouring of the Holy Spirit on Jesus' disciples in the Upper Room. At the same time that the priests were praising God and holding up the grain from the field in blessing, the Holy Spirit was across town manifesting the first yield from God's own Seed and His cross.

Israel's early harvest came forth with the blessing of the early rains. Empowered by the outpouring of the Spirit, the early church saw its initial harvest.

God commanded Israel to celebrate Pentecost exactly 50 days (Pente means 50) after another Old Testament feast, Passover. Passover is another example of an ancient feast fulfilled in a spiritual event. This feast commemorated the death angel passing over Israelite homes marked with lamb's blood during the Egyptian plagues. Jesus, the spotless Lamb of God, fulfilled Passover in His death on the cross in a literal and obvious way.

Israel's seventh month (which roughly corresponds to mid-September through mid-October in our calendar) featured a cycle of three feasts. The month, called Tishri, began with the Feast of Trumpets (Rosh Hashana), Israel's ancient New Years Day. Long ago in the desert, a trumpet made from a ram's horn had alerted the people to get ready to move camp or prepare for battle.

Later, in the cities and towns of Israel, the ram's horn (shofar) still called men to battle. As a warning, its call struck at people's hearts. The shofar also sounded for joyous occasions. As a triumphant proclamation, the priests blew the ram's horn to summon the nation to the celebration of its feasts.

The merriment of Tabernacles, begun on the 15th day of Tishri, followed Israel's most somber day. On the 10th day of the seventh month, the whole nation had come to a halt for serious repentance and a 24-hour fast. The ram's horn had sounded to announce this sober moad, the Day of Atonement. Burnt offerings substituted for man's deserved death from sin. On this day, and on this day only, the high priest entered the holy of holies in the Jerusalem temple to sprinkle sacrificial blood on the mercy seat.

This repentance was a vital prerequisite to celebrating the Feast of Tabernacles. Calling a sacred assembly, as described in Joel 2, and mourning together for wrongdoing was a crucial preparation. God told the people, "For whoever is not afflicted (by fasting and penitence and humility) on this day shall be cut off from among his people." (Leviticus 23:29) Repentance—real changed hearts—brought the people into a position where God could bless them with the joy of the Tabernacles celebration.

Significance of the Feast

God will fulfill the harvest feast of ancient Israel in the spiritual life of the church. Today, as spiritual Israel stands at the hour of harvest, God has blown the trumpet to herald the transition to a new era.

Instructing His disciples on end-time events, Jesus told us to look at the fig tree (representing the nation of Israel). Israel is showing forth God's preparation work in the natural arena. Let's look at Israel to see a natural parallel to God's spiritual work in the church today.

In 1948, a dispersed Israel became a nation again. The 1967 six-day war united Jerusalem as a city under Israeli control in the political state of Israel for the first time since 70 A.D. The rebirth of an ancient nation occurred. Water began to transform arid waste into fertile crop land. A new time period began.

These events in natural Israel saw a spiritual parallel. A scattered and dispersed body of Christ, locked in denominational isolation, began to experience the life of God's Spirit. Healing ministries like Oral Roberts' sprang up in the late 1940s. The outpouring of the Holy Spirit flooded the church beginning in 1967-68 (and the new age movement, its counterfeit, arose). The Holy Spirit began to rebuild spiritual Israel as a holy nation. The trumpet of prophecy began to sound, with a revival of the prophetic and teaching ministry. The sleeping church began to rouse itself to answer the shofar call to "prepare" to enter into a new phase.

The prophet Joel long ago foretold the Spirit's outpouring, but he also sounded a call to repentance. "Blow the trumpet in Zion!" (Joel 2:1) Set apart a fast; call a solemn assembly. Let the people mourn for their sins.

The people of God today have heard a trumpet call. The clarion voices of prophets have announced a new "day" dawning, the Day of the Lord. Just as the Israelites experienced the call to repentance on the Day of Atonement, so God has passed His remnant people through a cleansing by fire, a sprinkling by blood and worldwide judgement and repentance in the body of Christ. Purity and righteousness now mark a cadre of believers 100 percent surrendered to Jesus. They stand prepared to keep a divine appointment.

The harvest feast ends and begins the Jewish calendar. It signifies the transition from one divine time period to the next. As the Israelites had crossed the Jordan to freedom, so the church has come out of sin bondage to freedom in the Spirit. A time of transformation has occurred in men's and women's personal relationship to God. A nation has assembled from a bunch of ragged, untaught slaves and become a unified people.

This people has embraced the ancient themes of the Great Feast: God's provision, His protection, His promises. Teaching in these areas has built faith to believe and receive. They have answered the call to enter into the "secret place of the Most High," to abide in the Almighty, to shelter in Him, to tabernacle with Him. They have rediscovered the joy of giving, opening the way to a new prosperity in the financial flow of His kingdom. They have done it all in the spirit of the Tabernacles feast, praise. This spiritual nation has begun to rejoice. Their blissful intimacy with God becomes a covert of protection, a place of power, a shelter, a tabernacle or succoth.

"Succoth," of course, means shelter. The language of the Bible in referring to God as our shelter draws on this succoth meaning. Peter, describing the faith-filled response to suffering, says that during suffering "the Spirit of glory, the Spirit of God, is resting upon you." (1 Peter 4:14) The literal translation is "covered with God's succoth." Psalm 31:20 promises a sheltering succoth for those who take refuge in God: "In the secret place of Your presence You hide them from the plots of men; You keep them secretly in your pavilion." Psalm 91, truly the Psalm for a time of gathering darkness, uses succoth language referring to the sheltering and protection we gain when we "dwell in the secret place of the Most High."

A key scripture highlighting atonement and tabernacling in God's presence, which ended the last chapter, is repeated below because it features succoth wording:

> When the Lord shall have washed away the filth of the daughter of Zion...by the spirit of judgement and by the spirit of burning.
>
> And the Lord will create upon every dwelling place

> of mount Zion and upon her assemblies, a cloud and smoke by day, and the shining of a flaming fire by night; for upon all the glory shall be a defense.
>
> And there shall be a **tabernacle** for a shadow in the daytime from the heat and for a place of refuge, for a **covert** from storm and from rain. (Isaiah 4:4-6 KJV Emphasis mine)

The glory of God will be a succoth shelter and abiding place in the spiritual celebration of the Great Feast.

Today, in this defining hour of the church of the Lord Jesus Christ, the Lord God proposes to celebrate with His purified people a feast of great, great joy.

Every feast of ancient Israel has been celebrated in the spiritual life of the New Testament church except the harvest festival, the Feast. I now propose and purpose to celebrate with My people this feast.

In the book of Joel, people were longing for a harvest destroyed by drought and locusts. Repentance had to come to loose the rain/reign. So be it today as we prepare for the spiritual celebration of the harvest feast. I would have My people speak and write about this to give understanding in the churches. So rejoice that seven years of the feast and rejoicing will parallel seven years of the tribulation. The two will happen at the same time, seven "days" set aside since the foundation of the earth.

So rejoice and be glad as you witness the onset of the Feast, for My people are called with the shofar to a feast-celebration "in the presence of their enemies." Harvest, coupled with the abundance and flow described in Isaiah 60 and 66, is what I purpose in My heart for My church and I do not falter or fail.

Through His present-day prophets and the witness of His Holy Spirit, God has pinpointed the current period as harvest time. Harvest offers not only bounty but a blaze of gold, orange, red to spotlight summer's curtain call.

You have seen the fire and light and color of autumn as the warm season goes out with glory, a final "hurrah!" to dazzle the people. It is a blessing, a grace. My church will go out with glory. Watch for it and believe Me for it. Just as you enjoy the natural nice weather and overflowing farm market fruits, vegetables and herbs, so will the joy and fruitfulness of My church be. So go forth in joy, My people, celebrating the feast in bounty and joy, in pleasure and play, because I AM says the feast has begun.

Isaiah described the blessing of this last days feast: "Then you shall see and be radiant, and your heart shall thrill and tremble with joy. As one whom his mother comforts so I will comfort you." (Isaiah 66:13) This comfort pours from a Father of blessing who delights in the fulfillment of the prophetic moment, the appointed time to bless His people. This radiance, joy and comfort will not be reserved for blessing in heaven. They are earthly blessings, promised to be given in a time of "indignation" against God's enemies.

Father God now unveils his heart of festival joy:

Know thee then, people of Zion, people of My joyous heart, city of our God, that I am the one of whom it is said, "And the Father will dance, as on a day of joy, of festival." That festival is the spiritual celebration of the Feast of Tabernacles, the high feast, the Great Feast, culminating in the wedding feast to come. The Father is dancing now as on a day of joy.

Come dance and rejoice with Me, oh, Zion of God. I call you forth now to joy, My people, as I prepare and register My people flowing in, as Psalm 87 describes, through the precious gates of Zion to attend My feast. A great throng from many nations is flooding in, as Isaiah 60 shows, bringing gifts and talents and joyful service to Zion, even to My temple. So go thy way rejoicing in your God, rejoicing in this, that Zion, the city of God, will see her day of joy, her great festival and there will be none like it in all the earth, saith the Lord God of Hosts who arranges all.

The time has arrived.

The Lord of Hosts wants His people eager and expectant, exuberantly awaiting the celebration of the Feast. He wants us to announce to family, friends, congregations: "A great time of God's blessing has arrived. Prepare your heart to receive. And rejoice!"

Blow the trumpet in the new moon for the feast to begin. Not the shofar of warning or battle but the horn of the feast of abundance, My harvest feast. For I am the God that blesses thee. I will bless thee mightily, with many things to make thy heart glad before Me.

Receive now your reward, My children, for I will acknowledge you before men, openly will I proclaim that you are Mine. ***Today*** *is the day of salvation and joy.* ***Now*** *is the word that I give you. Fill your heart with hope and joy, with no fear of disappointment or misgiving for I promise that* ***today*** *is the day of fulfillment. Today! Enjoy it!*

The set time has arrived. A time set apart for joy, for rejoic-

ing, for rest, for music of praise, for dancing, for play. (I have taught My people all these expressions of joy.) A set time in history, a scheduled and appointed Feast. My people will fulfill this Harvest Feast, My Israel of the Lord. They will dance and rejoice before Me and enjoy the abundant fruit of the harvest festival. They will gather in, gather in, and rejoice.

As I AM, My people shall rejoice!

I have made it a statute and an ordinance for My people Israel and they will fulfill it. So rejoice for the Feast, the appointed time, is coming, is coming, is coming.

Blessings will overtake you. Mercy will flood upon you. Get ready! Get ready to get blessed and to rejoice. Prepare now for the Feast. Open your doors and windows. Be highly expectant and alert and ready!

Feast and Jubilee

At the time during the desert years that He established the Feast of Tabernacles, God also proclaimed the Year of Jubilee to be celebrated when the people finally entered the land of promise. During the Jubilee, a year of sabbath rest occurring every fiftieth year, possessions lost by families and individuals were restored to them.

The Lord plans to combine the Feast of Tabernacles festival with a full-scale restoration characteristic of Israel's year of restoration, the Jubilee year. The scripture promises a mighty time of "restitution of all things" by Jesus Christ. The promise from Acts 3:21, which this book quoted when discussing restoration, confirms a grand-scale Jubilee renewal:

> Repent then, and turn to God, so that your sins may be wiped out, that times of refreshing may come from the Lord and that He may send the Christ, who has been appointed for you—even Jesus. He must remain in heaven until the time comes for God to restore everything, as he promised long ago through his holy prophets. (Acts 3:19-21 NIV)

Jubilee is the time of remedy, the time of giving back things lost to their rightful owners and restoring loss or damage. The key to receiving spiritual restoration is repentance.

Jesus was anointed to restore. The major Old Testament passage which announced His anointing, Isaiah 61, heralded His mission to repair and bring back wholeness. In that prophecy the Holy Spirit linked the Jubilee celebration to the anointing of Jesus. In Section Five of this book we examined the anointing and we know it comes to bring restoration. Jesus' anointing flowed to heal blind eyes, make lame men leap, to open deaf ears and to proclaim the acceptable year of the Lord (the year of His favor, the Jubilee). (Isaiah 61:2) Every Jew would have recognized "the year of His favor" as the Jubilee year. The anointing will today renew families, raising up what Isaiah called "the devastations of many generations."

Origin of the Jubilee

The acceptable year of the Lord harks back to Leviticus 25 when God proclaimed the Jubilee, the fiftieth year. Every seventh year God designated as a sabbath year of rest for the land. After a cycle of seven sabbath years (49 years) came the Jubilee year of restoration. During this 50th year families exercised the Jubilee right to buy back land sold due to necessity; they could redeem houses sold; debts were cancelled; prisoners saw their sentences commuted; slaves and indentured servants went free. If an Israelite sold into slavery could not redeem himself, a relative acting as kinsman-redeemer could negotiate the slave's freedom.

Priests heralded the Jubilee year of rest and blessing with the shofar, or trumpet, a rousing cry through the land. During the Jubilee, and the Sabbath year which preceded it, Israel planted no crops. The land rested during the sacred year.

Today prophets are raising their voices like trumpets to proclaim restoration of all God's people have lost, full restoration of everything the enemy has stolen. Isaiah, the prophet, told us that this Jubilee "year of favor" would occur simultaneously with the day of vengeance from our God. (Isaiah 61:2) God has already unleashed judgement. The Day of the Lord has begun. The time of His favor has also begun.

The Lord rejoices that the day of restoration of all things has finally arrived.

Our Messiah, Jesus, will preside over the restoration. At Hebrew festivities, such as the seven-day wedding celebration, a master of ceremonies held the position of "lord of the feast." The celebration of Tabernacles ended with a public banquet.

Who is maitre d' of the spiritual Tabernacles banquet? Who is lord of this combined Tabernacles-Jubilee celebration? The Lord of Hosts, whom Isaiah 44:6 identifies as our redeemer, that is, the Lord Jesus.

I AM. I AM the Lord of the Harvest, Jesus, Lord of the Sabbath year, Lord of the Jubilee, Lord of the Feast.

I AM. I AM. I AM Lord of Life.

Now go forth knowing who is Lord over your Jubilee, your harvest, your feast-banquet of blessings. Now know ye, bond-servant of My heart, from whence your blessing came. For I will fulfill in My people (finally I have a people of My heart—how I rejoice!) all that I purposed for ancient Israel. Redemption of things lost; return of property, lands and houses; increase in crops and harvest for supply during a "year" of rest, sabbath rest; and restoration of the family on its ancestral turf, the "place" where I planted that family, i.e., their "land."

This is full restoration. Nothing left unrestored. And persons are brought back, those lost to slavery in other lands are brought back by their kinsman-redeemer, who is Jesus the Lord of the Harvest, the Lord of Hosts.

Know that as this harvest feast is celebrated, My arm of justice and redemption will sweep across the land to vindicate, justify, redeem and restore many. This is coming now soon.

The Lord of Hosts will prepare the banquet. There is another feast, carrion for the ravens, going on at the same time. Birds of prey will be glutted on carrion. Have you not seen the ravens? They are prepared for a banquet.

Know My heart of joy today "for all peoples." Yes, for Me too, a day of vengeance and sorrow and a "year of favor," bringing joy and delight and gladness to My heart.

The God of Love prophesies: No one has seen or heard what God has prepared for those who love Him. "Like nothing ever seen or heard" are the words of a popular praise song. They are true prophetic words. This banquet is a party, lasting for all eternity. The feast begins the tide of blessing and reward that builds and lasts...forever. Forever! Blessings forever from the heart of God who wanted to do this for all time. What joy characterizes the Father's heart over this matter. What indescribable deeply-delightful joy. What inspiring joy. For My joy begets joy.

Imagine the elation of celebrating the Great Feast during a Jubilee year. It's enough to set the feet of the Most High dancing. The angels will respond with their own revelry. God promises today this kind of festal gathering for spiritual Israel. Hebrews 12:22 describes Zion's celebration: "You have come to Mount Zion, even to the city of the living God, the heavenly Jerusalem, and to countless multitudes of angels in festal gathering."

The God of love and mercy speaks and says, Know My heart, children of Mine, know My father's heart. My desire to bless and restore. My will to repair the ruins and the "waste cities." My de-

sire to bring back and fulfill all I have wanted for My people since Adam. That is happening now, My children. My desire is finally fulfilled in My people Israel.

How the Father will dance! As on a day of joy, of festival, of the true Feast of Tabernacles. Oh how My heart now rejoices at the onset of the Feast, the appointed time, for this is the will of the Lord your God.

He reigns. He ***reigns*** *over His people Israel, His precious remnant, and in them He will restore all things. So get ready, get ready for the Feast of Tabernacles abundance and blessing: restoration and vindication, justice (in restoration of things lost unfairly) and a year of Jubilee from our God.*

Now let it begin! ***Let it begin!*** *says the Lord. Hold on! Plant your feet. Steady yourself in Me for the tidal wave of blessing and glory that's coming, says the Lord your God, and even the Lord of Hosts, Lord of the Feast and Lord of the Harvest.*

And the Spirit says, Come. Come partake of all the Lord of Hosts has prepared for those that love Him and minister love to Him. Come and taste the sweet wines, come and taste the fatness, like butter on the tongue. Come and eat, drink to your full, sample the banquet wares. Fine imported cheeses hidden in caves, mellowed and ripened, held back for you until this day. Wines, choice wines, to taste and drink. Abundance in grapes and fruits of the land. Choicest delicacies, held and aged and put away until this time. And I will release for you the wealth of the nations, yes, abundance released unto your holy and faithful hands.

And the Father will dance, as on a day of joy and spectacle, as the joyous procession comes into Jerusalem, My City of Peace, to celebrate the feast I have appointed this Day, says the Lord.

The body of Christ longs to hear this message of restoration. The Lord wants us to announce this festive celebration of joy to family, friends, co-workers, our worship community. It's good news!

Ring the bell, blow the trumpet, announce the feast for the appointed time, the moad has come. Now announce to My people the Feast, the glad tidings of Jubilee. Go forth and shout the news. Get thee up to the high mountain and broadcast the good news of My coming to rule the earth, says the Lord. Go forth to do all I have ordained you to do, without preconceived notions, for it will not be the way you imagined. Go forth now, I send you, saith the Lord.

The scripture summons us to the spiritual soapbox. We are anointed to proclaim the good news because we have the anointing of Jesus Christ to "proclaim the year of the Lord's favor." (Luke 4:19) The prophetic intercessors must call the celebration forth in the spirit. The people need to hear this happy news to prepare their hearts to receive and to lift their faith expectation.

> O Zion that bringest good tidings, get thee up to the high mountain; O Jerusalem that bringest good tidings, lift up thy voice with strength, lift it up, be not afraid; say to the cities of Judah, Behold your God! (Isaiah 40:9 KJV)

Zion needs to get up to the mountaintop and raise a voice like a trumpet to proclaim these glad tidings. The intercessors must call on the angels to carry out all that must be prepared. I AM lives in us. He has truly become Lord in our lives. He has anointed us to preach the Gospel of good tidings and restoration. (Expect the doors of people's hearts to be wide open.) And He has prepared for us a blessing feast, the Feast of Tabernacles, magnified in its bounty because it occurs during a time of rest and restoration, a spiritual Jubilee.

The same message I AM gave Moses, He gives to us now: "Say this to the Israelites, I AM has sent me to you." (Exodus 3:14) Now is the time to freely and exuberantly witness to I AM.

Go into the whole world teaching and preaching the Gospel of the Good News, that Jesus was anointed to bring healing and deliverance to the peoples and that Jesus is alive today, ministering through His people. Go forth now and tell them, saying "I am sent by Jesus, the Anointed One."

I AM. I am watching over you with great tenderness and love. I am guiding you daily to the blessings I have in store for you. I am preparing you to receive these blessings of healing, restoration, forgiveness, release from bondage. So make ready your heart, prepare your heart, stretch your heart to ***receive,*** *as Solomon received on his father's behalf, to receive on Jesus' behalf the blessings I will give you.*

Don't brush off or fail to fully receive or neglect to adequately rejoice in these blessings because you feel unworthy. You're not worthy—except in Jesus. Then you are very worthy, supremely worthy. Now know, know, know deep in the core of you that blessing is coming soon and that you are worthy in Christ Jesus to receive with exuberance and joy, participating fully, involved fully (as a whole person), rejoicing fully and giving away bounty in the fullness of the joy I want to give you.

Rejoice! Miracles—sheer, plain, outrageous, joyful miracles—are coming. Blessing! As Solomon was gifted, I gift you to-

day, My children.

The Day of the Lord will usher in a messianic age. We stand on its brink. Those in position to receive God's blessings see healing, prosperity, peace, love and joy appear on the horizon. Those who pray must faith-speak it into the earth in joyous proclamation.

God wants us to get our joy level up. He wants His spiritual Israel to rejoice in exultation, praise, singing and dancing. He will then "inhabit the praises of His people." He will manifest in the specific area of His people's praise and rejoicing. Glorify His name as the God of blessing.

Yes, I Am the God of Your Blessing. Yes, I Am the God of Love. You have called upon My name, praised My name. Oh, keep on doing that! I will inhabit your praises. I will give salvation to all who call upon My name. Provision—yes! Call on Me for it! I will ***give.*** *Now know Me in My munificence, My abundance, My lavishness for I would seriously give to My people in this messianic moment, this beginning of the messianic age. "The Spirit is poured out upon us from on high and the wilderness becomes a fruitful field. "(Isaiah 32:15) Read about it! It's* ***real.*** *Get excited with Me.*

Ephesians 1:3 declares that God has blessed us in Christ with every spiritual blessing in the heavenly realm. Now, at the harvest moment, He plans to show us His fullness, "the full measure of Him Who makes everything complete." (Ephesians 1:23)

All this spiritual blessing is given in Christ, the Anointed and in His anointing. His anointing, flowing in love, brings a manifestation of His goodness, in healing, deliverance, freedom.

I will make a banquet of fat things upon the lees, says the Lord. Yes, in the quiet places, protected from the wind, there I will make and lay a banquet for My beloved, serving up peace and joy in lavish portions, overflowing your cup with gladness, filling your plate with strength and providing oil, constantly flowing Zechariah-type oil, for the continual anointing. This is it—what I spoke of in the book of Zechariah, anointing that doesn't fail or falter. Receive it now today, not for once in a while, but a continuous flow and state of being in the anointing.

Oil is burned for incense but also for light. Oil was used as fuel for light. Be prepared for that light to shine. Now release—flow, flow, flow—continually release My anointing. It flows with love, love for others. You will be moved with concern, compassion, love for one another and that anointing will flow out of you.

Behold! Behold My glory in the anointing today, says the Father God of Love. Receive My love to do the harvest work.

For it is the Age of the Father's Love and the Father's love will be demonstrated in power in the earth today. Healings, deliverances, will be commonplace, everyday events. My people will be willing to walk in My power and that was not true yesterday. They are willing to pay the cost because the anointing costs. But you have paid the price in death, dying to yourselves and I have raised you up afresh to do My work.

Enjoy it! It will be fun, says the Lord. Rejoice! As I rejoice in you. Let us rejoice together. So be it.

Don't miss the party put on by the Lord of Hosts. God perfects the time. Praise seals His blessing work.

Chapter 19

God's Secret Intention

The Book of Revelation, Chapter 10, intrigues readers with a description of a mighty angel clothed in a glory cloud and crowned with a rainbow. His face shines like the sun. He plants his feet of fire, one on the sea and the other on the land. His stunning beauty matches the power of his voice, a lion-like roar.

John's word picture of this angel resembles his image of Jesus in Revelation Chapter 1 where John says that Jesus' face shone like the sun; his feet burned bright; his voice roared. Now John uses similar wording to describe this heavenly being:

> Then I saw a mighty angel coming down from heaven, robed in a cloud, with a (halo like a) rainbow over his head; his face was like the sun, and his feet (legs) were like columns of fire.
>
> He had a little book (scroll) open in his hand. He set his right foot on the sea and his left foot on the land.
>
> And he shouted with a loud voice like the roaring of a lion; and when he had shouted, seven thunders gave voice and uttered their message in distinct words.
>
> And when the seven thunders had spoken (sounded), I was going to write (it down), but I heard a voice from heaven saying, Seal up what the seven thunders have said! Do not write it down!
>
> Then the (mighty) angel...swore...that when the days come when the trumpet call of the seventh angel is about to be sounded, then God's mystery (His secret plan, His hidden purpose), as He had announced the glad tidings to His servants the prophets, should be fulfilled (accomplished, completed). (Revelation 10:1-7)

God's Secret Revealed

What is the secret that John could not record? Is it to be withheld for all eternity? Is it a punishment on sinful man so horrible that heaven refused to allow John to reveal it?

Or, is it the same "secret intention" that Paul mentioned in Ephesians—that the cross of Christ made salvation available to the Gentiles? The answer to this is no, because Paul had already published that secret when the Book of Revelation was written.

Is it the mystery that we shall not all die but will meet Christ in the air at His coming? No. Paul explained that mystery openly in 1 Corinthians 15:51-52 and 1 Thessalonians 4:15-17.

The passage from Revelation 10 itself reveals the answer. The message involves a plan already announced "to His servants, the prophets" but kept veiled. The secret will not remain hidden for all eternity. The angel thunders God's secret intention into the earth. The fulfillment of these glad tidings will happen on earth.

The message clearly comes from God Himself. Scholars tell us that the thunders, sounded in the heavenly number of seven, are the voice of God speaking.

The angel shouted like a lion roaring. The lion voice represents the voice of God. The prophet Amos tells us that. Amos 3:7-8 says, "Surely the Lord will do nothing without revealing His secret to His servants, the prophets. The lion has roared; who will not fear? The Lord God has spoken; who can but prophesy?"

The little book or scroll in the hand of the mighty angel lies open. The message, while openly available, has escaped our understanding.

Daniel, who received powerful insight into the end times, learned that his visions would be shut up and sealed "until the time of the end." Then "those who are wise shall understand." Specifically, the wise are those who "purify themselves and make themselves white and be tried, smelted and refined." The purified remnant will understand and will teach others. (Daniel 12:9-10)

So God's secret in Revelation 10 will not remain secret forever! And what exactly is this happy plan, already revealed to His prophets? What is this glad work, prepared to be accomplished while God is judging sin and demolishing the old order of human government?

Could the happy secret be news of the blessing feast, the spiritual celebration of the Feast of Tabernacles? Could it be an outpouring of the Father's love and blessing so strong that it matches Tribulation intensity? One of the angel's clues was that God had announced the secret to His prophets. Let's see if we can find the secret in the Old Testament.

God Promised a Feast to Moses, David and Isaiah

Moses

Hidden in God's word lies the promise of the feast. Long ago God proposed this feast. He told Pharaoh through Moses, "Let My people go, that they may hold a feast to Me in the wilderness." (Exodus 5:1) Unbelieving Israel never held that feast. His people today, released from bondage, will experience a spiritual fulfillment of that promised feast.

David

In the poetic language of Psalm 23, the Holy Spirit spoke through David about the promised feast. He linked the blessing banquet to a time when our enemies would flourish. He also linked the feast to the anointing, a theme of this book. Psalm 23 says:

> You prepare a table before me in the presence of my enemies. You anoint my head with oil; my (brimming) cup runs over. (Psalm 23:5)

The *Living Bible* translation of the same verse gives flavor to the feast image:

> You provide delicious food for me in the presence of my enemies. You have welcomed me as your guest; blessings overflow. (Psalm 23:5 LB)

Neither power nor position will earn an invitation. Those invited to the banquet have demonstrated diligence in seeking God. David prophesied:

> The poor and afflicted shall eat and be satisfied; they shall praise the Lord—they who (diligently) seek for, inquire of and for Him, and require Him (as their greatest need)...
>
> All the ends of the earth shall remember and turn to the Lord, and all the families of the nations shall bow down and worship before You.
>
> For the kingship and the kingdom are the Lord's, and He is the ruler over the nations.
>
> All the mighty ones upon earth shall eat (in thanksgiving) and worship... (Psalm 22:26-29)

Isaiah

Looking toward a messianic time, Isaiah prophesied a restoration feast when "Your God shall rejoice over you." (Isaiah 62:5) The joyous feast will be celebrated at a time of spiritual harvest. The Holy Spirit used harvest images to make this promise through Isaiah:

> ...they who have gathered it shall eat it and praise the Lord, and they who have brought in the vintage shall drink it (at the feast celebrated) in the courts of My sanctuary (the temple of My holiness). (Isaiah 62:9)

The spiritual harvest feast will take place in the wilderness. The wilderness, a place of intimacy with God, lacks the world's comforts. But those drawn out into the wilderness find God there. The desert flourishes with covenant love.

God told Isaiah:

> The wilderness and the dry land shall be glad; the desert shall rejoice and blossom like the rose. (Isaiah 35:1)

Not only love but God's protection characterizes the time of the feast. The Book of Revelation speaks of the Day of the Lord and His protection of His people during satanic harassment:

> And the woman (herself) fled into the desert (wilderness), where she has a retreat prepared (for her) by God, in which she is to be fed and kept safe... (Revelation 12:6)

God plans to recompense, vindicate and reward His people, as their enemies undergo vengeance against their rebellion.

> Behold, your God will come with vengeance; with the recompense of God He will come and save you. (Isaiah 35:4)

God will give Zion a banquet against a backdrop of "gloom, judgement and terror," Isaiah 25:6 prophesies. Despite the fear and blackness upon the earth, God's people will overflow praise saying, "This is the Lord, we have waited for Him; we will be glad and rejoice in His salvation." (Isaiah 25:9)

The Holy Spirit gave Isaiah a detailed picture of the blessing feast. Isaiah Chapter 25 is a key passage illuminating the festivity. Surprisingly, Isaiah 25 shows us a messianic banquet which occurs during Judgement, a joyous feast held at the incongruous hour of midnight.

This is Isaiah's picture: the feast, like the big banquet that culminated the Feast of Tabernacles, gathers a multitude on Zion. The *maitre d'* is the Lord of Hosts. The richest foods and finest wines weigh down the well-laden table. The spiritual banquet abounds with healing, deliverance, freedom, restoration and prosperity, all complemented by the wine of gladness.

One might think this banquet will happen in heaven. But the background of judgement and terror can only arise here on earth. Let's see how the prophet Isaiah describes this heaven-on-earth festivity:

> And on this Mount (Zion) shall the Lord of hosts make for all peoples a feast of rich things (symbolic of His coronation festival inaugurating the reign of the Lord on earth, in the wake of a background of gloom, judgment, and terror), a feast of wines on the lees—of fat things full of marrow, of wines on the lees well refined.
>
> And He will destroy on this mountain the covering of the face that is cast over the heads of all peoples (in mourning), and the veil (of profound wretchedness) that is woven and spread over all nations.
>
> He will swallow up death (in victory; He will abolish death forever). And God will wipe away tears from all faces; and the reproach of His people He will take away from off all the earth; for the Lord has spoken it.
>
> It shall be said in that day, Behold our God upon Whom we have waited and hoped, that He might save us! This is the Lord, we have waited for Him; we will be glad and rejoice in His salvation. (Isaiah 25:6-9)

The rich foods, understood in their spiritual sense, are God's best to meet our needs. First God meets our deepest need, our yearning for relationship with Him. He is our great reward. He Himself is the blessing of the blessing feast. Then He satisfies our hunger for physical and emotional wholeness, financial soundness, family restoration, blessing in our work. This is God's fatness and fine marrow.

Refined wines represent joy. The "lees" or dregs, strained out, do not taint the clarity of its joy. More than the transitory happiness we seek in material possessions or physical gratification, this joy is real, lasting and deeply satisfying.

The feast setting appears more splendid because it takes place against "a background of gloom, judgement and terror." (Isaiah

25:6) The hour on the world's clock strikes midnight.

Jesus gave us the same picture in different words when He told His parable of the ten virgins who waited so long at night for the arrival of the bridegroom. At the darkest hour, a cry rings out: "Behold, the bridegroom! Go out to meet him!" (Matthew 25:6) The five virgins who prepared wisely go in to feast with the Bridegroom.

The author received the following prophetic word regarding Isaiah's promise of a banquet during a time of darkness and gloom.

Is this to make a feast in the darkness? Yes, this is a big thing. But Daniel says that in the last days the wise shall understand. So you, whom I have made wise, shall understand.

Remember My scripture from Proverbs? "Lean not on your own understanding?" Here is My wisdom: there shall be a banquet, a feast upon the lees, a table set in the wilderness, a place reserved for the people of God.

Remember Revelation 3 "I will keep you in the time of trouble?" The place I will keep you is in the secret place of the Most High, in God, in His sanctuary, where feasting and riches and gladness are available to the people of God.

What a party! I am arranging it, says the Lord of Hosts. My party, My table, My hosted banquet. Prepare your heart for joy unspeakable, a feast in the midst of your enemies.

Destruction, Apollyon, where is your locust sting? Death, where is your sting? No longer among **My** *people, says the Lord.*

Hallelujah! "God's secret intention" of Revelation 10 is now revealed Amen!

Two Concurrent Moves of God

The Revelation 10 message has two sides. When John takes the little book, open on the hand of the angel, and eats it, the message tastes sweet as honey in his mouth, but it sours in his stomach.

The two sides of the message are the two sides of recompense. Recompense means repayment. In the sense of reward, recompense is a welcome paycheck. In the sense of retaliation, recompense is vengeance against evil. For those who yield to Him, the holy Judge destroys the evil altars within but preserves the person for restoration to righteousness.

Every mountain, high thing, idol and evil, including institutions and other power structures, will come crashing down to make way for Christ's reign of peace and justice—which from the world's point of view appears as suffering, wrath and destruction. But with that justice comes another kind of recompense: a rich compensation to His faithful people. Righteous judgement has two sides. One is punishment for evil. The other is remedy for the wronged.

The scripture highlights this two-pronged move of God in the great and awesome Day of the Lord. Isaiah 34:8 pinpoints the duality: "The Lord has a day of vengeance, a year of recompense for the cause of Zion." Two parallel moves of God's recompense are unfolding: one is vengeance; the other is a feast of blessing.

Jesus was anointed "to proclaim the acceptable year of the Lord (the year of His favor) and the day of vengeance of our God." (Isaiah 61:2. See also Luke 4:19) The Day of the Lord involves two separate but concurrent works of God, wrath and reward.

It consoles the Father to reward His obedient sons and daughters. His father's heart is torn by witnessing the consequences of wrong choices in the lives of His children who choose to stay in the world. They face judgement suffering. It satisfies His justice to recompense double back to His faithful children for everything the enemy stole. It rejoices His heart to bless Zion in a time of Tribulation. He says:

> As a mother comforts her child, so I will comfort you...the hand of the Lord will be made known to His servants, but his fury will be shown to his foes. (Isaiah 66:13-14 NIV)

Jesus, the Lord of Hosts, Hosts God's Great Party

God's succoth, the rest in the secret place of the Most High, with His glory as our shelter and covering, will never be more evident than in coming days. The church has long held onto the promise of Revelation 3:10. There Jesus told the faithful church at Philadelphia, "Because you have kept My word of patient endurance I will also keep you (safe) from the hour of trial which is coming on the whole world."

Some church teachers assure us that this promise guarantees that the rapture—the snatching away of the church to meet Jesus in the air when He comes—will happen before God's wrath occurs. But the wording of Revelation 3:10 is unsure. We have to "pump" it a little to derive the satisfying certainty of rapture from the words "I will keep you safe **from** the hour of trial," or **in** the time of trial, as some translations put it. Peter reminds us that God kept Noah safe **in** the flood and preserved Lot **from** the fire and brimstone that destroyed Sodom and Gomorrah (2 Peter 2:6-7) Jesus also used Noah and Lot as examples when He instructed His disciples about end time events. Both Noah and Lot witnessed the destruction around them, but they and their families remained unharmed.

Jesus clearly promised the rapture of the church and Paul confirmed the promise to "meet Him in the air" when the archangel shouts and the trumpet sounds. Paul also warns us to stay alert so that the day will not "overtake you by surprise like a thief." (1 Thessalonians 5:4) We know that "God has not appointed us to (incur His) wrath." But we don't all agree on exactly when the promised translation from earth to His presence will happen.

The Rapture Transports "A Moveable Feast"

The tight hold we have on the hope of escaping before tribulation via the rapture relaxes in the happy news of God's secret intention. God plans a blessing party here on earth. Despite darkness, the true church will be rejoicing. The rapture will be a happy surprise marking what Jesus plans as a "moveable feast." It will transport us to the Marriage Supper of the Lamb. The rapture will mark the transition of the feast from earth to heaven.

The Lord wants us to rejoice in faith, believing Him for the joyous celebration of this promised feast. He spoke this to me:

Give the Lord glory for what's coming, beyond what you could ask for or imagine, beyond your wildest dreams or imagination, a true champagne feast in the wilderness, a time for the people of God unprecedented in human history. Yes! Even in the time of Solomon, My child. This is what I have planned and preordained for My people. My wonderful secret! Now it is known to you. I reveal it to you, a banquet, a table, a feast for My people against a background of gloom and judgement. They will be vindicated! Mark My words, they will be vindicated.

Don't Fear the Lord's Day

The Lord has said that this spiritual celebration of the Great Feast will coincide with the worst time the world has witnessed, the time of wrath. The people of God will abound in good things while the world gnashes its teeth in darkness.

The following are three prophetic messages received by the author from the Holy Spirit regarding the coming Judgement. God promises blessing for His true church as the judgements unfold.

My people will flee from the camp of the enemy (Isaiah 33:3) when I raise up My voice to judge. People movements will occur, each one returning to his home base or shelter. Displaced people will go "home" because of economic crash or judgement siege.

Now know ye, chosen, Jezreel, Jacob, Israel, that I am God of all and the changes to come are of Me. All that I told you will come to pass. My people will have a banquet against a backdrop of gathering doom and darkness from the abyss. (Revelation 9:3) I will feed them on choicest delicacies and sweet wines while the others suffer. Mark My words!

Know that this will come to pass and watch for events leading to the death of the two witnesses (Revelation 11:3), the king and the priest figures who will die in "Jerusalem." Know Me now in this as a holy and mighty God.

God wants us prepared to receive His blessing.

I am the Lord God, Elohim, the Most High, Elyon, the Holy One of Israel and I speak now a message to My people: prepare! Prepare your hearts and your minds and your bodies (yes, even your bodies—weaned, stripped and readied) for the time coming when I will bless you. For I will bless you amid signs of coming tribulation. I will bless you in the distress that is to come upon the whole earth. And in the darkest hour I will take you home. At midnight the Bridegroom comes. My timing is never too late.

Know ye generation of the present, today, that My hand will fall in judgement in the coming days like never before. Earthquake. Economic disaster. Refugees suffering from war. And more. Behold and see. I have spoken. Credit card debt will be a problem. Isolated deaths, then death becoming widespread.

But for My people: joy! Deliverance! Freedom! Health! Prosperity! All in time of famine and darkness. Rejoice, oh people of God for what is laid out before you: feast in the wilderness, a desert blossoming as the rose, an abundance unheard of, unseen, given bountifully by the Lord God.

Rejoice Zion! Rejoice, My people, for this abundant life, which Jesus came to bring is yours now, today! Hallelujah!

While the celebration of the Feast of Tabernacles in spiritual Israel will involve spiritual harvest joy, material blessings will also flow.

Oh be joyful, for the best is yet to come. Psalm 37 says you will inherit the land, the earth.

When I say "the earth" I mean the land or earth in its abundance and fruitfulness, the way I made it, a good earth pro-

grammed and planned to produce good things. It still has this capacity to produce good, despite man's evil to it. (Even the unrighteous understand and recognize this truth.)

So hold on! Your blessing is coming, magnanimous, large-scale, pressing and growing, mushrooming, expanding like a big bubble ready to explode and shower you with champagne zest.

Oh, it is the best. I have "saved the best wine for the last." It is the champagne of our wedding feast. Drink, drink deeply, My love, My bride, for this is the day of My yearning and the day of My joy.

See it! Behold it in the spirit world. And enter into My love, oh beloved, oh bride of Mine, My own. Come, enter into the feast in an attitude of joy and rejoicing in Me.

Heaven On Earth

It may sound preposterous to some, but what God plans to give is heaven on earth. He wants to restore what Adam lost: a garden of delight, an abundant garden, a place to work happily and rest peacefully. But most important, a place to nurture a relationship with the God of our blessing. We will live in the joy of His presence, participate in our daily activities in Him and praise Him as our greatest treasure and richest reward.

The Lord wants His people to begin now to behold His beauty, without waiting for heaven when we will see Him face to face. We can enjoy His goodness right now by moving into the awareness of His presence. The more we behold Him, the more we find heaven on earth. He is our great reward.

Here is the Lord's invitation to know Him in this intimate way in a prophetic message given to the author:

I *AM a God of grace and beauty and love. All these things are Me. Know Me, that I am beautiful. Oh, good to gaze upon and enjoy. I want you to enjoy Me. Know Me today as beauty, for I am beautiful and I desire you to gaze upon Me and enjoy Me for all eternity. I am your great Reward, your exceeding Great Reward. I AM.*

Know Me as God of your everything; your all, every detail and every moment of your life. I want to infuse all with My glory, My presence, even the most mundane. Yield to Me these precious moments for they are precious to Me and I will infuse them with My presence, for I want to give you heaven on earth. Thus says the Lord, God of Israel, My people.

When Jesus taught us how to prepare for His coming, He framed it in the story about ten virgins touched on earlier. Remember, each of those waiting was a virgin, that is a blood-cleansed believer. Each one had a lamp, though some were constantly tending, trimming and filling the lamp. This equates to pressing in to God, seeking Him daily in prayer and in His word. But what the Bridegroom said to the virgins who failed to keep their lamps ready during the long wait for His arrival was "I do not know you." Knowing God, beholding His beauty, seeking intimate relationship with Him is the perfect state of preparation for His return.

Entering this deeply into His presence, even while we're still on earth, yields a joy that nothing can dismay. "In Your presence is fullness of joy" Psalm 16:11 says. Dwelling in His presence, beholding Him in His glory, fills us with peace, harmony and joy. Every problem melts in the beauty of His presence. Every care lifts.

His presence becomes a place of protection, "He who dwells in the secret place of the Most High abides under the shadow of the Almighty." Then God becomes a refuge and a fortress. (Psalm 91:1) We rise far above our enemies in His presence. They simply fall, as they did before Joshua, because of God's presence.

This place of joy in Him, where our hearts delight to minister to Him, also yields back blessing to us. "Delight yourself in the Lord and He will give you the desires of your heart." The God of blessing wants now to give the desires of their hearts to those ministering love and worship to Him.

I am getting ready to rend the heavens and come down like nothing ever seen or heard. And then My people shall rejoice! Houses and trees and gardens shall be theirs and wells, yes, wells of water and fields with streams running through and meadows with ponds. And dreams realized. Each one has a dream and I know it. And it will be a time of dreams come true. Heaven on earth. Dreams realized.

So let My people feast, says the Lord, and dance and celebrate, for My hand is active among them doing restoration. And you shall rejoice! says the Lord of your Blessing.

Double Sabbath Rest

During the Feast of Tabernacles, the people rested. Though the feast occurred during harvest, a busy time in an agricultural society, the Israelites honored God's command to enjoy a full day of rest the first and last days of the Feast. During the interim days, workers celebrated half holidays. Only necessary tasks were completed. Children free from school played amid the decorated booths. Some businesses closed; others kept shorter hours.

During the spiritual celebration of the Feast, harvest also peaks. The harvest is spiritual—salvation of people. The Spirit is stirring people's hearts. The Spirit is pressing in on them, weighing on them to repent. We need to work His harvest fields. Yet the feast calls for celebration and rest.

We can adopt an *attitude* of rest. Rest can underlie peak activity. The Holy Spirit will bring us opportunities to do His work. We can accomplish them "in Him," using His methods obtained in prayer and carry out His plans with joy. We don't need to fret, worry or drive ourselves but to accomplish everything in a relaxed obedience with the glad heart of a child picking flowers for the family table. We can work in a spirit of rest.

During the Jubilee, the land enjoyed a double sabbath rest. Israel, when faithful, followed God's rule to let the land lie fallow every seventh year. In the 50-year Jubilee cycle, seven sabbaths occurred. The last was year 49, followed by another year of rest, the Jubilee. So it was not until the end of the third year, the planting season after the Jubilee year, that the people reaped a harvest. God said, "I have ordered My blessing to be on you every sixth year, which will provide for you..." (Leviticus 25:21) During the time of rest, the people depended on God's provision.

Ancient Israel failed to embrace God's plan of rest. The nation fell away from faith in God's plan and neglected the sabbath rest for long periods. In fact, during deportation to Babylon, Jewish prophets forecast 70 years of exile to give the land its missed sabbaths.

Paul told the Hebrews that a spiritual rest remains for the people of God. For a people who *listen* to God, who willingly *learn His ways* and who *refuse unbelief*, walking in obedience before Him, that rest remains available.

> So then, there is still waiting a full and complete Sabbath rest for the (true) people of God; For he who has once entered God's rest has ceased from (the weariness and pain) of human labors, just as God rested from those labors. (Hebrews 4:9-10)

One element of rest lies in choosing to overcome our enemies. Jesus has already won the victory. We can choose to believe this and act it out—or not. Acting out our belief in His victory means remaining unruffled in the face of pressure.

Take the land and enter into your rest.
What does this mean? Use the spoken word of power to sub-

due your enemies and actively, by choice, enter into My rest.

There remains a rest for the people of God and ***now is the time****. Absolute, exhilarating rest. Do it now for Me. Submit everything to Me. Rejoice in all things. Praise. Trust. Overwhelm the enemy with your joy and worship and love and peace and trust. This no foe can withstand.*

Jesus' friends, Martha and Mary portray striving and rest. Jesus said that Mary chose the better part. Martha fussed in the kitchen, perspiring under the demands of preparing a meal for Jesus and her other guests. Mary sat at Jesus' feet, listening to Him and watching His expression.

Could the same Lord who fed 5,000 men, not to mention women and children accompanying them, feed Martha's guests? Yet the pressure of the situation cost her the life-changing experience of calmly beholding the Most High God in the awesome location of her own home. Choosing to rest in His presence is more crucial than any of the day's demands.

Enter into the rest. Let all your enemies be quelled as you sit in the secret place of the Most High, beholding Me. Any work you do will be easy and light, like a child floating balloons. I make it that way for you. Now I AM God and I command it: enter into My rest. Amen.

How do we rest? Like Mary, we first adopt an attitude of rest from striving and human effort. Second, we enter into the spirit of the Feast. Praise and rejoice. Dance, sing and worship before God. Let Him pour forth His abundant blessing. Psalm 81, the psalm for the Feast of Tabernacles, instructs us in rejoicing:

> Sing aloud to God our Strength! Shout for joy to the God of Jacob! Raise a song, sound the timbrel, the sweet lyre with the harp. Blow the trumpet at the New Moon, at the full moon, on our feast day...

After the praise comes the provision:

> I am the Lord your God, Who brought you up out of the land of Egypt. Open your mouth wide and I will fill it...God would feed (Israel now) also with the finest of the wheat; and with honey out of the rock would I satisfy you." (Psalm 81:1-3, 10, 16)

The psalm tells the people to open their mouths; God promises to fill them. The feast overflows with blessing. The

Holy Spirit explained to the author what Psalm 81's Feast of Tabernacles language means to convey.

Yes! I AM. And I am a Rewarder of those who diligently seek Me. Open your mouth wide and I will fill it. Expand your desire and believe Me for "the max" and I will do it! Because I want to! And the time is right.

Blessing is the word that I proclaim for you today. Rich, rich blessings, beyond your imagination or wildest dreams. Such peace, such joy, such love as you have not dreamed. For am I not a God of blessing? Will I not pour out blessing in the time of wrath? And have I not promised a spiritual rest for the people of God, a rest not yet fulfilled? So rest, rest, rest in Me as I pour out blessing upon you.

Ask and you shall receive. Give and it shall be given unto you, pressed down shaken together, overflowing will My blessings come upon you and overtake you. Cover it all with prayer and with My blood.

I am rejoicing now over My people Israel. "The Father will dance." I will celebrate the feast amid My people. I will show up for their party, their festal rejoicings. I am coming for this one. So celebrate My feast. Blow the trumpet and tell all about it as I teach you, for it is the message of the times.

The Feast and the Year of Jubilee celebrated simultaneously in the spiritual realm means that we are experiencing a unique time in God's spiritual history. Natural Israel, which became a nation again in 1948, in 1998 celebrated its fiftieth year. The Holy Spirit sees it as a Jubilee for the church of the Lord Jesus Christ as well.

I am your God. You have no other. See what I will do. Watch what I will do, now in the day of your redemption. It is your Jubilee, the time of your redemption, the fiftieth year for Israel and for the Church of the Firstborn, Jesus Christ. Now hallowed, rejoice. The time of your Jubilee has begun. Now holy ones, praise! The time of your redemption has come. Oh, My people, rejoice in Me, the Spirit!

Now come! Come to the Feast in the Year of Jubilee. I call you! I woo you, with precious things, offering the delights of My Feast in My invitation. Yes, come! Those who do not go up to the Feast of Tabernacles will have no rain.

It is an eternal Feast, to last for all time, to take us into the new rain of blessing, a reign of blessing, joy and righteousness. Go up!

Vindication

The Lord of Hosts wants to make the wealth of the nations flow into Zion. He plans to give us the treasures of darkness, to unlock revelation regarding spiritual and earthly scientific and technological mysteries. He is now saying through contemporary prophets that the church will not have to work to win the lost; instead they will pour in waves into meetings, church services, rallies because they'll be hungry for God. This is Sabbath rest!

God will recompense rest, provision, joy and glory to His people. He also promises vindication. To the faithful church at Philadelphia, Jesus proclaimed:

> Take note! I will make those of the synagogue of Satan, who say they are Jews and are not, but lie—behold I will make them come and bow down before your feet and learn and acknowledge that I have loved you. (Revelation 3:9)

The prophet Isaiah promised vindication:

> All those who despised you shall bow down at your feet, and they shall call you the City of the Lord, the Zion of the Holy One of Israel. (Isaiah 60:14)

While the unrepentant world experiences judgement and death, God's people will receive the recompense of blessing and abundant life. In the past, Christians have felt society's scorn and pressure to keep quiet. Expect this to change!

I am the God of victory in love and vindication for My people. Because I love them I protect them. Because I cherish them I vindicate them. And before men I will vindicate you and compensate for all you have lost. Before men I will do this and they will see it and know that I am your God, the God of My people. So know now that vindication is coming for My people and coming soon, says the Lord. I will show My love openly. Openly. Wait and receive in joy, says the Lord.

God will demonstrate His love openly. All the love He showered on Adam and Eve, the love He demonstrated for Israel in their exodus from Egypt, the blessing He showed during Solomon's reign, He wants to pour out now. All flesh shall see the glory of God—on us!

I AM God; there IS no other. Rejoice, O earth, for the Lord comes to rule the land. His people have gathered in praise, true praise. They have worshipped in spirit and in truth. Now the Lord comes to save.

See what I will do in the lives of those who worship Me. I am your God alone and now I will fulfill all that I have promised: recompense and reward in this earth now.

Realize it and proclaim it, for it is truth, hidden truth ready to be brought out now. The God of Recompense will recompense in this hour.

Prepare for heaven on earth reward. Joy unspeakable and full of glory. Soundness, health, wholeness, freedom from bondages. Love. Happiness. Peace. Wells filled and overflowing. Vats full. Barns bulging. Good to excess, so there is waste because it overflows. Pressed down, shaken together, overflowing abundant life. Restored life and wholeness.

Oh, you say, it sounds like a dream, too good to be true. But I say, eye has not seen, nor ear heard, nor has it entered into the heart of man to imagine what the Lord will do for those who love Him. Amen. I have spoken.

Jesus Arrived Midway Through the Feast

God has a way of showing up for the Feast of Tabernacles. When King Solomon (a pre-figure of the messianic reign of King Jesus) dedicated the newly-built temple in Jerusalem, God arrived on the scene and poured out His glory in the same way He plans to do in our day.

In Solomon's time, God prepared for the glory just as the Lord of Hosts has prepared everything today. Solomon's father, David, who was God's anointed, had cleansed the land of its enemies. He had replaced the rebellious reign of his predecessor, Saul, with submission to God. Today the Lord of Hosts has cleansed the church, judging its evil, running off its enemies.

David had gathered gold, precious stones, cedar from Lebanon and all the treasure necessary to build and decorate a temple of unprecedented beauty. It became one of the marvels of the ancient world.

The temple was dedicated during the celebration of the Feast of Tabernacles in Jerusalem. Solomon watched as the priests brought the ark of the covenant into the holy of holies. As they did, God filled the temple with His shekinah glory. (Shekinah means God's manifest presence.) "And the priests could not enter in to the house of the Lord because the glory of the Lord had filled the Lord's house." (2 Chronicles 7:2)

The king and all Israel offered sacrifice to the Lord. The number of burnt offerings exceeded anything that generation knew. Today His people offer their lives as a continual sacrifice—a multitude of burnt offerings.

Then Solomon hosted a great celebration:

> At that time Solomon held the feast for seven days and all Israel with him, a very great assembly, from the entrance of Hamath to the Brook of Egypt. (2 Chronicles 7:8)

This historic temple dedication and Tabernacles feast foreshadow the manifest presence God plans to demonstrate today. Another indicator lies in the behavior of Jesus when He Himself kept the feast in Jerusalem.

In actions that may reveal His coming for us today, He put off His arrival at the feast until the festivity reached its midpoint. He appeared, not with His disciples, but quietly slipped into Jerusalem and entered the temple court to teach.

Why the delay? Not because the Jews planned to kill him—which they did. They could do nothing until His hour came. Jesus tarried, He explained, "because My time is not ripe." (John 7:8) Perhaps that is why Jesus tarries today, at the time of God's great harvest. "Ripe," a harvest word, might apply to the peoples of the earth today, a harvest of souls that Jesus, Lord of the Harvest, discerns for ripeness.

Jesus showed Himself at the feast in the temple, specifically in the temple's court. The court represents the place of praise, according to Psalm 100. Today praise is drawing the coming of the Lord. God has ordained that His work requires the joyful participation of His people. Praise, specific praise of His kingship, draws His soon-coming reign with a magnet-like force. The reason for this is one of His kingdom principles: He has ordained that He inhabits the praises of His people. His reign just won't happen without a heaven-and-earth chorus of worship thundering before His throne as Revelation 5:11-13 pictures.

The Feast of Tabernacles crowds in Jerusalem argued about Jesus' origins. Did this man fulfill scriptural prophecy regarding the Anointed One? they asked. He ignored their squabbling and He taught them about His own anointing, explaining, "I come from His (very) presence." (John 7:29) It was God who sent Him, Jesus said. In response, some in the crowd cried, "This is the Christ (the Anointed One)!"

God is doing the same thing now. The message of the anointing rings like a trumpet in the earth today. Men of God, such as Kenneth Copeland, are proclaiming the anointing all over the earth. The message that Jesus preached at the Great Feast is being repeated today, at the time when God promises a spiritual fulfillment of that feast.

On the last and greatest day of the feast, the people commemorated the water gushing from the rock in the desert and they prayed for the late rains. Jesus identified Himself as the source of living water.

> He stood and cried in a loud voice, If any man is thirsty, let him come to Me and drink! He who believes in Me (who cleaves to and trusts and relies on Me) as the scripture has said, From his innermost being shall flow (continuously) springs and rivers of living water. (John 7:37-38)

Some believed. But others countered, "What? Does the Christ come out of Galilee?" Some demanded His arrest, but no one laid hands on Him. (John 7:41, 44) Similar squabbles erupt in the church today.

Jesus will come in glory to this spiritual celebration of the Feast. Will He come at this time to get His bride? These are questions we cannot answer because Jesus Himself said no one but the Father knows the hour. However, we can know the season or general time of His coming. And we can increase the alertness of our watch because we have prophetic knowledge of our times.

You were destined, or predestined, for glory. Think about it! Glory!

During the Harvest Feast, the glory of God in its fullness, ripeness, repleteness will be demonstrated in My people. My glory fest, My feast. Just as God came into the newly-built temple during Solomon's reign, during the celebration of the Harvest Feast, so I will come into My living temple, My spiritual temple during the Great Feast of Tabernacles. Amen!

Just as the Feast of Tabernacles reached its jubilant peak in a huge festival banquet, so God's spiritual celebration will culminate in a gala supper that every Book of Revelation reader knows. This prophecy distills God's plan for a final Feast of Tabernacles:

I AM. Hear Me, Oh Israel, I AM.

I am coming. I AM is coming back for His church, His people, to gather them from the far corners of the earth, the four winds, to His bosom, to His heart, to rejoice together with them for all eternity. Be glad then church, gathering of My elect, My chosen; rejoice then for this is soon-coming. I am soon-coming. Delight in this knowledge and in the word "soon."

And the Marriage Supper of the Lamb, the festal dinner, will be unlike any celebration you have known. Rejoice with Me in the preparation of this feast, this Harvest Wedding, this festal gathering, this joyous event.

Be thou holy as I am holy. Be thou set apart and virginal before the King. (Psalm 45) Be thou loyal and faithful to Him alone, not drawn or seduced by any other thing but fresh and new and prepared as bride unto Him. Keep thyself for thy Master, Lord and Husband.

The seven days of the feast correspond to the seven years of tribulation. I will make great the Harvest Feast and celebrate the Succoth with My people. I will prepare a banquet beneath the eyes of My enemies, your enemies (for they are Mine!). You will walk in the joy of the Feast, the festal gathering and your "tabernacle" or tent shall be lovely and fulsome. Believe Me for it. People will move into the "tent" of My choosing.

Now the devil is thrown down upon the earth, knowing his time is short. The heavens are cleared for the exodus of My people. All things are coming to fruition.

Chapter 20

The Wedding Feast

Praise Calls Forth The Marriage Supper of the Lamb

God plans to make the Feast of Tabernacles like the seven day wedding celebration of ancient times. The party that begins here on earth will escalate in joy, exultation and high praise until it moves into the Marriage Supper of the Lamb. The people of God need to rejoice, raising the praise level until it brings forth the glory God intends.

Your praise will usher in My coming. Your praise will usher in the Marriage Supper of the Lamb. For I will come when a mighty chorus of praise rises, when the whole people of God united in praise, His church on earth, give Him mighty worship, glory and praise.

A resounding symphony of worldwide worship is prophesied:

> After this I heard what sounded like the shout of a vast throng, like the boom of many pounding waves, and like the roar of terrific and mighty peals of thunder, exclaiming, "Hallelujah (praise the Lord)! For now the Lord our God, the Omnipotent (the All-ruler) reigns!
>
> Let us rejoice and shout for joy (exulting and triumphant)! Let us celebrate and ascribe to Him glory and honor, for the marriage of the Lamb (at last) has come, and His bride has prepared herself. (Revelation 19:6-7)

The Holy Spirit expanded for me the significance of Revelation 19:5 concerning this last days praise.

Praise from the body of Christ will usher in the Marriage Supper of the Lamb. Specific praise.

God is hearing a thunderous voice of many waters, from a multitude of His people over all the earth saying, "Our God reigns!"

Yes! You have done this. Your voice has been part of the

thunderous chorus heard in heaven. And so the Marriage Supper of the Lamb is prepared and ready.

Come. Enter in. The Feast, like the old-time Hebrew wedding, will last for seven "days." It will be "a moveable feast." The Feast of Tabernacles, celebrated on earth, is the onset of the Great Feast, the holy Marriage Supper. Know that the two are tied together, merged into one. The moad, appointed time, for the beginning of the feast has come, for the mighty chorus of praise has perfected the time. My Spirit has done this in My people. My Spirit! Rejoice! Rejoice with Me in the work My Spirit has done!

Come now and celebrate the Feast, the Feast of Tabernacles, the Harvest Feast with Me, the banquet in the midst of your enemies, (Psalm 23), the feast of fat things in the presence of background of gloom and darkness, My Feast. Come!

I anoint your head with oil daily, anointed revelation knowledge of Me and My kingdom. I prepare a banquet for you in the midst of your enemies. Dress up in My clothes of ardor, praise and love—you're going to a party, beloved!

Put on the garment, the wedding garment. Remember what Jesus said about the garment? Put it on now. Dress up in Me. Study it out. Prepare!

A Garment Represents a Lifestyle

What is the wedding garment? Like the garment of praise mentioned in Isaiah 61:3, the key passage on the anointing, it is something we choose to put on. In God's word, the garment represents a behavior pattern or a life state. Ephesians 1:12 describes praise as a lifestyle, encouraging us to "live for the praise of His glory." God puts on a garment of vengeance in Isaiah 59:17, taking up a behavior pattern of wrath. Those who conquer wear white garments in Revelation 3:5.

The garment also denotes an attitude.

Jesus pinpointed the importance of the wedding garment when He described a king who gave a wedding banquet for his son. "Tell those who are invited...everything is prepared; come to the wedding feast." The parable in Matthew 22 tells how the king scrapped the original invitation list.

> The kingdom of heaven is like a king who gave a wedding banquet for his son
>
> And sent his servants to summon those who had been invited to the wedding banquet, but they refused to come.
>
> Again he sent other servants, saying, Tell those who

> are invited, Behold, I have prepared my banquet; my bullocks and my fat calves are killed, and everything is prepared; come to the wedding feast.
>
> But they were not concerned and paid no attention (they ignored and made light of the summons, treating it with contempt) and they went away—one to his farm, another to his business,
>
> While the others seized his servants, treated them shamefully and put them to death. (Matthew 22:1-6)

When the intended guests ignored his summons, He sent servants out to the crossroads to gather both bad and good to fill the banquet hall.

> But when the king came in to view the guests, he looked intently at a man there who had on no wedding garment. And he said, Friend, how did you come in here without putting on the (appropriate) wedding garment? And he was speechless. Then the king said to the attendants, Tie him hand and foot, and throw him into the darkness outside; there will be weeping and grinding of teeth. For many are called (invited and summoned), but few are chosen. (Matthew 22:11-14)

The wedding garment is white, representing purity, and is fashioned from fine linen, indicating righteousness.

> She has been permitted to dress in fine (radiant) linen dazzling and white—for the fine linen is (signifies, represents) the righteousness (the upright, just and godly living, deeds and conduct and right standing with God) of the saints (God's holy people). (Revelation 19:8)

Jesus' story stresses that we need to put on the wedding garment. When we dress in the morning, we take deliberate action to put on our clothes. It's simple, but crucial, that we make a conscious choice to put on the wedding garment—or be found in our spiritual pajamas in the Day of the Lord. Will He find a sleeping church? Praise is a behavior pattern and a lifestyle. It flows from us on bad days and good, in crisis and tranquility.

Ephesians 4:24 admonishes, "Put on the new nature created in God's image in true righteousness and holiness." It is not a passive state but an active decision played out in moment-by moment-choices to live fully in our new nature—and the natural result is praise, joyous, jubilant praise.

The Holy Spirit has prepared a bride. And she has *chosen* to dress in fine linen. The Lord of Hosts has purified her with holy refining fire. Pressing in to Him daily, she has found intimacy with her Bridegroom. She is prepared.

Now only radiant final enhancements remain. Will the bride allow the Holy Spirit to complete the finishing touches to her beauty before her presentation to her King? Will she accept her crown? Or does she respond, "No, I am too weak, too unworthy, to wear this crown and rule with My Lord."

Balky Bride

The Holy Spirit is speaking to the intercessors now to pray for the bride because she balks in false humility at these final preparations. She has yielded to His destruction of unholy altars within her and allowed him to rebuild an altar of true worship. She has surrendered to cleansing and refining. But she refuses to accept the rich accoutrements of her position as bride—arrangement of her train, acceptance of the bouquet, the jewels, the luminous veil and crown.

Jesus Himself will lift her veil. Then she will behold Him face to face. She must not try to remove the veil herself but wait upon His move. Again, she must yield to this holy ritual. The time has come for the bride to be bride. No longer maidservant, she becomes the wedded wife.

The Holy Spirit says this to the bride:

I am God. I am your God. I am holy, the Holy One of Israel. I call forth holiness in Christ Jesus in My anointed people, who are kings and priests in their land, after the order of Melchisedek. For if you are the branch of Jesus, are you not also after the order of Melchisedek?

Bride, wake up! Acknowledge who you are in Christ Jesus, acknowledge who I say you are: you are priests and kings. Rulers with dominion. Priests with access to the holy of holies and the Holy One of Israel.

You have free access! Free movement on Zion, My holy mountain. Unquestioned authority and privilege of position.

Arise, bride, to this calling!

The Holy Spirit has given a prayer for His intercessors to proclaim over the bride:

The Lord has spoken His express purpose in this hour, a prayer for the bride. Pray it. Repeat it to Me. Let me hear these words from My church. Let me hear these sweet words and I will do it! I will do all, says the Lord your God.

The Proclamation Prayer:

Now let the veil be lifted. Behold your King, unfettered by shrouded vision. Clear-eyed, gaze into His face, even His eyes. And beholding Him, you go from glory to glory in Christ Jesus. Know your King by looking into His face.

As a handmaiden, you have watched His hands. When they moved, you moved. As bride you read every expression on His face and respond with your heart.

Oh, bride, arise now! I call you forth to arise from shame and unworthiness. Leave your past and all its association with death (death-things, negativity, woundedness) behind you. (Psalm 45:10) Forget where you came from, Shulammite woman (Song of Solomon 1:6 and 6:11-13), and accept the love of the King. Be bride, as you are called to be bride. Rejoice and accept.

So arise. Be glad that the King has chosen thee, above all women the fairest. Go and do valiantly what He has called you to do. Like Esther, you are called for the salvation of your people. Amen! Oh, amen!

We must prepare our hearts by yielding to what God says about His bride: that she is beautiful, spotless, unblemished and worthy to be a resplendent, radiant, exuberant bride. When He hears us rejoicing in praise that He has made us truly worthy, truly ready, truly beautiful, He will no longer tarry. He will sound the call.

Now the bride must allow the Spirit to complete His work. Just as Esther submitted to Hegai's beauty treatments of myrrh oil and sweet spices and perfumes, the bride must surrender to the Holy Spirit's preparations.

While the bride prepares, so does the Bridegroom. He prepares gifts for His beloved and selects the finest for the wedding celebration.

Jesus Has Saved the Best Wine for Last

You are not only priests, you are My bride, My wife. The praise I bring you into will be a deep praise expressed through the Spirit with deep words of love, words of love so deep they must be expressed through the Spirit. Oh, how I long for this intimacy with My bride.

You will see yourself in beauty through My eyes, Yes, you will see it, the clothing, the garments. This is My gift to you, oh My beautiful bride.

As they serve champagne at weddings, My anointing is the champagne at our wedding. You have the taste for My love and

My anointing, not the love of the world. This is why you have come through. You have forsaken the flavor of the world for My sake. I have saved the best wine for the wedding feast, the champagne of the Spirit, and this is what you have the taste for.

Jesus performed His first miracle at the Cana wedding feast. He turned water into wine. This wine far surpassed that served earlier. He will again reserve the best for last, for His own wedding celebration.

The beauty and valor of the bride, in her intimacy with her Lord, makes her powerful in Him. In her worship, she finds glory and victory in the battle with the enemy.

I will do mighty things upon the earth through you, My children, My chicks, that I gather in before the coming storm. I have seen your surrender and marked in the Book of Life that you embraced death to gain life.

I am coming soon. Praise has been perfected in the earth. I am coming to get My bride and then—hallelujah!—this thing will wind up in glory!

Prepare for storm, for battle before My coming. But the glory will increase to obliterate any dirt, dust of battle. Just as in the "Battle Hymn of the Republic" song you sing so sweetly to Me, the battle will take place in the "glory of the Lord."

The anointing will energize and give you rest. Oh, the love, the healing, the satisfaction, the greatness of it. Enter into this with Me. Oh be with Me. I long to be with you. It's the great warfare, our intimacy together, our bond together. It is what you were created to be, bound together in the heart of God.

I love you. I am drawn to you, My bride, like a magnet. When the obstacles (or demagnetizing elements) are removed, we are just drawn together in My coming. You will meet Me in the air, drawn to Me by our love and free of the restraint of the flesh—because the flesh will be overcome and transparent in the glory.

Our bondedness to the Lord Jesus makes us a powerful combination with Him, both in battle and in support of Him as the holy judge. He has earned the right to open Revelation's seven seals during the time of wrath that coincides with the combined Jubilee and Feast of Tabernacles celebrations.

We have already entered this time of duality, a time of both comfort and correction. The Holy Spirit promises through Isaiah:

> As one whom his mother comforts, so will I comfort you...When you see this, your heart shall rejoice...the

> (powerful) hand of the Lord shall be revealed and known to be with His servants, but His indignation (shown) to be against His enemies. (Isaiah 66:13-14)

Solace the Heart of the Savior

Jesus is appointed both savior and judge. His role as saviour confronted Him with a price—a bloody, brutal death on the cross. Yet He set His face like flint, for the joy that lay ahead—His redeemed people. His role as judge also demands from Him a brutal toll. He must set His face like flint again, to unleash wrath upon an evil world, a place where His own sinful loved ones dwell. Again His heart is grieved to the point of Gethsemane anguish. The Lord of Hosts, who is our Jesus, asks for His bride's solace during the Judgement, a judgement grievous to His heart.

I must clothe Myself in zeal because My heart is not a heart of judgement but of love for My children, who will go into perdition, whose blood is on MY garment. (Isaiah 63) Their blood is on My garment, just as Jack Kennedy's blood spilled on the suit of his wife, Jackie.

Those judged are My children, the ones I loved and made and formed and cherished. Do you see why Judgement is delayed? Why I am slow to anger—and justice? Why I say justice comes swiftly? Look at My loss: My own children, the work of My hands. Yet the time has run out and opportunity for choices, to choose life, has been given over and over. Now, Judgement begins. Stay with Me. Stay at My side, bride of Christ, and see Me through.

Nowhere, nowhere in this great universe is solace available to God's heart except from His beloved children. Nowhere is comfort available to the Savior-Judge except from His bride. The angels can't do it because they haven't suffered. But you have and can. So I say to you now, "thank you." Stay with Me through this thing, beloved, beloved people of My heart, and I will reward you with My own comfort, says the Lord.

Despite the Lord's grief at carrying out judgement, His purpose remains firm. He will not turn back from this prophesied last days Judgement. We should be careful about even asking Him to delay or turn back His judgements. The Judge, who is Jesus, will use His bride *in the Holy Spirit* to proclaim and call forth certain judgements. But it must be only at the Holy Spirit's direction. We can, and should, pray for His mercy to operate within the framework of judgement.

We also must praise the holy and righteous Judge. When darkness gathers and the earth begins to shake, we won't feel like praising. This is just the time when praise is most powerful.

I AM. I AM. I AM. Know Me today in might and power, not as your gentle and merciful friend—though I am that—but as a mighty, powerful and glorious God-and-Judge. I rise up to judge. My judgements are just and true. Praise Me for that. Let the earth erupt in praise!

What is coming is heavy and hard. Keep that praise up. Keep the praise coming. I need the praise support of My people who are "with Me." They are pictured following on white horses, coming with Me to carry out My just judgements upon the earth, their earth. I need the kings and priests of the land (just like the Gulf War coalition) to back up and support Me.

An awesome time is coming. Awesome. So rejoice in the Lord your God that His judgements are just and true. Some of these judgements are for your vindication.

Certain areas will be judged because they have not been turned back to Me in prayer. The kings and priests have not torn down the altars of idolatry. The people—even a fraction of them—have not changed or turned to Me. So I must judge.

The time of mercy—a time of repeated chances to turn and repent—is over now. I arise to judge. I stand up, stand up from My throne of mercy and grace. I leave that mercy seat, and I will not sit down upon it until the Judgement is over. Hear Me! I will not relent or turn back from My expressed desire and purpose until this great work, this cleansing work is done.

And I need you, My people, to praise Me for what is being done. Amen. Alleluia.

We need to prepare now by entering into that spiritual rest described earlier. The spiritual rest remaining for the people of God will keep their hearts in peace during distressing times to come. The real test of peace comes in the storm.

There's a story about a fine art painting competition. Its theme was "Peace." Many entries portrayed sylvan scenes radiating peace. The winner, however, showed a wild storm in the woods. In the crook of a tree wedged a nest. There a mother bird, wings outstretched, protected her young in calm, despite the raging wind.

The kingdom of God, Jesus had already instructed them, comes not by observation. It resides in men's hearts. So it is in men's hearts that Jesus' millennial reign will begin. His reign is one of peace, blessing and joy.

A swell of richness in our love for God, love for those around us, harmony with creation and hope for the future will lift God's people to a new level of life in Him. This fullness of the feast, this abundance of goodness, is coming.

Joy Unspeakable

Hear Me. Oh Church, oh Israel, My people, My own, My chosen race and nation, My cherished little ones, My heart children, beloved, My very own, hear Me!

I will do all I have promised to you in My word in one single, short hour. All I have promised you from My heart, My heart of hearts, My fond-Father promises, dear to My heart as they are to you, ***all*** *that I have promised will be done now in one short time period.*

Get ready to excel, excel in abundance, luxury, joy in the Spirit. Luxurious, abundant peace; excellent joy; ecstasy; forever-fervent power in praise; joyous release to My Spirit; hope, abounding hope; faith to believe for miracles; reaffirmation of My love wherever you look; on all sides comfort—because you were willing to acquiesce to Me, your God.

Prepare for joy unspeakable and full of glory. Prepare your heart to expand, receive fullness, be exuberant with flowing life as I am ***exuberant****! Rejoice! For all this is coming, says the Lord.*

The days have arrived for the fulfillment of God's promises. We become so accustomed to thinking that fulfillment lies in the far-off future that we forget the prophetic moment on today's time clock. Though we live in a time of judgement to come upon the whole earth, we also live in an earth-stopping hour. We will witness the onset of Christ's prophesied reign. What a moment! When God says His words will be fulfilled now, He means it.

Heaven rejoices at the beginning of the full reign of the Lord Jesus Christ. This word from the Lord, received by the author, describes it:

I am mighty God and King, a king to satisfy the desire of your heart for a glorious, respected leader. For I will be King, with all the delightful pomp and pageantry My people desire.

Now know, My children, that I am coming to reign in the fullness of My reign. The millennial time has begun. Know children of the King, My own beloved and favored children, that I am coming into My reign. All is set and nothing will stop Me from fulfilling My plan. You will see it with your own eyes.

Come now, beloved, into the circle of My love and My reign. My devoted people will be drawn in even closer to Me in this time. For the coming of the King brings everyone together and they all draw close to Him, joyously celebrating.

Festival! Yes, the coming of the King is cause for festival and rejoicing. Amen.

God is excited about what He's doing and He wants us to share in the anticipation. The words of Ezekiel expose a nagging attitude of unbelief that we should avoid:

> Son of man, what is this proverb that you have in the land of Israel, saying, The days drag on and every vision comes to nothing and is not fulfilled!
>
> ...Thus says the Lord God: There shall none of My words be deferred any more, but the word which I have spoken shall be performed, says the Lord God. (Ezekiel 12:22, 28)

God is wrapping things up. Even the Tribulation, fearful as it sounds, is a merciful attempt by a merciful God to get the attention of His people and to bring down every high, rebellious fortress to clear the way for the excellent reign of a righteous and holy King. We can view Tribulation as the back side of a beautiful tapestry called "Restoration."

This is what's happening now. We see signs of Tribulation already in the earth—earthquakes, violence, plagues, ethnic hatred. We also witness signs of millennial reign, signs of the coming kingdom—the mighty praise chorus, outpouring of the Holy Spirit, signs, wonders and miracles, heightened pace in the spiritual realm, fulfillment of ancient prophecy. These accelerate in timing and increase in significance, like birth pangs. They serve as signs, easy to read for those who watch, that Almighty God will fulfill His word in this "day."

The Day of the Lord ushers in Christ's absolute kingship over all things in heaven and on earth. What a mighty time we live in. The Scriptural promise that has awed us every time we hear it is now being fulfilled in our lifetime:

> For He (the Father) has put all things in subjection under His (Christ's) feet...However, when everything has been subjected to Him, then the Son Himself will also subject Himself to (the Father) Who put all things under Him, so that God may be all in all. (1 Corinthians 15:27-28)

God showed Daniel the might and splendor of earth's great empires. These empires, the Babylonian, Medo-Persian, Greek and Roman, crushed and conquered nations. But when the Ancient of Days gives judgement to the saints of the Most High (Daniel 7:22), a final and lasting kingdom will emerge. Today, the Lord is calling upon the intercessors to declare His judgements, expressed in the scriptures, into the earth. It is a calling not taken lightly by those commissioned to do it. We saw in earlier chapters that Psalm 149 and Psalm 110 commission the saints to execute judgements. Daniel confirms the assignment:

> ...Judgement was given to the saints of the Most High (God) and the time came when the saints possessed the kingdom. (Daniel 7:22)

Judgement will restore righteousness and right order. When righteousness springs up, Jesus will take up His full reign.

> I saw in the night visions, and behold, on the clouds of the heavens came One like a Son of man and He came to the Ancient of Days, and was presented before Him.
>
> And there was given Him (the Messiah) dominion and glory and kingdom, that all peoples, nations, and languages should serve Him. His dominion is an everlasting dominion which shall not pass away, and His kingdom is one which shall not be destroyed. (Daniel 7:13-14)

When the seventh trumpet of Revelation sounds, the Lord Jesus Christ will begin this reign. We will hear the happy and long-awaited words, "The kingdom of this world has become the kingdom of our Lord and His Christ, and he shall reign forever and ever." (Revelation 11:15 RSV)

The words of this passage, in their amplified version, are awe-inspiring:

> And the seventh angel blew (his) trumpet and there were mighty voices in heaven, shouting, the dominion (kingdom, sovereignty, rule) of the world has now come into the possession and become the kingdom of our Lord and of His Christ (the Messiah), and He shall reign forever and ever. (Revelation 11:15)

The time we have awaited has almost arrived. To be chosen to live on the earth in this pivotal moment is a great blessing. We will see the reality of words that have made generations ache with yearning for their fulfillment:

> The government shall be upon his shoulder and his name shall be called Wonderful, Counselor, the Mighty

God, Everlasting Father (of Eternity), Prince of Peace. Of the increase of his government and peace there shall be no end. (Isaiah 9:6-7)

"Behold, I Have Prepared My Banquet"

Those who are wise, who maintain the Holy Spirit oil in their lamps, pressing in to seek intimacy with Him, will witness the onset of Christ's reign and the coronation of the King. At the Marriage Supper of the Lamb, a vast heavenly assembly will watch radiant as the royal diadem is brought forth. He is the great I Am and He wants to be I AM fully in us, becoming our All in All, and to reign as King of our lives.

The Holy Spirit has moved on the body of Christ to herald the coming reign of Jesus Christ. Through songs sweeping through the church, through scriptures and through declaring praise, the Holy Spirit has prompted us to proclaim "Our God reigns." This praise arises like a mighty shout to God from every part of the body, echoing Revelation 19:6, "Hallelujah! For the Lord our God, the Almighty reigns!" God inhabits these praises. He manifests their reality, His reign.

Our loving praise and ministering worship will draw the Bridegroom.

This moment of closeness, love and glory is just the beginning of our close relationship, our succoth of tabernacling and dwelling together. When people live together, they know one another intimately. So know, know the richness of this feast of our love, the closeness, the power that results, the glory of My presence on you and in you. Know it and rejoice.

The finest aged things held back, good things prepared and mellowed, these are the things I have prepared for you to feast on in the feast of My love.

The Bridegroom will appear and open for us a door to the long-awaited wedding feast, the Marriage Supper of the Lamb, and the coronation of our King. Let us maintain the alertness and the discipline to be ready. Remember that in the Song of Solomon, the Beloved arrived and went to open the door to His beloved. He found the door locked.

Part of keeping the door unlocked is a watching our attitudes. The Lord encourages us:

First, watch expectantly. Don't say, "It's not time yet" and forget to watch.

Second, be ready to go out. Have your preparations complete and your "shoes" on. Be **all** *ready. Don't be tied up in the things of this world. Free yourself up. Be* **ready**.

Third, have the door unlocked, not as the bride in the Song of Solomon who had latched the door for the night. His scent was on the latch, but she missed him because it was dark and she was sleepy.

Even the expectant need to unlock ourselves from the iron grip of our daily lives. Just as a child leaves his indoor play and waits on the front steps the day grandpa and grandma are coming to visit, so we must distance ourselves mentally and emotionally from our goals and activities, loosening their hold on us so that we're ready. We must uproot and destroy any hold that sin has on our lives because it causes us to fear His coming.

Know that My anxious people, My waiting people, must come out to meet Me on the day of their visitation.

When Abraham received a visitation from heaven, Sarai hid inside their tent. When God called for Adam in the garden, he and Eve both hid.

In contrast, when Moses saw the burning bush, the scripture says he "turned aside." Although intent on reaching a destination, he turned aside.

My people hide from Me today, for they do not know Me and so remain "within" on the day of their visitation. They do not come out to meet Me.

Abraham **ran** *to meet Me. See this as an example of My coming, for there are those who are hiding in fear. They will not come out to meet Me. And others will run at the moment of My appearing. Take this to heart.*

Peter stripped down to his loincloth and dove into the water when he caught a glimpse of Me.

And the gospel story of the Bridegroom's coming said the virgins "went out to meet Him." Anyone anxious for someone to come waits and watches, then runs out to meet that person, as you go out to meet a son or daughter returning home after a long absence.

It's a mind-set. Lot wasn't ready to leave Sodom. I am the Lord, thy God; thou hast no other. If need be, I would lead thee by the hand as I did Lot. But My desire is to have you more responsive than that. I said to Abraham, would I not tell My friend and servant (about Sodom's judgment)? Would I not fully disclose to My friend and intimate, who has been obedient to Me, the fullness of My will and My thoughts toward the earth?

Yes! Surely the Lord will do nothing without informing His servants, the prophets.

So know surely that I do this thing plainly in your sight. My coming is imminent. So be it. My coming is soon and quickly. And then you must go out, go out to meet Me.

Yes, to meet Me in the air, as the scripture proclaims, but also to meet Me in the earth, the place of My visitation. For I will visit the earth in judgment and I want you involved. I will visit the earth in My mercy and I want you involved.

So "going out" means leaving behind your regular work and activities to actively wait on Me. It means being alert. The householder in My parable was not alert because of a delusion about when I would come. Don't be that way. Stay actively alert. Expectant. Tuned in. Don't get swept up in your lifestyle. Put all that aside now.

Chapter 21

Prepared For Rapture

We have discovered that the Feast of Tabernacles celebrates the Person of Yahweh, I AM, the personal God of Israel, who abides in each of us. It recalls Succoth, when the people of Israel dwelt in wilderness tents, or tabernacles, sheltered in the manifest presence of the One Who revealed Himself to Moses as I AM.

The fulfillment of the Great Feast in spiritual Israel today will demonstrate the fullness of I AM dwelling in us. The Feast completes all the messianic prophecies envisioning the fullness of His presence shown forth in an obvious way. Those who have surrendered, allowing the Lord of Hosts to refine them in fire reserved for the purest silver, have become sacred human vessels, holding the full presence of God. This presence will be so full and intense that it will shine through our flesh for others to see.

God's presence shining through our flesh transfigures our flesh. Resurrection glory will transmute bodies that have died to sin and corruption so thoroughly that they can be instantly transformed at the rapture of the saints.

The Apostle Paul, in a prophetic leap across the centuries to our messianic time, describes this "resurrection, even while in the body." He identifies it as a "hope." He says he hasn't reached the goal, but he runs his race to strive for "the resurrection (that lifts me) out from among the dead (even while in the body)." We studied this scripture when we looked at transfiguration. Here, we'll relate it to the rapture. Another translation says:

> I want to know Christ and the power of his resurrection and the fellowship of sharing in his sufferings, becoming like him in his death, and so, somehow, to attain to the resurrection from the dead. (Philippians 3:11 NIV)

Paul goes on to say that Jesus Christ "will transform our lowly bodies so that they will be like his glorious body." We might think that this refers to the final resurrection at the end of time. That is true. But a generation of believers, those who maintain their virginity and keep their lamps supplied with oil, will not experience death. They will undergo immediate translation at the rapture from a natural physical body to a glorified resurrected body.

The way the Lord will achieve this glorious transformation and the timing of it, lie in the last few words of the verse. The scripture says:

> The Lord Jesus Christ (the Messiah)...will transform and fashion anew the body of our humiliation to conform to and be like the body of His glory and majesty by exerting that power which enables Him even to subject everything to Himself. (Philippians 3:20-21)

We know from 1 Corinthians 15:28 that Christ will subject all things to Himself, then in turn subject all, including Himself, to the Father. This will happen while the world as we know it still exists, because in heaven no evil power usurps His reign. He will "abolish every rule" through the initiation of His reign in His people and through events described in the Book of Revelation.

The transformation of our bodies so that they will be like His glorious body is a process that perfects and completes the indwelling of Christ in us, our hope of glory. The fullness of Christ, the Anointed One, the Messiah, dwelling and tabernacling in us, attains our hope of glory.

This same person, Jesus, the Christ, said to us, "I AM the Resurrection and the Life." He is the I AM who is our hope of resurrection glory. And this resurrection glory, Paul says, can occur while we are still in our bodies.

Something deep inside of us aches, even groans, to be fully alive. The word of God promises this life. The promise will become reality. Jesus and the Father gave us their own Spirit as a guarantee of the achievement of our hope of glory. We should pray for "glory clothes" because this is just what God promises:

> Here indeed, in this (present abode, body) we sigh and groan inwardly, because we yearn to be clothed over (we yearn to put on our celestial body like a garment, to be fitted out) with our heavenly dwelling.
>
> For while we are still in this tent, we groan under the burden and sigh deeply (weighed down, depressed, oppressed)—not that we want to put off the body (the clothing of the spirit) but that we would be further clothed, so that what is mortal (our dying body) may be swallowed up by life...
>
> Now He Who has fashioned us (preparing and

making us fit) for this very thing is God, Who also has given us the (Holy) Spirit as a guarantee (of the fulfillment of His promise). (2 Corinthians 5:3-5)

Here is the crux of what these scriptures promise: the glory will prepare God's people for the rapture. The refining work of the Lord of Hosts and the effect of Christ's manifest presence in us transforming our flesh will bring us to such a point of pre-resurrected life that we can go "in a twinkling." Our bodies will be on the verge of resurrection. The perfect fulfillment of Jesus' words, "I AM the Resurrection and the Life," will begin at the Rapture when resurrection without physical death will occur.

"The last enemy to be subdued and abolished is death," according to 1 Corinthians 15:26. What a testimony to that truth the Rapture will be!

Take notice! I tell you a mystery (a secret truth, an event decreed by the hidden purpose or counsel of God). We shall not all fall asleep (in death), but we shall all be changed (transformed)

In a moment, in the twinkling of an eye, at the (sound of the) last trumpet call. For a trumpet will sound, and the dead (in Christ) will be raised imperishable (free and immune from decay) and we shall be changed (transformed).

For this perishable (part of us) must put on the imperishable (nature) and this mortal (part of us, this nature that is capable of dying) must put on immortality (freedom from death)

And when this perishable puts on the imperishable and this that was capable of dying puts on freedom from death, then shall be fulfilled the scripture that says, Death is swallowed up (utterly vanquished forever) in and unto victory.

O death, where is your victory? O, death, where is your sting? (1 Corinthians 15:51-55)

The Holy Spirit has put such richness into the word of God. We will soon discover that richness as He begins to reveal the fullness, completeness and perfection of the scriptures. When God told Ezekiel to prophesy life, to speak life into bones long dead and wasted, the prophet gave us an example of the power of speaking I AM's life words. God plans to resurrect the whole of His nation, spirit, mind and body.

Ezekiel 37 refers to resurrection, that is, being raised from the dead. It is a prophecy of the Resurrection, a prophecy for the nation of Israel and a prophecy for today.

It is working on three levels.

Physical resurrection

Bringing the national soul of Israel back to life

And the spiritual resurrection of the new messianic Israel, bringing a people to the point of new life even in the flesh, so that they can go "in a twinkling."

Do you see why conquering the flesh is so important right now? Yes! It is a process of the Holy Spirit, the Spirit of Life.

Yes, I AM the Resurrection and the Life, says the Lord Jesus, and you will see that played out in the physical realm. Amen! I have spoken.

Our life in Christ in glory has so far remained hidden. We already live the identical life He lives in heaven. But the scriptures promise this will be revealed—in this life, in this world. It will happen at His "coming," at the time when Christ is "revealed."

> For (as far as this world is concerned) you have died, and your new, real) life is hidden with Christ in God.
>
> When Christ, Who is our life, appears then you also will appear with Him (in the splendor of His) glory. (Colossians 3:3-4)

When Christ, the Anointed One and His anointing, is revealed in His glory, His excellence, then His own will be revealed. Every prophet of God is now declaring the advent of His glory poured out upon the earth. The very issue we are discussing, the redemption of our bodies, is the pivotal issue that will reveal His own people as God's sons, according to Romans, chapter 8. The scripture there says that all of creation awaits the revealing of God's sons. It identifies the same Holy Spirit who raised Christ from the dead as the one who will enliven our perishable bodies.

> But if Christ lives in you (then although) your (natural) body is dead by reason of sin and guilt, the spirit is alive because of (the) righteousness (that He imputes to you).
>
> And if the spirit of Him who raised up Jesus from the dead dwells in you, (then) He Who raised up Christ Jesus from the dead will also restore to life your mortal (short-lived, perishable) bodies through His Spirit Who dwells in you.

> For all who are led by the Spirit of God are sons of God.
>
> For (even the whole) creation (all nature) waits expectantly and longs earnestly for God's sons to be made known (waits for the revealing, the disclosing of their sonship).
>
> For the creation (nature) was subjected to frailty (to futility, condemned to frustration) not because of some intentional fault on its part, but by the will of Him Who so subjected it—(yet) with the hope
>
> That nature (creation) itself will be set free from its bondage to decay and corruption (and gain an entrance) into the glorious freedom of God's children.
>
> We know that the whole creation (of irrational creatures) has been moaning together in the pains of labor until now.
>
> And not only the creation, but we ourselves too, who have and enjoy the firstfruits of the (Holy) Spirit (a foretaste of the blissful things to come) groan inwardly as we wait for the redemption of our bodies (from sensuality and the grave, which will reveal) our adoption (our manifestation as God's sons). (Romans 8:10, 11, 14, 19-23)

When Christ, who is our life, appears, then we will witness this glory and bodily redemption. "Spirit, mind **and body**" will be preserved "blameless unto the coming of Our Lord Jesus Christ," Paul tells us in 1 Thessalonians 5:23.

Scripture scholars call the time when Christ "appears" or is revealed the *parousia*. It means "presence." In the Greco-Roman world, *parousia* referred to visits by royalty. Early Christians adopted the word as a term for the glorious coming of Christ. Its meaning is not limited to Christ's final coming but also refers to the power He will display when He comes to establish His messianic kingdom. When the disciples asked Jesus in Matthew 24 about the events of His coming, He told them of famines, earthquakes and ethnic group rising against ethnic group. The Greek word used there for His "coming" is *parousia*. When Jesus is fully revealed as the Christ, the Anointed One, revealed in His glory as completely as the Book of Revelation prophesies, then our own glory will be made manifest.

The glory is the outward demonstration of His presence or *parousia*. It completes and perfects "Christ in you, the hope of glory."

He is coming again in glory, but He won't come as we expect. He will come in glory in us, His people. Don't miss His parousia, His coming, as the Pharisees did, because of rigid expectations. Look for Christ to return in glory in His people.

Glory Is Our Destiny

Know in your heart that the glory is your destiny. I have given you a future and a hope. (Jeremiah 29:11) You have learned that this word "hope" also means "destiny." Now meditate on this: Christ in you, the hope of glory the hope of meeting your destiny. Christ, the Anointed, in you, the hope of glory. What is glory but the manifest presence of God? So, Christ revealed in you is glory.

Scholars call this time of fulfillment the messianic age, the Messiah or Anointed One's age.

What was He anointed to do? To release captives, give sight to the blind, deliver the oppressed. And more. Jesus was anointed to do these things, which He did in His earthly ministry. But, we have learned, His anointing will also accomplish all that Isaiah 61 foretells for an era beyond Jesus' earthly ministry: to proclaim the Jubilee, to console, beautify, strengthen, to rebuild ancient ruins, the devastations of many generations, to recompense, prosper and bless Zion, that God might be glorified.

This is the messianic age, the age of the anointing, a time of the manifest glory of God, with His goodness and excellence expressed. It is His reign of love.

Glory is coming, unprecedented glory. More than Solomon's temple and reign. More than Jesus' miracles. More glory than the world has ever seen. Greater than Nebuchadnezzar's splendor or Pharaoh's majesty will be the kingship and kingdom of the Lord Jesus Christ.

It will express His nature—to love, to heal, to suffer and die for another, to give sacrificially, to bear burdens for another's sake, to comfort, to mourn with, to rejoice with. This is His kingdom: to care. This kingdom of love is at its onset and the glory (manifest goodness, excellence of God) will be highly visible. "All flesh shall see the glory of God" is true. All flesh, all humanity, will see it.

What does this mean to you? Get ready for healing. Get ready for comfort and restoration. Get ready for the great I AM-ing of the Great I AM. Life! Life more abundantly. What Jesus came to bring and do will be brought and done.

This is a turning point. Rejoicing will be heard in My courts, and thanksgiving, untold joyous thanks. The glory will outshine imagination, exceed anything you've thought. I am veritable, truthful and reliable. This will come to pass.

Temple

The prophets foretold a last-days rebuilt temple. Jesus spoke of the temple of His body. Peter said that we are living stones being built into a spiritual house. Paul said that we

> ...all grow into one holy temple in the Lord; and you too, in him, are being built into a house where God lives, in the Spirit. (Ephesians 2:21 JB)

We understand that natural Israel represents the physical demonstration of God's work in history and that the church represents His spiritual work. The prophets envisioned a material temple to rise in the ancient city of Jerusalem, but their words at the same time described a spiritual temple to outshine any other in its glory.

> The latter glory of this house...shall be greater than the former, says the Lord of hosts: and in this place will I give peace and prosperity, says the Lord of hosts. (Haggai 2:9)

The temple, as well as the new Jerusalem where it resides, is a spiritual reality. The awesome picture of the new Jerusalem portrayed by the Book of Revelation is rising in the spirit realm now. We perceive it in stillness in the secret place of the Most High.

Perceive the imperceptible with Me. See the unseeable, the hidden. I will show you. In the spirit world, defenses are arising, even now. Your world is changing for the better. Walls of defense and protection are going up. Jerusalem is being rebuilt. And all is being made ready for the King to occupy the city.

Know and trust and believe now, My children, that all is glorious within, within the temple of our God, in the supernatural temple. It has been rebuilt first, not the city, and it is all glorious within, stunning in beauty, richness and purity. It is the new temple of our God, His new residence and dwelling place. Finishing touches are taking place now and God will soon inhabit His temple.

Yes, I will inhabit, indwell, appear in manifest glory in My new temple, says the Lord, just as My prophets have spoken. I will dwell there and manifest My glory. Amen. I have spoken and I will do it.

Just as the glory of God filled His ancient temple, His glory will also fill the spiritual temple of Christ's body. His glory descended to fill Solomon's temple during the Feast. He plans a parallel outpouring of His glory today.

Understand that when the glory fills My church, when the glory fills the rebuilt temple, then I will come in during the celebration of the Feast of Tabernacles. Yes, the feast of Yahweh, I AM. Know Me as I AM, that you might celebrate fully with Me My Feast. Know the "who" of who I am as a person. Know Me. Celebrate Me. Rejoice in Me. That is the Feast, the Great Feast, the great party celebrating God, I AM. Hallelujah. When My people know Me, we can celebrate!

The glory of God is His excellence. That resides in a person, the Lord Jesus Christ. He is "the sole expression of the glory of God." (Hebrews 1:3) The glory of the Father is the Son. When the scriptures describe the Lord Jesus Christ as the mirror of the Father's glory, their words inspire awe:

His beauty…

> …in that (future Messianic) day the Lord of Hosts shall become a crown of glory and a diadem of beauty to the (converted) remnant of His people. (Isaiah 28:5)

His splendor…

> His brightness was like the sunlight; rays streamed from His hand, and there (in the sunlike splendor) was the hiding place of His power. (Habbakuk 3:4)

His radiance…

> He is the sole expression of the glory of God (the Light-being, the out-raying or radiance of the divine), and He is the perfect imprint and very image of (God's) nature, upholding and maintaining and guiding and propelling the universe by His mighty word of power. (Hebrews 1:3)

Jesus, the glory of the Father, will fill the temple, culminating the promise, "Christ in you, the hope of glory."

Oh, yes! Yes! Yes! Yes! My glory shall fill My temple, My church, My people. Arise, shine, for your light has come. The glory of the Lord Yahweh I AM has risen upon thee.

And what is the glory of God? The Son. He is the radiance, the best expression of the glory of the Father. He is the Sun of Righteousness who rises with healing in His rays or wings. You know Him. He is your Jesus. But more, saith the Lord, much more than "your Jesus." He is the Lord of Hosts, Yahweh Sabbaoth, the Most High, Holy One of Israel, Lord God, Sovereign Lord of Eternal Glory. He IS.

Who has risen upon you? The Sun, the Son of Righteousness. Your light has come. A new Day is dawning. Be not afraid of the Day of the Lord. It is a Day of blessing and righteousness.

Know that in the fullness of time Jesus, your Jesus, will come and fill the temple of His Body with His glory, for ***all*** *to see. All flesh will see the glory of God-in-you. For Jesus said, "In them My glory is achieved." (John 17:10) The Father's glory revealed in the Son. The Son's glory revealed in you, My people.*

It's simple. It's easy. It's God mixing with man. It's love. It's light. It's life expressed at its best, as the glory of I AM Life, Light, Love.

Rejoice, My people. This "Day" (this light period) is coming!

Grace

Who can stand when the glory of the Lord comes on the scene? Moses had to hide in the cleft of the rock only to observe a glimpse of the glory. Those who touched the Ark in procession died. The temple priests could not minister because of the glory. Those who will stand in the wind of God's glory are those who have already stood in the stripping storm-wind of His judgement. If they have stood there, they will stand in the glory. But even that is not enough. The only true source of our ability to stand will be grace.

> And he shall bring forth the finishing gable stone (of the new temple) with loud shoutings of the people, "grace, grace to it!" (Zechariah 4:7)

Grace will be our byword.

The voice of the Lord is upon the waters; the God of glory thunders. (Psalm 29:3)

Yes, I am your God. I roar, My voice sounding like a trumpet, a mighty, thunderous noise of many waters, saying, "Yes! I am coming into My temple to ***fill*** *it, fill it up with My glory. Even the wooden bowls and vessels will be sanctified, holy unto the Lord. (Zechariah 14:20) So know, children of Mine, that I roar My message (the prophets speak it), saying, "Behold My glory!"*

And the priests could not minister because of the glory. They could not stand up. What do you say, oh wise-in-your-own-sight man about standing in My glory? It will be grace, grace only, that allows you to stand and to minister. It will be Me standing up inside you!

This day I shout "Grace" to the capstone of the temple, My rebuilt temple, My dwelling place, My ark, My sanctuary. Amen! "Grace!" will be the byword for My temple, saith the Lord. And see: all this written happens in the spiritual realm before it happens in the natural. See with the eyes of your understanding.

The Holy Spirit didn't inspire the Bible's great messianic prophecies for their fulfillment in heaven. The wilderness will blossom like a rose here on earth. (Isaiah 35) The oil of gladness will be traded for mourning (Isaiah 61) during a time of vengeance against God's enemies here on earth. The anointing will overflow as we initiate Jesus' full reign. To reign, Jesus has needed a people to reign over and with. This people has been formed, to the joy and jubilation of the Lord.

I am your God; you have no other. I am well pleased with you, My children, as I open the door to a new Day. Rejoice with Me, Oh Israel, My people, for a new Day has dawned. A new beginning. A new era. My time clock is not off. I know what time it is! I am saying "New Day." and you are here to see it. You are brought through, over the Jordan and into the land to inherit it.

Am I happy? Yes! My messianic reign will now begin, for I have a people to call upon My Name. Hallelujah! Know now, children of Mine, that things will be drastically different. Drastically. Because My reign begins now.

Your prayer now should be pure praise. Just praise and the rest will be done.

Look up! Your salvation is nigh. Yes, these are rousing words: Look Up! Your salvation, your final salvation (wholeness, healing, restoration, righteousness, vindication) is nigh!

Oh, yes. Yes! My big word to My people is Yes! Yes to your prayers. Yes to your hopes. Yes to your dreams. Yes to the impossible. Yes, yes, yes. I, the Lord God Almighty, am now, today, saying Yes to My people. Hear Me. I say one giant, joyous YES. Make it a billboard in your mind, a roar in your ear. Carve it into your imagination. YES! The God of Love and Mercy reigns!

We see the kingdom of heaven not by natural observation but by reading people's hearts. His own anticipate His appearing. Expectation runs high. Those who watch in the Spirit will not miss His coming.

Times are coming to a close. Eras end. Times change and dissolve. One melts seamlessly into another. Who will notice that the Day of the Lord has arrived? Not the world, though they know something is going on. Not the church Christians, for they are not Mine; they do not hear My voice.

Then who does know? My beloved, who watches and waits for Me. She is not asleep but awake and alert, waiting for My very footfall, the least rustle of My garment. She awaits in the utter darkness of the world—but she has her lamp. She will see My arrival by night, even at midnight, because she has her lamp, earnestly tended, wick shortened, oil filled. The time is short and all that will be done for you will be done quickly. Amen!

Love Letters From Jesus

If you haven't yet accepted Jesus, He wants to say...

My heart is a heart of love and mercy toward you. Yes, I stand up to judge and you can see judgement upon the earth in natural disasters—earthquakes, floods, hurricanes—that is Me pulling back My hand of protection against the judgement sin has brought on the land. Yet **all** *who call upon the name of the Lord shall be saved. Yes, all!*

Call upon My name as Jesus, Savior, your salvation. Call upon My name as Provider. I AM your provision. It's one of My names, Yahweh Provides, given to My people Israel in the Old Testament. Look it up and see. (Genesis 22:14)

Call upon My name as your protector. I have said in My word that all who call upon the name of the Lord shall be saved. Joel 2:31-32 speaks of "the great and terrible day of the Lord" and says "whosoever shall call on the name of the Lord shall be delivered." I have promised it and I stand behind My promises.

Now know ye, peoples of the earth, that the Great Day of the Lord shall come, is coming and has already come. It has begun. Have you not eyes to see and observe the signs of My coming? Do you brush aside earthquakes, coming in waves as I, Jesus, the Word, described them, as pangs of childbirth, increasing in intensity and severity. (Yes! To birth a new government, a new reign upon the earth!

So know now, people of My heart, that I love you and even as great judgment comes upon the earth and its inhabitants (those dwelling in the earth and not in My kingdom), so does My love and protection increase for those who call upon My name.

Yes! Call upon My name and I will show you great and mighty things! (Jeremiah 33:3) I will show you the Father's love, reveal it to you in full. I will show you the cross where Jesus died for you, gave up His life amid insult, mockery and great physical suffering. I will show and introduce to you My Spirit who is sent to you by the Father and Jesus to be your Comforter and your Helper. (John 14:16, 26 and John 16:7)

I Am God and there is no other. Know Me, that I Am God. Recognize, understand, perceive and comprehend that I am God.

I am God of Israel, the believers, the "nation" that believes in Me. For I had and have a physical Israel and a spiritual "Israel," that nation of believers who believe in Me. The people of faith. And you can join that people of faith any time by entering in and believing, accepting the cross and participating as one of Christ's kingdom and reign. For the kingdom of God comes not by observation (by seeing it), but it is in men's hearts. (Luke 17:20-21) Someone might look like they belong to Me and not be one of Mine. It's what's inside that counts and you can't see it. But it does bear fruit and that you should be able to see.

Know now that it is your **heart** *that matters, not outward appearances. You don't have to be like others you see as "Christians." No carbon copy. No formula. You just have to turn your heart to Me, give over your heart to Me, and I will do the rest by My Holy Spirit working within you to establish My kingdom in your heart.*

Recognize Me, My people, as the God of your heart, the One that your heart loves and serves out of love, not out of law. For My law is written in your heart (Psalm 37:31a) when you love Me and doing right comes easily when done with love and joy.

Oh, yes! My burden is light. My yoke is easy. (Matthew 11:30) It's all done with joy and love. It's just as a mother gets up in the morning when she hears her baby stir. It's a little hard for her to be roused, but she rises with joy to see her child new each morning and goes to her child in love.

Oh, I am like a mother too! My Spirit hovers over, listens, protects, nurtures, feeds and teaches. My Spirit inspires with His vision for the beloved. My Spirit sees deep into the child and calls forth greatness, goodness, love to compensate for all the world's evil. To make just one "child" a candle to a family, a light to a community, a torch to the nations.

Go now, go thy way and listen for Me. Listen to Me, speaking to your heart as never before, wooing you and calling you to Myself. Just as a mother hen calls her chicks to beneath her wing before a storm, so I am calling you before the great and terrible Day of the Lord to come and hide in Me. I have a safe place for you, a place of peace hidden from the storm where you can rest and take respite in Me.

If you're a believer, but separated from Jesus, He says...

I Am. I tell you, I Am. Know Me. Know My heart. I am God, but I am a gentle person, interested in you, loving you. I sent My son, My beloved son, the son of My heart to die on a cross for you.

My people answer, "God, you say you love me. But you are in control of the universe and the holocaust happened...or my marriage broke up...or my son died. How could you let that happen? If you love me, how could you let that happen?"

Remember, My people, that I sent My son, My beloved son, the son of My heart, to die on a cross for you. I gave My only son for you. I removed Him from the happiness of heaven, our sweet life together, and sent Him to earth, to live in flesh, to bear insults, spitting, bruising and finally the cross. My son died with His precious blood dripping into the dust of Calvary. They pounded nails into His hands. They rammed a crown of thorns into His beloved brow. With great anguish I gave Him for you.

I love you. I love you with an everlasting love. I want you to relate to Me, to have fellowship with Me, sweet communion, friendship, sonship, daughterhood. Pleasant conversation. Enjoyment of one another. Love. I want that for you and Me.

Hear Me: I need you. I am your God and I need you.

Let Me say it simply: You are My child. I cannot divorce Myself from you. I cannot forget you or turn away from you. You are always in My thoughts. I made you and planted Myself inside you. Oh, hear Me: I love you. I need you to be a part of My life.

Now, I know that this impassioned plea from your God is not what you expect. Many of you think of Me as a far-off God. Master of the Universe. Creator. The One who set things in motion eons ago and then sat back with folded hands to watch impassively.

No! I am involved! I care deeply. I am with you constantly. I made you, formed you in the womb, rejoicing. I watched you every step of the way and sent My angels to care for and protect you.

But I have established certain laws. They are written in the Bible. I do not act outside these laws (and neither should you). These laws call for faith, prayer, walking righteously and speaking My word over your life, as sprinkled seed to make the blessings of My promises grow. I do not act outside these laws for I am a righteous God, a holy God. If you don't walk in My ways, protecting and blessing yourself and your loved ones with My word, you are open to cheating, stealing and killing by the enemy of your soul. I don't do bad things to you nor do I disobey My own laws. Sin opens the door for bad things to happen, even to "good" people.

I AM. Know Me. Who I am is I AM.

I exist. I've existed forever. I exist today for you. I Am and I am available to you. Know Me as One who is ***available*** *to you. I am yours and you are Mine, forever. Forever we are together. As a mother cannot break the bond, the relationship, with her baby (she will always be that child's mother, no matter what) so I cannot break or change My relatedness to you. I will always be your Father, your Abba, your Daddy-God. It will never change on My part, no matter how far you run, no matter how bad you are. I will always be related to you, bonded to you as Father. Some-*

times brokenhearted Father but always Father, loving Father.

Men, hear Me: I am your Father. I have loved you always with a Father's heart, cherishing you, holding you always in My heart. I have trained you, provided experiences to help you grow, instructed you with My eye upon you.

Women, hear Me: You are My cherished, lovely daughters. I am your doting Father. I have watched you grow with great awe and love. I honor you, My beloved. I treasure and cherish you. You're not junk. Don't believe that. Each and every one of you is My treasure.

Now children and young people, hear Me: I am going to set fire to this world and use you, My young ones, to do it. You are My mouthpiece, My firebrand. I will light you like a torch and send you shining to the nations. Know Me, My children, as the One-Who-Sends-You-Forth. I am preparing you, equipping you, arming you. And don't forget that I love you. I am sending you forth with love. My heart and My name are a seal upon your forehead. You will go in My authority.

Arise!

If you're a Christian, but not intimate with Jesus, He says...

Know Me. Know Me in My Word. Know Me in My reflections in the world around you. I desire to be known, not a lofty and remote God but One who is very present and wants to be known, yearns to know.

Know Me. I plead with you: Know Me. I want to be known. I made you. I love you. I want relationship with you. Hear Me: I love you, cherish you, cradle you fondly in the palm of My hand. Please look at Me. Please see Me. I am a person who loves you.

I beg you to know Me. I am meek and humble of heart, though I am your God. I desire, passionately desire, desire with all My heart, to fellowship with you, to relate to you, to talk with you. I would instruct you, heal you, restore you, shower My love upon you. Yes! I would!

I showed you a picture of Myself in the Bible, the Song of Solomon, as the stag, peering in at the lattice, looking through your fences, calling you to My presence. Again in Solomon's Song, I appeared as the Beloved with His hand on the door handle, the door that was latched as the loved one slept.

Awake to Me. Open the door that I might come in and commune with you.

My heart is aching for My people, My family, My beloved, My bride, to come unto Me. Aching. Deep desire unsatisfied. Where do you think romantic love came from? It is an expression of My passionate love for My own, My insistent love, My everlasting love, My longing and yearning for My beloved.

I find My beloved asleep. I find My beloved too busy. I hear My beloved say, "Later. Later I will come to you. Later!"

Sometimes My beloved hears My wooing and cries, "No! I can't. It means turning away from something or someone here in the world. I can't. No, don't ask that of me."

Now My heart has found the one it loves and she is beautiful, set apart for Me, refined in splendor, beautiful and flawless in her perfection before Me. She is My bride. She is ready, prepared for Me by My Holy Spirit. I will lavish her with blessings, carry her away to the marriage bed, make her to reign with Me. Forever I will enthrone her in majesty alongside Me.

"And what of me?" you say. Oh, I have invited you. I have wooed you. I have called you from afar to come to Me and drink of Me, to drink at the river of My life forever. And I still invite you. There is still time, just a little time, to say, "Yes!" I will come.

Say "yes" today to Me, says the Lord. Say "yes" before My coming. Say the "yes" that will delight and satisfy My heart with joy no earthly lover has ever seen or imagined. Know Me today and accept Me as I AM.

Index

NOTES

NOTES

Order Other Books by Mary Ellen Gilliland

THE SUMMIT HIKER

___Quantity@ 14.95
Colo. only tax .45

THE VAIL HIKER
• And Ski Touring Guide •

___Quantity@ 15.95
Colo. only tax .48

SUMMIT

___Quantity@ 19.95
Colo. only tax .60

BRECKENRIDGE!

__Quantity@ 4.95
Colo. only tax .15

Postage & handling per book 2.00

Total Enclosed $_____

By Mail: Send to

Alpenrose Press
P.O. Box 499
Silverthorne, CO 80498
Check or Money Order Only

By Telephone:

Toll Free: 1-800-579-1179
Credit Card Orders

Name ____________________
Address ____________________
City ____________________ State ________ Zip ________

__Author: Please autograph my copy.